PHILOSOPHICAL PAPERS

J. L. AUSTIN

PHILOSOPHICAL PAPERS

THIRD EDITION

EDITED BY

J. O. URMSON

AND

G. J. WARNOCK

Oxford New York Toronto Melbourne

OXFORD UNIVERSITY PRESS

1979

Oxford University Press, Walton Street, Oxford OX2 6DP

OXFORD LONDON GLASGOW
NEW YORK TORONTO MELBOURNE WELLINGTON
KUALA LUMPUR SINGAPORE HONG KONG TOKYO
DELHI BOMBAY CALCUTTA MADRAS KARACHI
NAIROBI DAR ES SALAAM CAPE TOWN

© *Oxford University Press 1961, 1970, 1979*

First published by the Clarendon Press 1961
Second edition 1970
First issued as an
Oxford University Press Paperback 1970
Second impression 1976
Third edition 1979

British Library Cataloguing in Publication Data

Austin, John Langshaw
Philosophical papers. – 3rd ed.
1. Philosophy – Collected works
I. Urmson, James Opie
II. Warnock, Geoffrey James
192'.08   B1618.A8   79–40630
ISBN 0-19-824627-7
0-19-283021-x Pbk

Printed in Great Britain
at the University Press, Oxford
by Eric Buckley
Printer to the University

FOREWORD
TO THE SECOND EDITION

SINCE 1961, when Austin's *Philosophical Papers* was first published, three further papers by him have appeared in print. Two of these are included in this new edition, and are further mentioned below. The third is 'Performatif-Constatif', which Austin. presented at a (predominantly) Anglo-French conference at Royaumont in March 1958, and the original French text of which was published after his death in *Cahiers de Royaumont, Philosophie No. IV, La Philosophie Analytique* (Les Editions de Minuit, 1962). The editors felt in 1961 that this piece was too closely similar in content to 'Performative Utterances' for it to be reasonable to include both in a single volume, and of the two preferred 'Performative Utterances'— partly, of course, because Austin's own English text of that paper was available. There seems no reason now to change that view; however, it should be noted that 'Performatif-Constatif' is now in print, and also that it has been translated into English (by G. J. Warnock, in *Philosophy and Ordinary Language*, edited by C. E. Caton, University of Illinois Press, 1963).

Of the two papers now added to this collection, 'ἀγαθόν and εὐδαιμονία in the *Ethics* of Aristotle' is much the earlier in date. It was written before 1939, when Prichard, on whose views it comments, was still alive; but it was not published then, and there is no reason to think that in later years Austin intended that it should be, though he made in it certain changes and additions. That is largely why it was not included in the original edition of this book; another factor was that its text was imperfect in some passages. However, it has now appeared very fittingly in the collection *Aristotle*, edited by J. M. E. Moravcsik (Doubleday, New York, 1967: Macmillan, London, 1968), and should now be included with Austin's other published papers. 'Three Ways of Spilling Ink' is a rather different case, since, as the introductory note to that paper explains, Austin's manuscript was obviously unfinished and incomplete. Professor Forguson, however, found it possible to produce a text which, though certainly rough, is both authentic and intelligible; and since it adds valuably to Austin's previously available papers, publication seemed justified. This piece appeared in the *Philosophical Review* in October 1966. In each case we are grateful for permission to reprint.

In the present volume, then, all Austin's previously published papers are included with the exception of 'Performatif-Constatif'—perhaps we should mention also his reviews, and two short notes on *Analysis* competitions (*Analysis*, vol. xii, No. 6, 1952 and vol. xviii, No. 5, 1958). 'Ifs and Cans' (1956) was published in the *Proceedings of the British Academy*. 'A Plea for Excuses' was his Presidential Address to the Aristotelian Society in 1956. 'How to Talk—some simple ways' (1953) was also published in the *Proceedings of the Aristotelian Society*. 'Are There *A Priori* Concepts?' (1939), 'Other Minds' (1946), 'Truth' (1950), and 'Pretending' (1958) were all contributions to symposia of Joint Sessions of the Mind Association and the Aristotelian Society, and were published in the Supplementary Volumes of the *Proceedings of the Aristotelian Society*. We thank the editors for permission to reprint.

Three further papers appeared for the first time in the first edition of this book. 'The Meaning of a Word' was read to the Moral Sciences Club in Cambridge and to the Jowett Society in Oxford in 1940. 'Unfair to Facts' was read to the Philosophical Society in Oxford in 1954, and is a sequel to Austin's symposium on Truth, with P. F. Strawson and D. R. Cousin, in 1950. 'Performative Utterances' is a transcript, with minor verbal corrections, of an unscripted talk delivered in the Third Programme of the B.B.C. in 1956, and our thanks are due to the British Broadcasting Corporation for their permission to publish it here.

All the papers in this volume are now arranged in chronological order of composition—on the supposition, where it

applies, that that was the same as the order of their public
presentation in print or otherwise.

J. O. URMSON
G. J. WARNOCK

Oxford 1969

NOTE TO THE THIRD EDITION

ONE further paper is included in this edition; it is called
'The Line and the Cave in Plato's *Republic*'. It was recon-
structed by J. O. Urmson from notes; further details are
given in an editorial note prefixed to the paper.

J. O. URMSON

Stanford 1979

CONTENTS

I

ΑΓΑΘΟΝ AND *ΕΥΔΑΙΜΟΝΙΑ* IN THE *ETHICS* OF ARISTOTLE[1]

THIS article takes its start from an article by Professor H. A. Prichard (*Philosophy*, x [1935], 27–39) on 'The Meaning of ἀγαθόν in the *Ethics* of Aristotle'. It will be seen that I disagree with him, but I think his article has the great merit of raising serious questions.

Statement of Professor Prichard's conclusions. Professor Prichard begins by stating his 'heretical' conclusions, as follows:

1. Aristotle really meant by ἀγαθόν 'conducive to our happiness'.

2. Aristotle maintained that when a man does an action deliberately, as distinct from impulsively, he does it simply in order to, i.e. from the desire to, become happy, this being so even when he does what is virtuous or speculates.[2]

(2. 1) A corollary: Aristotle, being anxious to persuade men first and foremost to practice speculation and secondarily to do what is virtuous, conceived that, to succeed, what he had to prove was that this was the action necessary to make a man happy.

---

[1] Originally published in *Aristotle: A Collection of Critical Essays* edited by J. M. E. Moravcsik, published by Doubleday & Co., Inc., New York, 1967, and Macmillan & Co. Ltd., London, 1968. Copyright © 1967 by J. M. E. Moravcsik. Reprinted by permission of the editor and publishers. Footnotes other than Austin's are by Professor Moravcsik, and the translation used is that of Sir David Ross. Additional editorial work on the text was done by J. O. Urmson.

[2] This distinction between 'speculating' and 'doing what is virtuous' is not strictly Aristotelian: θεωρία is ἐνέργεια κατὰ τὴν τελειοτάτην ἀρετήν.

(The corollary Professor Prichard ignores, and, at least for the present, I shall do the same.)

His reason for excluding certain passages from consideration invalid. We must first direct our attention to a curious and important reservation, which Professor Prichard makes in stating his view. Aristotle, he says, means by ἀγαθόν conducive to our happiness 'in the *Nicomachean Ethics* [abbreviated *NE* hereafter —Ed.] except in the two discussions of pleasure—where ἀγαθόν is opposed to φαῦλον and μοχθηρόν'. We are not here concerned with the restriction to the *NE*, but it is necessary to examine the further restriction, by which we are precluded from using *NE* VII. xi–xiv and X. i–v.

The argument implied in Professor Prichard's words seems to be as follows:

(a) In these passages ἀγαθόν means something different from what it means in the rest of the *NE*.

(b) This is shown by the fact that it is, in these two passages, opposed to φαῦλον and μοχθηρόν.

With regard to (*a*), it is most unfortunate that Professor Prichard does not tell us what ἀγαθόν *does* mean in these two passages.

As to (*b*), we clearly need further explanation. I hope that the following is a correct expansion of Professor Prichard's argument.

1. Throughout the *NE*, with the exception of these two passages, ἀγαθόν is never opposed to φαῦλον or μοχθηρόν, but to something else, presumably κακόν.

2. In these two passages alone, ἀγαθόν is opposed, not to κακόν, but to φαῦλον and μοχθηρόν.

3. Since we know on independent grounds that κακόν has a different meaning from φαῦλον or μοχθηρόν, it follows that ἀγαθόν, in these two passages, must have a meaning different from that which it has throughout the rest of the *NE*.

(To take a parallel case. Suppose that I do not know the meaning of the adjective 'green': and that throughout a certain work

I find it opposed to the adjective 'experienced', except in two passages where it is opposed to 'red' and 'yellow'. Then if I know on other grounds that 'experienced' means something sufficiently different from 'red' or 'yellow', I can infer that 'green' must, in these two passages, have a meaning different from that which it has throughout the rest of the work.)

If this is actually the sort of argument on which Professor Prichard is relying, I think there are considerations which will lead him to abandon it.

1. ἀγαθόν is opposed to μοχθηρόν elsewhere in the *NE*—e.g. in IX. viii. 7—where pleasure is not under discussion. (Not to mention passages in other works, e.g. *Met.* 1020ᵇ21.) I have not found a case of ἀγαθόν being explicitly opposed to φαῦλον elsewhere, but cf. (3) *infra*.

2. ἀγαθόν is constantly opposed to κακόν in the two discussions of pleasure: VII. i. 1–2, xiii. 1 and 7, xiv. 2 and 9, X. ii. 5. In VII in particular, the discussion is introduced and terminated by an opposition between ἀγαθόν and κακόν, and in xiv. 2 we read: κακῷ γὰρ ἀγαθὸν ἐναντίον.

3. I do not know of any clear distinction between the meaning of κακόν and the meanings of φαῦλόν and μοχθηρόν (or πονηρόν) any more than I can clearly distinguish between ἀγαθόν, ἐπιεικές, and σπουδαῖον. The words seem to be used almost indifferently, or at least for 'species' of one another which would be equivalent in certain contexts.

Very many passages in the *NE*, such as III. v. 3, are evidence of this. But the point seems clear even from the two discussions of pleasure. σπουδαῖον seems equivalent to ἀγαθόν in VII. xiv. 4, ἐπιεικές to ἀγαθόν in X. ii. 1, μοχθηρόν seems equivalent to or a species of κακόν in VII. xiv. 2, φαῦλον to κακόν in X. i. 2. Pleasures are called ἀγαθαί, σπουδαῖαι, ἐπιεικεῖς (also καλαί, etc.) in apparently the same sense or senses not sufficiently distinguished: and similarly οὐκ ἀγαθαί, μοχθηραί, φαῦλαι (also αἰσχραί, etc.) in apparently the same sense. And these adjectives seem opposed to one another indifferently, cf. e.g. X. v. 6. (It must be admitted that Aristotle does not use the expression κακαί ἡδοναί: if this requires some explanation, I think one could easily be found.)

It is, of course, possible that some distinction can be drawn between κακόν on the one hand and φαῦλον and μοχθηρόν on the other. But (*a*) it is clearly incumbent on Professor Prichard to draw it—which he does not do. (*b*) Even so he would by no means be out of the wood, for (i) it does not seem to be true that ἀγαθόν is, in these passages on pleasures, more commonly opposed to φαῦλον and μοχθηρόν than to κακόν. μοχθηρόν only occurs *once* in each book, and is only used as opposite of ἀγαθόν in VII. xiv. 2: and there it is only so opposed because it is equated with κακόν. φαῦλον is opposed to ἀγαθόν only once in x. i. 2, a rather popular passage: and there, as section 5 of the same chapter shows, it is equivalent to κακόν. (ii) Actually ἀγαθόν is in these same passages much more commonly opposed to κακόν, and so presumably has its 'normal' sense. (But we shall see that it is vital for Professor Prichard that, when Aristotle says 'ἡδονή is an ἀγαθόν', ἀγαθόν should *never* have its 'normal' sense of 'conducive to our happiness.') (iii) In a most important passage, x. ii. 1, exactly the same remarks are made about ἀγαθόν as in I. i. 1, a passage on which Professor Prichard relies in arriving at his interpretation of it as 'conducive to our happiness'. Here then ἀγαθόν must presumably have that meaning: but this is one of the places where ἡδονή is said to be an ἀγαθόν, which, on Professor Prichard's interpretation of ἀγαθόν, does not make sense. *v.i.*

It would seem then that Professor Prichard's ostensible argument for excluding these two discussions of pleasure from consideration will not bear examination. And it is in any case so very recondite that we may be tempted to think he would never have chanced upon it, unless he had been *searching* for some reason to justify the exclusion of these passages.

Why does he wish to exclude these passages? His interpretation of εὐδαιμονία. Why then, we must ask, should it be important for Professor Prichard to secure the exclusion from consideration of the two discussions of pleasure? In order to understand this, we must first understand that the whole argument of Professor Prichard's paper is based upon a premiss which is never expressed, no doubt because it seems to him obvious; namely, that 'happiness' (his translation of εὐδαιμονία) *means* a state of feeling pleased. This may be shown as follows:

1. On p. 39, line 16, 'causing happiness' is substituted without remark for 'causing pleasure', which was the expression used in the parallel argumentation on, e.g., pp. 35–6.

2. On p. 38, at the bottom we read 'what he means by ἀγαθόν is productive of a state, or rather a feeling, of happiness, i.e., as I think we may say in this context, a feeling of pleasure.' This remark is interesting, since it seems to imply that 'in other contexts' being happy does *not* mean feeling pleased. However, we need not worry, I think, about these other contexts, for it is quite essential to Professor Prichard's argument at a crucial point that the word εὐδαιμονία, or in English 'happiness', should be and should be known by all to be, at least for purposes of Ethics, entirely clear and unambiguous in meaning: so that, if being happy means feeling pleased in some contexts in the *NE*, it clearly must do so in all thought that concerns the moral philosopher.[1] (The crucial point referred to is found on p. 37 at the bottom, and repeated on p. 39 at the top. Professor Prichard there maintains that Aristotle cannot be really asking the question he 'ostensibly' asks, viz. 'What is the nature of happiness?' for there is no uncertainty about that—'the nature of . . . happiness is known to us, for we all know the nature of that for which the word "happiness" stands'.)

3. On p. 39, in summing up his own contentions, Professor Prichard says that he has in effect represented Aristotle as a psychological *hedonist*; i.e., I understand, he claims that, according to Aristotle, all deliberate action is done from a desire to produce in ourselves feelings of *pleasure*. Now on p. 27, quoted

---

[1] Prichard's reservation 'in this context', whatever it means, is not important here; nor is the contrast between state ('disposition') and feeling. Similarly, on p. 38, a distinction is drawn between 'happiness' and 'some particular state of happiness': but I do not think that concerns us here.

above, Professor Prichard said that, according to Aristotle, all
deliberate action is done from a desire to become *happy*. Hence
being happy and feeling pleased are evidently, for Professor
Prichard, equivalent expressions. (And this enables us to see
why he considers his view, as he says on p. 27, 'heretical',
although, at first sight and as here stated, it does not appear very
extraordinary: if we realize that 'become happy' means 'feel
pleased' the view certainly is very strange.)

It is, therefore, clear that Professor Prichard does not distinguish what we call 'being happy' from what we call 'feeling
pleased': and he has in fact been good enough to tell me that
that is so.

It now becomes evident why the two discussions of pleasure
in the *NE* should have a peculiar interest for him.

For if *ἀγαθόν* means 'conducive to our happiness', and if
'happiness' is equivalent to 'pleasure'—then how *can* we ask,
as Aristotle does in these passages, whether *ἡδονή* is an *ἀγαθόν*?
For *ἡδονή must* presumably be translated 'pleasure': so that the
question we are asking becomes 'Is (our) pleasure conducive
to our pleasure?', which is absurd, or at least absurdly limited.
Further similar difficulties arise, if we ask, for instance, what
could be meant by saying that some *ἡδοναί* are *ἀγαθαί*, and,
odder still, that some are *not ἀγαθαί*.

Hence it is essential for Professor Prichard to maintain that
ἀγαθόν has in these passages a meaning different from 'conducive
to our happiness': but, as we have seen, his reason for saying
ἀγαθόν has a new meaning in these two passages is invalid (nor
does he explain what *ἀγαθόν does* mean in them).

But Professor Prichard has another and quite radical difficulty
to face in connexion with Aristotle's discussions of pleasure,
which in his paper he appears not to appreciate. For Aristotle
there discusses the relation of *ἡδονή* to *εὐδαιμονία* in such a
manner as to make it quite plain that *these*.two Greek words do
not mean the same.[1] Whereas Professor Prichard's whole
argument depends on translating *εὐδαιμονία* 'happiness', and

[1] *εὐδαιμονία is τὸ ἄριστον, ἡδονή* is *not τὸ ἄριστον*: and so on.

taking 'happiness' to be equivalent to 'pleasure' which *must* (we assume) be the translation of ἡδονή: so that ἡδονή and εὐδαιμονία ought to mean the same. Hence Professor Prichard must hold that, in these discussions, not merely ἀγαθόν, but *also* either εὐδαιμονία or ἡδονή changes its meaning from the normal. Otherwise his view is untenable. As to which alternative he would choose, I do not know: but both are very difficult. He can scarcely hold that εὐδαιμονία changes its meaning, for, as we shall see, much of his argumentation depends on his view that the meaning of εὐδαιμονία was clear and unambiguous. As to ἡδονή, he does hold, as we shall see, that the word is sometimes used in a special restricted sense to include only the σωματικαὶ ἡδοναί: but it is obviously quite impossible to hold that it has only this restricted sense throughout the two full-dress discussions of pleasure. Unfortunately, Professor Prichard does not notice this additional difficulty.

Even the exclusion of these passages would not suffice to save Professor Prichard's view from refutation. It would still be open to Professor Prichard to maintain (and in view of his low opinion of Aristotle's *Ethics*, I think it possible he might do so) that, even apart from other arguments such as that about φαῦλον and μοχθηρόν, these very facts which I have just mentioned are themselves sufficient to show that the two discussions of pleasure are inconsistent with the rest of the *NE* and may therefore be neglected. It need scarcely be pointed out how dangerous this would be: for we are trying to discover the meanings of ἀγαθόν (and εὐδαιμονία) and it is scarcely permissible to eliminate a large part of the evidence, not otherwise known to be incompatible with the rest, on the ground that it will not square with our interpretation of those meanings. At least it would be necessary to *prove* that εὐδαιμονία *must* elsewhere mean 'pleasure': but, it seems to me, Professor Prichard does not prove this, he assumes it.

However, it would in any case be of no use to exclude from consideration the 'two discussions of pleasure'. For pleasure is mentioned in many other parts of the *NE*, and precisely the

same difficulties for Professor Prichard's view are to be found
in them also.

Let us confine ourselves to book i, since it is upon that book
that Professor Prichard principally relies, including chapters
v and xii, which he cites.

In i. v we are told that οἱ πολλοὶ καὶ φορτικώτατοι maintain
that εὐδαιμονία is ἡδονή and that Aristotle himself *rejects* this
view. According to Professor Prichard's interpretation, it
would seem that he ought to accept it, as tautological. Professor Prichard did reply, when faced with this, that ἡδονή here,
being the end of the ἀπολαυστικὸς βίος, has a special restricted
meaning which includes only the σωματικαὶ ἡδοναί (cf. VII. xiii.
6).[1] This is scarcely obvious, and we should have expected
Aristotle's rejection to take a rather different form, if he himself held that our end *is* ἡδονή, although not merely the σωματικαὶ
ἡδοναί. However, we need not insist on this passage; others are
plainer.

In i. xii. 5, what Eudoxus said about ἡδονή is compared with
what Aristotle himself says about εὐδαιμονία: clearly, then,
ἡδονή and εὐδαιμονία are distinct. And, whatever may be true of
Sardanapallus, there is no reason whatever to suppose that
Eudoxus meant by ἡδονή merely the σωματικαὶ ἡδοναί.

Finally, in i. viii the relation of ἡδονή to εὐδαιμονία is discussed very much as in books VII and X: εὐδαιμονία is μεθ'
ἡδονῆς ἢ οὐκ ἄνευ ἡδονῆς,[2] but quite clearly it is distinct from it.
(Even if they are necessarily connected, we must not confuse
one with the other: cf. *EE* i. ii. 5.)

We do not, naturally enough, find in book i a discussion
as to whether ἡδονή is an ἀγαθόν. But the views that it is τὸ
ἀγαθόν or τὸ ἄριστον are mentioned, and, though rejected,
not rejected as absurdities (i. v and xii). Moreover, as was
pointed out above, Eudoxus' views are mentioned in i. i and xii

---

[1] Just as, when Aristotle says ἡδονή is ἀγαθόν, Professor Prichard says ἀγαθόν
has a meaning different from the ordinary, so, when Aristotle distinguishes
ἡδονή from εὐδαιμονία, Professor Prichard says ἡδονή has a meaning different
from the ordinary.

[2] 'Accompanied by pleasure or not without pleasure'.—Ed.

in pretty much the same words as in x. ii, so that it would seem
that the meaning of ἀγαθόν ought to be the same in each case.

We see, then, that Professor Prichard cannot exclude VII.
xi–xiv and x. i–v from consideration, and that they are fatal
to his view. But even if we do exclude them, other passages,
equally fatal, can be produced even from book I, on which he
relies. So that, if he still maintains the view, it would seem that
he must be prepared to attribute to Aristotle even more and
graver inconsistencies and oversights than those, already so
numerous, which he attributes to him in his article. Myself,
I am not yet prepared to do this: though I am only too well
aware how imperfect the *Ethics* is in these respects.

Present state of the problem. So far our results are negative.
εὐδαιμονία does *not* mean a state or feeling of pleasure and
ἀγαθόν does *not* mean conducive to our pleasure. (It is, however,
still possible that ἀγαθόν may mean conducive to our *happiness*,
if 'happiness' is not equivalent to 'pleasure'.) It certainly is
important to discover, therefore, what these two words *do*
mean. Of the two, εὐδαιμονία is, for reasons which will appear,
considerably the easier to elucidate, and accordingly I shall
consider it first.

Τί ἐστιν εὐδαιμονία; the meaning of the question. Once again I
shall take my start from Professor Prichard's article. In a
passage extending from p. 36 at the bottom to p. 38, he argues
that evidence for his view is to be found in *NE* I. iv. I must
quote, I am afraid, at some length.

At the beginning of Chapter IV he [Aristotle] directs his hearers'
attention to the question . . . 'What is it that is the greatest of all
achievable goods?' and he proceeds to say that while there is general
agreement about the name for it, since both the many and the
educated say that it is happiness, yet they differ about what happiness
is, the many considering it something the nature of which is clear
and obvious, such as pleasure, wealth, or honour, whereas, he implies, the educated consider it something else, of which the nature
is not obvious. Then in the next chapter he proceeds to state what,
to judge from the most prominent types of life, that of enjoyment,

the political life, and that of contemplation, various men consider that the good or happiness is, viz. enjoyment, honour, and contemplation. And later he gives his own view ... that happiness is ψυχῆς ἐνέργειά τις κατ᾽ ἀρετὴν τελείαν.

Here it has to be admitted that Aristotle is expressing himself in a misleading way. His question, 'What is the greatest of goods?' can be treated as if it had been the question, 'What is man's ultimate end?' ... And his answer to this question, if taken as it stands, is undeniably absurd. For, so understood, it is to the effect that, though all men, when asked 'What is the ultimate end?' answer by using the same word, viz. εὐδαιμονία, yet, as they differ about what εὐδαιμονία is, i.e. really, about the thing for which they are using the word εὐδαιμονία to stand, some using it to designate pleasure, others wealth, and so on, they are in substance giving different answers, some meaning by the word εὐδαιμονία pleasure, others wealth, and so on. But of course this is not what Aristotle meant. He certainly did not think that anyone ever meant by εὐδαιμονία either τιμή or πλοῦτος; and he certainly did not himself mean by it ψυχῆς ἐνέργειά τις κατ᾽ ἀρετὴν τελείαν. What he undoubtedly meant and thought others meant by the word εὐδαιμονία is happiness. Plainly too, what he thought men differed about was not the nature of happiness but the conditions of its realization, and when he says that εὐδαιμονία is ψυχῆς ἐνέργειά τις κατ᾽ ἀρετὴν τελείαν, what he really means is that the latter is what is required for the realization of happiness ... his meaning is similar to that of the man who, when he asks 'What is colour?' or 'What is sound?', really means 'What are the conditions necessary for its realization?'

Here is the passage, 1. iv. 1–3: Λέγωμεν ... τί τὸ πάντων ἀκρότατον τῶν πρακτῶν ἀγαθῶν. ὀνόματι μὲν οὖν σχεδὸν ὑπὸ τῶν πλείστων ὁμολογεῖται· τὴν γὰρ εὐδαιμονίαν καὶ οἱ πολλοὶ καὶ οἱ χαρίεντες λέγουσιν, τὸ δ᾽ εὖ ζῆν καὶ τὸ εὖ πράττειν ταὐτὸν ὑπολαμβάνουσι τῷ εὐδαιμονεῖν. περὶ δὲ τῆς εὐδαιμονίας, τί ἐστιν, ἀμφισβητοῦσι καὶ οὐχ ὁμοίως οἱ πολλοὶ τοῖς σοφοῖς ἀποδιδόασιν. οἳ μὲν γὰρ τῶν ἐναργῶν τι καὶ φανερῶν, οἷον ἡδονὴν ἢ πλοῦτον ἢ τιμήν, κτλ.[1]

---

[1] 'Let us state ... what is the highest of all goods achievable by action. Verbally there is very general agreement; for both the general run of men and people of superior refinement say that it is happiness, and identify living well

Whence does Professor Prichard derive his confidence that Aristotle is misrepresenting his own problem? If he is, it must be admitted that the misrepresentation is pretty consistent. Right through to book x Aristotle always purports to be telling us 'what εὐδαιμονία is'. (He summarizes the present passage in almost the same words again in I. vii. 9.)[1] Moreover, Aristotle is, of course, aware of the very kind of misrepresentation of which Professor Prichard accuses him: compare what he says about *pleasure* in VII. xii. 3 and X. iii. 6, rebuking those who maintained that pleasure *is* a γένεσις, when they really meant that a certain γένεσις is the condition of the realization of pleasure.

The real reason for Professor Prichard's confidence is to be found in his unquestioned assumption that εὐδαιμονία means pleasure. This assumption is stated in the passage above: 'What Aristotle undoubtedly meant and thought others meant by εὐδαιμονία is happiness.' (This is, of course, rather odd as it stands, since Aristotle did not know English: it would lose its plausibility if we substituted ἡδονή for 'happiness'.) For if εὐδαιμονία were the Greek word for 'pleasure', it might well be contended that to ask τί ἐστιν εὐδαιμονία; *must* be misleading: for it might very well be held[2] that 'pleasure' stands for something unanalysable and *sui generis*, which we either know, and know with entire adequacy, from experiencing it, or do not know at all. Pleasure might, on these lines, very well be considered to be in the same case as colour and sound, to which, accordingly, Professor Prichard without hesitation compares εὐδαιμονία. In such cases, one who asks 'what is so-and-so?' will very probably be found to be asking 'what are the conditions for its realization?' And whether or not 'pleasure' could in any sense be analysed, at least, e.g., the

and doing well with being happy; but with regard to what happiness is they differ, and the many do not give the same account as the wise. For the former think it is some plain and obvious thing, like pleasure, wealth, or honour, etc.'—Ed.

[1] The only reasonable alternative is to hold that in both passages it is really τὸ ἄριστον ἀνθρώπῳ which is being elucidated.

[2] I do not inquire whether this would be correct.

person who said pleasure is honour or wealth would obviously be suspect of only really intending to give conditions of realization.

However, εὐδαιμονία does not mean pleasure, as we have seen. And this very passage proves as well as another that it does not. This is not merely because the theory that εὐδαιμονία means or 'is' ἡδονή is rejected, but also because in a most important clause omitted in Professor Prichard's paraphrase, εὐδαιμονία is said to be equivalent to τὸ εὖ ζῆν καὶ τὸ εὖ πράττειν, which cannot mean 'feeling pleased'. To this we shall return shortly.

Professor Prichard seems to make out that, apart from the fact that the Greeks did not disagree about what εὐδαιμονία stands for, Aristotle's actual presentation of his question makes it in general an absurd one. Certainly, Professor Prichard's ostensible argument for maintaining that Aristotle here misrepresents his own problem is not very explicit. According to him, Aristotle says that men agree only on the *name* for the τέλος, viz. εὐδαιμονία, but disagree about what it is used to stand for, or to designate. This, he says, is undeniably absurd. Now why? Has Professor Prichard any other reason for saying so, except his belief that there could, in fact (owing to the unanalysable nature of what εὐδαιμονία does stand for), be no disagreement about what εὐδαιμονία stands for?

He seems to suppose that, according to Aristotle, (1) men agree *only* on the name; (2) that is a substantial measure of agreement; (3) what is being (mistakenly) asked for is some *synonym* for εὐδαιμονία, in the simplest sense—some other word or phrase which stands for precisely the same as εὐδαιμονία stands for. (Somewhat as though, when asked for the answer to a mathematical problem, all should agree that the name for the answer was '*k*' while disagreeing as to the number which '*k*' stands for.) I do not know whether even this would be undeniably absurd (always assuming that in fact all did *not* know εὐδαιμονία to stand for 'pleasure'): but in any case Aristotle does none of these things.

1. According to Aristotle, men agree, not merely on the name εὐδαιμονία, but also that εὐδαιμονία is equivalent to τὸ εὖ

ζῆν καὶ τὸ εὖ πράττειν. (This statement Professor Prichard omits in his paraphrase.) Moreover, it transpires later that they also agree on a number of other propositions about the characteristics of εὐδαιμονία, which are listed in chapters viii and ix–xii.

2. As is shown by I. vii. 9, Aristotle does *not* think that the agreement on the name alone is very substantial. And indeed it is clear even from chapter iv that this agreement could cover most radical disagreements.

3. Aristotle is not, I believe, searching for some simple synonym for εὐδαιμονία, but rather for an 'analysis' of its meaning. While satisfactory as a preliminary statement, this does not make it sufficiently clear what exactly Aristotle is doing.[1] All men know more or less *vaguely* what is meant by εὐδαιμονία or τὸ εὖ ζῆν καὶ τὸ εὖ πράττειν, and agree on many propositions about it: but when they attempt to *clarify* that meaning, they disagree. Cf. I. vii. 9: ἀλλ' ἴσως τὴν μὲν εὐδαιμονίαν τὸ ἄριστον λέγειν ὁμολογούμενόν τι φαίνεται, ποθεῖται δ' ἐναργέστερον τί ἐστιν ἔτι λεχθῆναι.[2]

To search thus for an analysis of the meaning of εὐδαιμονία does not seem to me absurd, except on the false assumption that its meaning was, and was known to be, simple and un-analysable. We might, to take a similar case, agree that the aim of the statesman is 'liberty' or 'justice', and yet, in a perfectly intelligible sense, disagree about 'what liberty is' or 'what justice is'.

** There is no doubt, however, that this account of what Aristotle is asking when he asks τί ἐστιν εὐδαιμονία; is far from entirely satisfying. For we need to distinguish from the analysis of the meaning of εὐδαιμονία another procedure altogether, namely the 'discovery' of those things, or that life, as he would rather ordinarily say, which satisfy the definition of εὐδαιμονία when that has been discovered. As Moore has insisted in the

---

[1] At this point, in view of the state of the manuscript, some editing by Mr. Urmson was required.—Ed.

[2] 'Presumably, however, to say that happiness is the chief good seems a platitude, and a clearer account of what it is is still desired.'—Ed.

** See below under the same sign.

case of 'good' (which will occupy us later), it is important to distinguish the discovery of what a word means from the discovery of those things in which the characters meant by the word in fact reside. (Of course this latter procedure is still not what Prichard means when he speaks of discovering 'the conditions for the realization' of something.) This is too simple a view for modern times, since few will accept that goodness is a character in this simple sense. But we still would distinguish the meaning of εὐδαιμονία—the best life for man, etc.—from what we may call the specification of the good life: what the good life allegedly consists in concretely. The whole problem arises over the connexion between these two.

There is justice in Prichard's remark that Aristotle 'certainly does not think that anyone ever *meant* by εὐδαιμονία either τιμή or πλοῦτος'. They were capable of having *said* that they meant this, but would have more plausibly claimed that τιμή or πλοῦτος was what satisfied the specification of εὐδαιμονία. But it is not so clear that 'he certainly did not himself mean by it ψυχῆς ἐνέργειά τις κατ' ἀρετὴν τελείαν', at least ἐν βίῳ τελείῳ. It is hard to discover, especially in I. vii, where the analysis ends and the other process begins. It is perhaps impossible to judge how much is meant to be analysis. Certainly εὐδαιμονία is analysed (ταὐτὸν ὑπολαμβάνουσι) as τὸ εὖ ζῆν καὶ τὸ εὖ πράττειν. Then ἐν βίῳ τελείῳ (ambiguous phrase!) also seems clearly part of the meaning of εὐδαιμονία. I *believe* that the whole of I. vii. 9–16 is intended to be an analysis of that meaning. And it results, as it should, in a clear and full definition, referred to as ὁ λόγος of εὐδαιμονία or of τὸ ἄριστον. Moreover EE II. i. 10 says that ψυχῆς ἐνέργεια κατ' ἀρετήν is τὸ γένος καὶ τὸν ὅρον εὐδαιμονίας. If it had been said that Aristotle did not *mean* by εὐδαιμονία θεωρία, that would, I think, be certainly true: and it is θεωρία which, in Aristotle's theory, occupies the place of ἡδονή and πλοῦτος in rival theories, as chapter v plainly shows.

But when Aristotle discusses what are in fact the special virtues, and which is the most perfect, he cannot be said any longer to be analysing the meaning of εὐδαιμονία. He is asking τί ἐστιν εὐδαιμονία; in a different sense: what are the virtues that fill the bill. Even in x. viii. 8, where the conclusion is reached: ὥστ᾽ εἴη ἂν ἡ εὐδαιμονία θεωρία τις, it is evident that εὐδαιμονία does not mean θεωρία—ἐφ᾽ ὅσον δὴ διατείνει ἡ θεωρία καὶ ἡ εὐδαιμονία, καὶ οἷς μᾶλλον ὑπάρχει τὸ θεωρεῖν καὶ εὐδαιμονεῖν οὐ κατὰ συμβεβηκὸς ἀλλὰ κατὰ τὴν θεωρίαν.**

So Aristotle's distinction between analysis and specification is most unclear. But there is some excuse for Aristotle perhaps, in that εὐδαιμονία does not stand for some character, such as goodness might be, but for a certain kind of life, or ἐνέργεια (Aristotle is unclear as to which): in such a case it is not so easy clearly to observe Professor Moore's distinction, or even one such as Hare's or Urmson's between meaning and criteria. Suppose we were to ask, for instance, 'What is golfing?'. But there is this finally to be said. If Aristotle had thought that εὐδαιμονία, like golfing, resided in fact in only one activity of one kind of creature, there would have been more excuse for him than is actually the case. For actually he does think that εὐδαιμονία is achieved, in different ways, by gods and by men: hence εὐδαιμονία cannot mean those activities in which human εὐδαιμονία is found. (Unfortunately, of course, his statements on divine εὐδαιμονία are rudimentary, and it is very doubtful, e.g., how ἐν βίῳ τελείῳ can be a part of the meaning of εὐδαιμονία if the gods are also εὐδαίμονες!)

Some distinctions, however, though not this requisite one, Aristotle does draw: in a way he was perhaps on his way to it. In *Rhet.* I. v *ad init.* he says we must ask: τί ἐστιν εὐδαιμονία καὶ τὰ μόρια αὐτῆς; and this distinction is common, though not in the *NE.* In *EE* I. v. 13–14, he calls the particular virtues μόρια τῆς ἀγαθῆς ζωῆς, which συντείνουσι πρὸς εὐδαιμονίαν. (This does

** The material included between the double stars required extensive editing by Mr. Urmson because the manuscript on these pages was complicated by notes, corrections, and revisions. Ross's translation of this Greek passage reads: 'Happiness extends, then, just so far as contemplation does, and those to whom contemplation more fully belongs are more truly happy, not as mere concomitant but in virtue of the contemplation; . . . Happiness, therefore, must be some form of contemplation'.—Ed.

not, of course, mean that they are 'the conditions for the realization' of εὐδαιμονία: in *NE* 1129ᵇ18, where the μόρια εὐδαιμονίας
are mentioned, they are distinguished from τὰ ποιητικὰ καὶ
φυλακτικὰ εὐδαιμονίας [cf. VI. xii. 5], a distinction insisted on in,
e.g., *EE* I. ii. 5. There is a similar distinction in *EE* I. i of ἐν
τίσι τὸ εὖ ζῆν from πῶς κτητόν; compare also *MM* I. ii. 9–11:
οὐ γὰρ ἐστιν ἄλλο τι χωρὶς τούτων ἡ εὐδαιμονία ἀλλὰ ταῦτα.)¹ Now
in effect, the discovery of the μόρια εὐδαιμονίας is the discovery of the activities which together make up the life which,
for man, satisfies the definition of εὐδαιμονία; and we can in
a sense say, as Aristotle does, that this life *is* εὐδαιμονία. Nevertheless, εὐδαιμονία does not *mean* that life, and its discovery is
posterior to the analysis of the meaning of εὐδαιμονία. Two
erroneous presuppositions were, however, encouraged by
Aristotle's failure to be clear what question he is asking when
he writes τί ἐστιν εὐδαιμονία; first, the presupposition that
εὐδαιμονία— the ideal life—is not a will-o'-the-wisp, and that
there is only one possible ideal life; second, that the question
of what fills the bill is throughout purely factual.

Summing up then, the question τί ἐστιν εὐδαιμονία; is
sensible but ambiguous. Aristotle means to ask firstly: what
is the analysis or definition of εὐδαιμονία? and secondly: what
life, in particular for man, satisfies that definition or specification? (A subsidiary and distinct question is: What are the
conditions ὧν οὐκ ἄνευ, and the methods necessary for the
realization of such a life?)

What does εὐδαιμονία *mean? Some general considerations.* We
must now concern ourselves with the first of these questions:
What does εὐδαιμονία mean in Greek and incidentally what is
its translation in English? But I cannot enter into details of
Aristotle's own analysis: I shall only attempt to show what,
according to him, was the vague and common notion of
εὐδαιμονία from which his analysis starts.

¹ It is important to remember this when interpreting such a passage as
I. vii. 5. Compare *EE* II. i. 12, a better statement. [Austin's *MM* is a reference
to *Magna Moralia*.—Ed.]

According to I. iv. 2 τὸ εὐδαιμονεῖν was admittedly equivalent to τὸ εὖ ζῆν καὶ τὸ εὖ πράττειν. (In I. vii. 4 there is a weaker statement: it is admitted 'that the εὐδαίμων lives and acts well'—but, as Aristotle remarks, on his own account εὐδαιμονία is living and acting well: and in both the other *Ethics* the statement is given as in I. iv. 2; cf. *MM* I. iii. 3; *EE* II. i. 10 and I. i. 7.) εὐδαιμονία, then, *means* living a life of a certain kind—of *what* kind can of course only be discovered by analysing the word εὖ, and hence ἀγαθόν (so that the full analysis of εὐδαιμονία includes that of ἀγαθόν). εὐδαίμων, I suppose, means literally or, what is often the same, etymologically, 'prospered by a deity': and what the deities prosper is lives or careers or activities or parts of these. Aristotle insists on two further points—εὐδαιμονία means a *complete* life of *activity* of a certain kind. On the latter point, that the reference is to ἐνέργεια not to ἕξις, he is always firm (cf. also I. xii).[1] On the former point he is not so happy: not only is βίος τέλειος hopelessly ambiguous (cf. *MM* I. iv. 5), but Aristotle often omits to remember this qualification. So much so that in the end he never explains how the βίος *is* made up—only the ἀρεταί which predominate it.

At any rate, what is important in all this is, that, though of course we can speak of a *man* as εὐδαίμων, the substantive with which εὐδαίμων naturally goes is βίος or a similar word: a man is only called εὐδαίμων because his life is so. Hence the discussion in chapter v of the various βίοι which lay claim to being εὐδαιμονία.[2] And hence the saying 'call no man εὐδαίμων until he is dead' (I. x. i).

[1] On p. 38, Professor Prichard makes what seem to me serious misstatements about I. xii. 'In other words . . . everything else.' The contrast in the first sentence I, of course, consider mistaken. As for the rest, the quotation given is actually from section viii where εὐδαιμονία is not contrasted with ἀρετή at all. The contrast with ἀρετή is in ii. and vi: ἀρετή is ἐπαινετόν qua τὸ ποῖον καὶ πρός τι εἶναι—viz. the ἐνέργειαι (πράξεις, ἔργα) which are εὐδαιμονία: the ἐνέργειαι are τίμια and the εὐδαιμονία. Professor Prichard talks as though in xii ἐνέργειαι κατ' ἀρετήν were ἐπαινετά: they are τίμια!

[2] And when in I. iv the suggestion is made that εὐδαιμονία *is* ἡδονή or πλοῦτος, that is loose language (as v shows) for the life in which most pleasure or most wealth is gained.

Similarly the forms εὐδαιμονίζειν and εὐδαιμονισμός, which seem to mean 'to congratulate', 'congratulation'. That whereon I congratulate someone is an *achievement*, an activity and normally a completed one (though normally also, of course, of less extent than his whole career). With reference to this point consider I. v. 6 and viii. 9.

These considerations show conclusively that εὐδαιμονία could not *mean* 'pleasure': pleasure is a *feeling*, not a life of a certain kind nor an achievement: nor do I congratulate someone on his feeling pleased: and it would be silly to say 'call no man pleased until he is dead'.

There is, however, Aristotle's own remark in I. iv that many people do maintain that εὐδαιμονία is ἡδονή, as others πλοῦτος or τιμή. This is a loose remark— as Professor Prichard claims, though not in his way. His explanation, that Aristotle meant that some maintain that εὐδαιμονία is *produced* by ἡδονή, also πλοῦτος, etc., is incorrect. Aristotle himself shows what he meant more fully in chapter v. The view was that εὐδαιμονία is the ἀπολαυστικὸς βίος, the life in which most pleasure is felt. Likewise the identification with πλοῦτος should be taken as 'the life in which most wealth is gained' (not, of course, 'is by definition' but 'in fact resides in').

If we want a translation of εὐδαιμονία which will not mislead, as 'happiness' appears to mislead Professor Prichard, we might use as a prophylactic 'success'. 'Success' is at least a word of the same *type*, so to say, as εὐδαιμονία. 'Success' does mean living and acting well: a life or a part of it is 'successful': and with some hesitations I do congratulate on 'success'; it might well be said 'call no man successful until he is dead'. Furthermore, success demands just that fortunate supply of εὐτυχία, εὐημερία, which Aristotle admits in I. viii. 15–17 is also a necessary condition for εὐδαιμονία.

It is true, however, that 'success' is not a moral notion for us. Perhaps this is no great disadvantage, for it is doubtful how far a pagan ethic, such as the Greek (or the Chinese), gains by a translation which imports our own moral notions:

εὐδαιμονία is certainly quite an unchristian ideal. Still, we do require a word to import some form of *commendation*, as εὐδαίμων did, and certain non-personal standards.

**That εὐδαιμονία did mean life of *activity* of a certain kind is almost certainly the correct analysis; and that it did further mean life of ἀρεταί seems equally correct. So we may say that the analysis in I. vii. 8–16 is correct and is supported by I. viii. However we must also say: (*a*) That roundabout way of bringing into the discussion ψυχή and ἔργον is a piece of unnecessary Aristotelian metaphysics. It is not really made use of until the very end, in the argument for the supremacy of θεωρία; the argument proceeds straight on to the ἀρεταί. (*b*) The whole discussion here is *not* purely factual; its nature is disguised by the transference of commendation to the ἀρεταί. (*c*) Of the three lives suggested none accords with the popular view which was that of Tellus the Athenian.[1] His ideal is omitted altogether except when allowed in by the backdoor suddenly in book x. (*d*) It might be argued that he omits to give sufficient consideration to μεθ' ἡδονῆς ἢ οὐκ ἄνευ ἡδονῆς and it might be argued further that not enough deference is shown to ψυχικόν—people may have meant by this something genuinely internal, as did later the Stoics. Quite possibly εὐδαιμονία *did* have this 'meaning' too.

Nevertheless, 'happiness' is probably after all to be preferred as a translation, partly because it is traditional, and still more because it is fairly colourless.[2] It seems to me very rash to assume that in common English 'happiness' obviously means feeling pleased: probably it has several more or less vague meanings. Take the lines:

** . . . ** This passage appears to be a later addition by Austin, which we inserted here in a somewhat expanded form.—Ed.

[1] Tellus the Athenian is mentioned by Plutarch in his *Life of Solon*, where Solon is said to describe him as a happy man on account of his honesty, his having good children, his having a competent estate, and his having died bravely in battle for his country. Tellus appears to have been a plain man whose happiness, nevertheless, Solon holds up to Croesus.—Ed.

[2] Success also does not always or usually refer to life *as a whole*: and it has perhaps a nuance of *competitiveness*.

> This is the happy warrior, this is He
> That every Man at arms should wish to be.

I do not think Wordsworth meant by that: 'This is the warrior who feels *pleased*.' Indeed, he is

> Doomed to go in company with Pain
> And fear and bloodshed, miserable train.

(Though no doubt his life is μεθ' ἡδονῆς ἢ οὐκ ἄνευ ἡδονῆς as Aristotle likes to assume or feebly to argue his own chosen one must be.) What every man at arms is being incited to wish, is not so much to get for himself *feelings* comparable to those of the paragon, as to imitate his *life*. I think, then, that if we are on our guard against misleading nuances, 'happiness' is still the best translation for εὐδαιμονία.

The question of the relation of εὐδαιμονία to ἡδονή has not, it should be noticed, yet been cleared up. It to a great extent coincides with the equally difficult problem of the relation of τὸ ἀγαθόν to τὸ ἡδύ. Both must be reserved for a separate discussion later.

ἀγαθόν—Does Aristotle tell us what its meaning is? Professor Prichard's contention is, it will be remembered, that Aristotle really means by ἀγαθόν 'conducive to our happiness'. Not concerning ourselves for the moment with the precise interpretation given, we may notice, *firstly*, that he is purporting to give Aristotle's answer to a question which Aristotle himself expressly declines to answer, viz. what is the meaning of ἀγαθόν? And *secondly*, that the answer given, implying as it does that ἀγαθόν does have a *single* meaning, is of a kind which Aristotle himself is at pains to prove impossible.

Let us take the translation of ἀγαθόν as 'good' here for granted, and let us once more, following Professor Moore, distinguish between two very different sorts of question, which are commonly asked in books on ethics. We are investigating, we may say, the Good: but we may intend to ask: (1) What does the word 'good' mean?[1] or (2) What things are good, and in what degrees? Of course, these two questions may be formulated in a variety of ways. For (1) we may substitute: What is the nature of goodness? or: In saying of anything that it is good, what am I saying about it? even: What sort of a predicate is 'good'? and so on. For (2) we may substitute: Of what things may it be truly said that they are good? And which is the best of them? and so on.

To these two different sorts of question, as Moore claimed, we shall get two correspondingly different sorts of answer. To (1) the answer might be: Goodness is a simple unanalysable quality like yellow, or: 'Good' means 'approved by me', or: To say of anything that it is good, is to say that it is conducive to happiness, or: 'Good' is an evaluative word. Whereas to (2), the answer might be: Friendship is good, or: Violence is better than justice, and so on. Note here that it is assumed that the only sense in which ἀγαθόν has a 'meaning' is some 'factual' sense. Aristotle assumes this too.

Now we must ask, on this distinction does Aristotle concern himself with both these questions or with one only? And if the latter, with which? And I think that we must answer, that he concerns himself professedly with the second only.[2]

For Aristotle himself is aware of and draws this distinction between the two questions, and says that, in the *Ethics*, he is concerned only with the second. This he does in the celebrated chapter I. vi. He there confutes those who had supposed that the word ἀγαθόν always stands for a single identical predicate.[3]

---

[1] Which is itself probably an ambiguous question, but we may let this pass for the moment. (We also have to distinguish (a) how to translate a word? (b) what does someone say about the analysis of the meaning or of the definition of a word? and both of these from (c) possibly different senses of 'mean'.)

[2] And with that only in the more special form: 'What particular things are good, and in what degrees, *for man*?'

[3] Compare H. W. B. Joseph, *Some Problems in Ethics* (Oxford, 1931), p. 75: 'That goodness is not a quality is the burden of Aristotle's argument in *NE* I. vi.': but this is not quite correct. Aristotle is anxious to say that ἀγαθόν has no

But in proving this, he does not tell us what are the various meanings of ἀγαθόν—the furthest he goes in that direction is to give us a hint as to how the various meanings may be related to one another, i.e. how the variety yet forms a unity. He then dismisses the matter, 1096ᵇ30: ἀλλ' ἴσως ταῦτα μὲν ἀφετέον τὸ νῦν. ἐξακριβοῦν γὰρ ὑπὲρ αὐτῶν ἄλλης ἂν εἴη φιλοσοφίας οἰκειό-τερον.[1] He then turns to his present problem: What is that good which is πρακτὸν καὶ κτητὸν ἀνθρώπῳ, that is: What particular things are good for man (and in what degrees)? Unfortunately, as is well known, he does not in fact discuss 'the meaning of ἀγαθόν' elsewhere.

It is clear, then, that Aristotle declines in general to discuss the meanings of ἀγαθόν but argues that it has no single meaning. In both respects Professor Prichard's view conflicts, *prima facie*, with Aristotle's statements. Nevertheless, it may be urged both that Aristotle is unjustified in declining to explain the meaning of ἀγαθόν, and that he must himself attach some meaning to it in using it throughout the *Ethics*, which we may be able to discover. And further, that meaning might be identical in all important cases (this will be explained later).

If asked to justify himself, there is no doubt how Aristotle would reply.[2] The *NE* is only intended as a guide for politicians, and they are only concerned to know what is good, not what goodness means. Probably Platonists would have said that I cannot discover what is good until I have found the definition of goodness, but Aristotle would claim that the definition, if possible at all, is only necessary if we wish to *demonstrate* scientifically that certain things are good. So much ἀκρίβεια is not called for in the *NE*, and in any case one can know what things are good without knowing the analysis of 'good'.[3]

single meaning— whether a quality, a relation, or anything else. As a matter of fact, he says it does sometimes stand for a quality.

[1] 'But perhaps these subjects had better be dismissed for the present; for perfect precision about them would be more appropriate to another branch of philosophy.'—Ed.

[2] Aristotle does to some extent reply to this objection in I. vi. 14–16.

[3] I do not, however, accept Burnet's exaggerated view of the 'dialectical' method of the *NE*.

Whether this reply is satisfactory is doubtful. Certainly there is much to be said on Aristotle's side. Firstly, as Moore pointed out, we can know something to be true without knowing its analysis. Secondly, as Aristotle pointed out in I. vi. 4, if goodness is an isolable, definable property we should be able to study it in isolation from all subject-matters, whereas in fact there is no such study. Thirdly, even those who, like Moore, find goodness 'unanalysable' still go on to discuss what is good. But in any case it must be admitted that his method has its dangers; and whether they are serious can best be judged by its results in the body of the NE. (In at least two cases, those of ἡδονή and φιλία and perhaps also in that of τιμή, the lack of a clearer account of the meaning or meanings of ἀγαθόν is in fact most serious.)

The extent to which Aristotle does in fact attach a discoverable, and even single, meaning to ἀγαθόν will, of course, concern us largely. But before proceeding, it is worth considering an example of the extreme lengths to which Professor Prichard is prepared to go in imputing inconsistency to Aristotle. His view, we said, implies that ἀγαθόν does have a single meaning, i.e. does always stand for an identical common character in the subjects of which it is predicated. (Note that we need 'character' here, not 'quality'; for, of course, one of Professor Prichard's main contentions is that Aristotle mistakes 'being conducive to our happiness' for a *quality* of that which is so conducive, whereas it is not.) And this, we said, conflicts with Aristotle's own statement that ἀγαθόν does not do this.

Now it may be thought that I have been wasting unnecessary words over this, since Professor Prichard himself notices this objection and answers it on pp. 32–3:

But Aristotle in saying, as he would have said, that in pursuing, e.g. an honour, we are pursuing it ὡς ἀγαθόν, could only have meant that we are pursuing it in virtue of thinking that it would possess a certain character to which he refers by the term ἀγαθόν, so that by ἀγαθόν he must mean to indicate some character which certain things would have. Further, this being so, in implying as he does

that in pursuing things of certain different kinds καθ' αὐτά we are
pursuing them ὡς ἀγαθά, he must be implying that these things of
different kinds have, nevertheless, a common character, viz. that
indicated by the term ἀγαθόν. It will, of course, be objected that he
expressly denies that they have a common character. For he says:
τιμῆς δὲ καὶ φρονήσεως καὶ ἡδονῆς ἕτεροι καὶ διαφέροντες οἱ λόγοι
ταύτῃ ᾗ ἀγαθά (*Ethics* I. vi. 11).[1] But the answer is simple; viz. that
this is merely an inconsistency into which he is driven by his inability
to find in these things the common character which his theory
requires him to find, and that if he is to succeed in maintaining that
we pursue these things of various kinds ὡς ἀγαθά he *has* to maintain
that in spite of appearances to the contrary they have a common
character.

We are not concerned for the moment with this doctrine
about 'pursuing things ὡς ἀγαθά.'[2] But what we must notice
is that Professor Prichard quotes the sentence about τιμή,
φρόνησις, and ἡδονή, as though it were an *unwilling admission*,
into which Aristotle's honesty drives him: as though Aristotle
is admitting that in certain cases he *cannot* find the common
character, which he *must* find. Yet a glance at the context
will show that, on the contrary, the whole passage is designed
to *prove* that there is no such common character: and the
sentence quoted clinches the argument.[3] It is not too much
to say that, if τιμή and the rest *are* possessed of a common
character denoted by ἀγαθόν, the whole argument against the
Platonists is undermined: and Professor Prichard must accuse
Aristotle not so much of inconsistency as of bad faith.

In any case, this passage cannot be thus lightly dismissed.
The objection retains, it seems to me, very considerable weight.

[1] 'But of honour, wisdom, and pleasure, just in respect of their goodness,
the accounts are distinct and diverse.'—Ed.

[2] ὡς ἀγαθά does not in Greek mean 'in virtue of their possessing a certain
characteristic, "goodness"'. It means rather 'pursuing them *in the way in which
we pursue things we say are good*'. Thus the phrase is noncommittal as to whether
there is a common quality or not. Cf. in English 'stating as a fact', 'stating as
a matter of opinion'.

[3] Aristotle does not say he 'cannot find' a common character denoted by
ἀγαθόν in these instances: he says that he knows ἀγαθόν stands for *different*
characters.

ἀγαθόν—Does it mean 'that which is desired' ? We may now turn to the main problem, the meaning of *ἀγαθόν*. It must, I think, be agreed, that there is some chance of our being able to discover what Aristotle does in fact believe about the meaning of the word: but, since Aristotle appears to decline to assist us, that chance is small.

It is on p. 31 that Professor Prichard begins his attempt to elucidate the meaning of *ἀγαθόν*: and he says that 'Aristotle's nearest approach to an elucidation' is to be found in I. vi. 7–11[1] and vii. 1–5. Certain statements there made, he says, 'seem intended as an elucidation of the meaning of *ἀγαθόν*': nevertheless they fail, even formally, to constitute such an elucidation: and moreover, if they *are* 'taken seriously as an elucidation', the result is to render absurd other well-known doctrines in the *Nicomachean Ethics*.

I suppose it cannot be denied that Aristotle is capable of getting himself into pretty tortuous confusions; but this time, at least, I think he can be exonerated.

In the first place, it seems to me that the statements in question are not intended at all as an 'elucidation of the meaning of *ἀγαθόν*' in Professor Prichard's sense.[2] It is, consequently, not surprising that they fail formally to constitute such an elucidation: what is surprising, I think, is Professor Prichard's reason for saying that they so fail. In the second place, if they are 'taken seriously as an elucidation', they do not so much render absurd the doctrines mentioned by Professor Prichard as others which it is easy to find. In these passages, says Professor Prichard, Aristotle

speaks of τὰ καθ' αὑτὰ διωκόμενα καὶ ἀγαπώμενα as called ἀγαθά in one sense . . . and he speaks of τὰ ποιητικὰ τούτων ἢ φυλακτικά πως as called ἀγαθά in another sense, and he implies that these latter are διωκτὰ καὶ αἱρετὰ δι' ἕτερον (*Ethics* I. vii. 4) . . . Further he appears to consider that the difference of meaning is elucidated [*sic*] by referring to the

---

[1] For '7–11' we should read '8–11'.

[2] If any passage deserves the description 'Aristotle's nearest approach to an elucidation' it is probably I. vii. 10 (not mentioned by Professor Prichard); on this *v.i.*

former as ἀγαθὰ καθ' αὑτά and to the latter as ἀγαθὰ διὰ ταῦτα, i.e.
ἀγαθὰ διὰ ἀγαθὰ καθ' αὑτά. But this unfortunately is no elucidation,
since to state a difference of *reason for calling* two things ἀγαθόν is not
to state a difference of meaning of ἀγαθόν, and indeed is to imply
that the meaning in both cases is the same. Nevertheless, these
statements seem intended as an elucidation of the meaning of
ἀγαθόν. And the cause for surprise lies in this, that if they are taken
seriously as an elucidation, the conclusion can only be that ἀγαθόν
includes 'being desired' in its meaning, and indeed simply means
τέλος or end.

It will, I am afraid, necessarily take some considerable space
to clear this matter up.

Let us, as a preliminary, remark that the passage vii. 1–5 is
not concerned with at all the same matter as vi. 8–11. In vii. 1
he asserts that τὸ ἀγαθόν of any activity whatsoever is τὸ τέλος
(incidentally this passage implies that τὸ ἀγαθόν and τὸ τέλος
do not *mean* the same): he then proceeds to ask, what is the
τέλος τῶν πρακτῶν ἁπάντων? And the word ἀγαθόν is not so
much as mentioned again. Moreover, though he does proceed
to distinguish a τέλος καθ' αὑτὸ διωκτόν (αἱρετόν) from a τέλος δι'
ἕτερον διωκτόν (αἱρετόν), he does not assert that the word τέλος
has (in any sense) two meanings, only that there are some
τέλη which are τέλεια (complete or final), others which are not.
Still less, of course, does he assert that τέλεια has two meanings,
or endeavour to elucidate its meaning: he says nothing about
it at all; just as, in vi. 8–11, no mention is made of τέλος
at all.

We may confine ourselves, therefore, to vi. 8–11. Upon
what is Aristotle there engaged? In the earlier part of the
chapter he has been arguing that ἀγαθόν cannot have always an
identical meaning. But now he produces an attempted answer
to his own objections, which is to be understood by referring
to his own logic (*Categories* 1ᵃ 1–15). A word (ὄνομα) may
be used either συνωνύμως, ὁμωνύμως, or παρωνύμως. If, on each
occasion of its use, its connotation (ὁ κατὰ τοὔνομα λόγος τῆς
οὐσίας) is identical, then the word is used συνωνύμως. If, on

different occasions of its use, its connotations are different, then the word is used ὁμωνύμως: e.g. κλείς may be used to mean 'key' or 'collarbone', ζῷον 'animal' or 'picture'. But there is a third possibility: on different occasions of its use, the word may possess connotations which are *partly* identical and *partly* different, in which case the word is said to be used παρωνύμως.[1] There are evidently many ways in which a word can be used paronymously: Aristotle names some of them, and gives examples (τὸ ὑγιεινόν in *Met.* 1003ᵃ33, τὸ ἰατρικόν and τὸ ὑγιεινόν in *Met.* 1060ᵇ37. Also notoriously τὸ ὄν, with which ἀγαθόν here is again compared, and τὸ ἕν. For more details, the reader may refer to those passages, or to Burnet's notes on p. 29 of his edition of the *Ethics*.)[2]

One such type of paronymity is known as the "πρὸς ἕν". When we speak of a 'healthy exercise' the word 'healthy' has a connotation which is only partly the same as that which it has in the phrase 'a healthy body': a healthy exercise is an exercise which produces or preserves healthiness in bodies. Hence healthiness[a], when predicated of an exercise, means 'productive or preservative of healthiness[b]', i.e. of healthiness in the sense in which it is predicated of bodies. Thus 'healthiness[b]' and 'healthiness[a]' have connotations which are partly identical and partly different.

Now, in our present passage, vi. 8–11, Aristotle is producing as an objection against himself the fact (admitted elsewhere, cf. *Rhet.* 1362ᵃ27) that ἀγαθόν is paronymous in this way. His opponents are supposed to claim that, although ἀγαθόν does not always have an identical meaning, that is *merely* because it is paronymous in the above manner. Sometimes it means 'x', sometimes 'productive, etc., of x', etc.; and clearly it is only the 'nuclear' meaning of 'x', which is common to both, with

---

[1] Compare the traditional classification of terms as *univocal, equivocal,* and *analogous.*—Joseph, *An Introduction to Logic* (Oxford, 1916), p. 46: 'analogous' is unsatisfactory, since κατ' ἀναλογίαν is only one form of paronymity.

[2] This supplements and amends *Cat.* I. a bit; homonymy and paronymy are defined by very limited examples there. Consider also *Rhet.* 1362ᵃ21 ff. with regard to this point.

which they are concerned. And it *is* always identical. To which Aristotle replies as follows. First, let us distinguish ἀγαθόν as used in the one sense, from ἀγαθόν as used in the other, by substituting for it, in the one case ἀγαθὸν καθ' αὑτό, and in the other ἀγαθὸν διὰ ἀγαθόν τι καθ' αὑτό.[1] Then let us disregard all cases where ἀγαθόν is used in the latter sense. And finally observe that, even in cases where it is used in the former sense only, it *still* has not always an identical meaning.

Now let us ask, with reference to Professor Prichard's argument quoted above, does Aristotle intend here to 'elucidate the meaning' of ἀγαθόν? It is clear that there is no simple answer, Yes or No, to this question. He does intend to point out that it has at least two meanings, at least in a reasonably strict sense, and to explain how those two meanings are related, and to show how they are in part identical. But he does not intend to elucidate that identical part. Moreover, he proceeds to assert that in fact ἀγαθόν, used in the nuclear way, has at least three different meanings (so that there may be at least six meanings of ἀγαθόν in general): but he does not mean to elucidate any one of the three, nor even to explain how they are related to each other. It is not, then, surprising that Professor Prichard should feel dissatisfied; if we ask his over-simplified question, the passage must 'seem intended as an elucidation' of the meaning of ἀγαθόν, and yet fail to *be* one—for plainly, Professor Prichard would only count as a *real* elucidation, an elucidation of the meaning of ἀγαθόν in the nuclear sense or senses, which Aristotle is not concerned to give him.

Professor Prichard's remark, that 'to state a difference of reason for calling two things ἀγαθόν is not to state a difference of meaning of ἀγαθόν, and indeed is to imply that the meaning in both cases is the same', remains to me obscure. But it seems clear that he has not appreciated the doctrine of παρώνυμα, since he uses the rigid dichotomy 'same meaning—different meaning' whereas παρώνυμα are words which have meanings *partly* the same and *partly* different. His 'difference of reason' might be

[1] πρός might have been expected rather than διά: but διά is more general.

the point about, say, healthy. Then Aristotle would accept the claim, and say that what he offers is *not* an elucidation and is not intended to be one. We have seen, however, that Professor Prichard is prepared to believe that the passage may be seriously intended as an elucidation of ἀγαθόν in the 'nuclear' sense. Seeing that he has already dismissed the distinction between ἀγαθὰ καθ' αὑτά and ἀγαθὰ διὰ ταῦτα as 'no elucidation', and seeing that Aristotle makes no attempt to elucidate the meaning of ἀγαθόν in the nuclear sense, and further states that it has at least three nuclear senses, it is clearly bound to be difficult for Professor Prichard to find anything in the passage which could be described as 'an elucidation of *the* meaning of ἀγαθόν'. He fastens upon the words διωκόμενα καὶ ἀγαπώμενα, διώκεται, διώκομεν and concludes that, according to Aristotle here, ἀγαθόν 'simply means τέλος or end'.[1]

Let us proceed to consider first Professor Prichard's arguments to prove that ἀγαθόν does *not* have that meaning. After asserting that it quite certainly is not used by Aristotle with that meaning [which in a way is true: but surely, then, it is unlikely that he intends to ascribe that meaning to it in this passage?] he proceeds as follows: 'Apart from other considerations, if he did [mean by ἀγαθόν simply τέλος], then for him to say, as he in effect does, that we always aim at ἀγαθόν τί would be to say nothing, and for him to speak, as he does, of the object of βούλησις as τἀγαθόν would be absurd.'

The first of these arguments is perhaps too concise to be clear. 'We always aim at ἀγαθόν τι' may perhaps mean

1. whenever we *act*, we aim at ἀγαθόν τι, or
2. whenever we *aim*, we aim at ἀγαθόν τι.

If (1) is meant, I very much doubt whether Aristotle would maintain it; for we sometimes act from ἐπιθυμία or θυμός, and then we aim at ἡδύ τι or at ἀντιλύπησις. But he might say[2] that in all *deliberate* action we aim at ἀγαθόν τι, as he implies in

---

[1] It sems to me doubtful whether τέλος means simply 'something desired': but for present purposes it will do no harm to suppose it does so.

[2] Wrongly.

the first sentence of the *Ethics*.[1] However, this qualification need not concern us here (though, since he *would* certainly have said that every action aims at some τέλος, it is clear enough that ἀγαθόν does not mean τέλος). If, then, (1) is meant, and if ἀγαθόν τι means τέλος τι, Aristotle will be saying 'Whenever we act, we aim at some end.' But to say that is not to say *nothing*: indeed, it is to say something which Professor Prichard declares, on p. 29, to be false.[2] At most the sentence is *pleonastic*: for we could write τινός for τέλους τινός (or ἀγαθοῦ τινός) without loss of meaning. But that is a very minor matter. And this would serve, e.g., to define ἀγαθόν.

If (2) is meant, the sentence is certainly emptier: 'Whenever we aim, we aim at some end.' It might be said to be a matter of definition. But it might well be said, for emphasis, in explaining the notion of 'aiming', or in otherwise explaining the use of words. However, for reasons similar to those given in the preceding paragraph, I do not consider that Aristotle would ever have made such a remark about ἀγαθόν, though he might well have made it about τέλος. If we change it to 'whenever we aim *deliberately*, and only then, we aim at ἀγαθόν τι', Aristotle might agree: but *then*, if we substitute τέλος τι, for ἀγαθόν τι, the statement would simply be *false*. Thus proving, though not by Professor Prichard's argument, that ἀγαθόν does not mean τέλος.

Now take Prichard's second argument. Here, no such objection applies as in the case of the first argument, for Aristotle certainly *would* say that the object of βούλησις is τἀγαθόν. If ἀγαθόν means τέλος, the statement becomes: 'The object of βούλησις is τὸ τέλος.' Now this is not, as a matter of fact, as it stands, absurd—it is in fact a remark which Aristotle often makes, with good sense (cf. e.g. 1111^{b}26, or 1113^{a}15, ἡ βούλησις τοῦ τέλους ἐστίν). However, τὸ τέλος is there being contrasted with τὰ πρὸς τὸ τέλος, and βούλησις with προαίρεσις: whereas

---

[1] The importance of which should not be exaggerated.

[2] Because he understands by τέλος only what Aristotle call a τέλος παρὰ τὴν πρᾶξιν, I confess that his criticism at this point seems to me perverse.

it is clear that Professor Prichard means, and fairly enough, to refer to a context where βούλησις is being contrasted with ἐπιθυμία and θυμός, and τἀγαθόν with τὸ ἡδύ and ἀντιλύπησις. In such a context, it is clear enough that we cannot substitute τέλος for ἀγαθόν. For in the case of the other two types of ὀρέξεις we are also aiming at a τέλος, and we need ἀγαθόν not τέλος to provide the contrast. Professor Prichard's arguments, then, reduce to one, which I think is sound: ἀγαθόν cannot *mean* 'that which is desired', because Aristotle holds that there are *other* objects of desire besides τὸ ἀγαθόν.

Apart from this argument, it is absolutely clear from I. vi itself that ἀγαθόν does not, for Aristotle, mean (or at any rate *merely* mean?) 'that which is desired'. It is not merely that he says that ἀγαθόν has *no* single meaning, and hence, *a fortiori*, not that suggested. But further, he says of τιμή, φρόνησις, and ἡδονή that they are all διωκόμενα καθ' αὑτά, so that, presumably, their λόγοι ᾗ διωκόμενα καθ' αὑτά[1] are *identical*: whereas their λόγοι ταύτῃ ᾗ ἀγαθά are *different*. So that being ἀγαθόν cannot mean being desired.

I expect the reader has found the proof of this tedious. But it is important to establish the point, since the relation between 'being ἀγαθόν' and 'being desired' is one of the most baffling puzzles in Aristotle's, or for that matter Plato's, ethical theory. This puzzle, like that of the relation between ἀγαθόν and ἡδύ, must be reserved for a separate discussion.

[1] 'Their accounts as things pursued for their own sake.' (Ed. transl.).

2

ARE THERE *A PRIORI* CONCEPTS?[1]

MR. MACLAGAN seems to have ransacked every available cupboard for skeletons to grace our feast: I hope I shall not be thought ungrateful for his assiduity, if I decline to pick with him the particular bones which he proffers to me. My excuse is that he, like Mr. Mackinnon, has touched only perfunctorily, if at all, on certain preliminary matters which deserve discussion. Frankly, I still do not understand what the question before us *means*: and since I hold, nevertheless, no strong views as to how it should be answered, it seems best to occupy myself primarily in discussing its meaning. I only wish I could do this more helpfully. I shall, therefore, first write something about *concepts*, and then something about their *existence* and *origin*: finally, because it seems an interesting case, I shall choose to argue with Mr. Maclagan about *resemblance*.

I

Neither Mr. Mackinnon nor Mr. Maclagan would claim, I think, to have told us carefully what they are talking about when they talk about 'concepts'. Both seem, however, to imply that the word 'concept' could not be explained without using the word 'universal':[2] and this seems also the common view, though how the two are related is no doubt obscure and controversial. I propose, therefore, to make some remarks about

[1] Reprinted from *Proceedings of the Aristotelian Society*, 1939, by courtesy of the editor.

[2] Mr. Maclagan perhaps denies this, in order to allow for the possibility of 'innate ideas': but he does not believe in these. Nor does he explain about them: his brief account of a 'concept' as an 'element in our knowing or thinking' will scarcely suffice for that.

'universals': because I do not understand what they are, so that it is most unlikely I shall understand what concepts are.

People (philosophers) speak of 'universals' as though these were entities which they often stumbled across, in some familiar way which needs no explanation. But they are not so. On the contrary, it is not so very long since these alleged entities were calculated into existence by a transcendental argument: and in those days, anyone bold enough to say there 'were' universals kept the argument always ready, to produce if challenged. I do not know if it is upon this argument that Mr. Mackinnon and Mr. Maclagan are relying. It may be that they do claim to stumble across 'universals' in some easy manner: or it may be that they rely upon some other argument which is admittedly transcendental.[1] But I propose to consider, not very fully, that celebrated argument which, above all, seems suited to prove the existence of 'universals' in the most ordinary sense of that word: it runs as follows:

It is assumed that we do 'sense' things, which are many or different.[2] Whether these things are 'material objects' or what are commonly called 'sense-data', is not here relevant: in fact the argument can be made to apply to the objects of any kind of 'acquaintance', even non-sensuous—although such applications were not originally envisaged. It is assumed, further, that we make a practice of calling many different sensa by the same single name: we say '*This* is grey', and '*That* is grey', when the sensa denoted by 'this' and by 'that' are not identical. And finally it is assumed that this practice is 'justifiable' or indispensable. Then we proceed to ask: How is such a practice possible? And answer:

(*a*) Since we use the same single *name* in each case, there must surely be some single identical thing 'there' in each case:

[1] For there are in fact several: see below.

[2] There is a constant and harmful ambiguity here: the sensa are commonly different *both* 'numerically' *and* 'qualitatively' (the former, of course, always). The 'universal' is alleged to be single and identical in *both* ways. Hence, from the start, that fatal confusion of the problem of 'genus and species' with the problem of 'universal and particular'.

something of which the name is the name: something, therefore, which is 'common' to all sensa called by that name. Let this entity, whatever it may be, be called a 'universal'.

(b) Since it was admitted that the things we sense are many or different, it follows that this 'universal', which is single and identical, is *not sensed*.

Let us consider this argument.

1. This is a *transcendental*[1] argument: if there were not in existence something other than sensa, we should not be able to do what we *are* able to do (viz. name things). Let us not consider here whether, in general, such a form of argument is permissible or fruitful: but it is important to notice the following points:

(i) The 'universal' is emphatically *not* anything we stumble across. We can claim only to know *that*, not *what*, it is. 'Universal' *means* that which will provide the solution to a certain problem: that *x* which is present, one and identical, in the different sensa which we call by the same name. Unfortunately, as so often happens, succeeding generations of philosophers fell naturally into the habit of supposing that they were perfectly well acquainted with these entities in their own right: they have any amount to tell us about them (partly this was due to a confusion of 'universals' in our present sense with 'universals' in other senses, as we shall see). For instance, we are told that they are 'objects of thought': and myths are invented, about our 'contemplation' of ursaneivls: and so on.

(ii) On the same grounds, it must be held that to ask a whole series of questions which have constantly been asked is non-sensical. For instance: 'How is the universal related to the particulars?', 'Could there be universals without instances?', and many others. For a 'universal' is *defined* as something which is related to certain sensa in a certain way. We might as well

---

[1] In Kant's sense. But it is also 'transcendental' in another sense, that o proving the existence of a class of entities different in kind from sensa.

worry about what is the relation between a man and his aunt, and as to whether there can be aunts without nephews (or nieces).

(iii) Here, however, a point to which I have already twice referred in anticipation, must be made: this will unfortunately be a digression. There are *other* transcendental arguments for 'the existence of universals'. I shall mention one: A true statement is one which corresponds with reality: the statements of the scientist are true: therefore there are realities which correspond to those statements. Sensa do not correspond to the statements of the scientist (exactly *why*, is rather too obscure to discuss here): therefore there must exist other objects, real but not sensible, which do correspond to the statements of the scientist. Let these be called 'universals'.

That this argument begs many questions, is evident. Are all sciences alike? Is all truth correspondence? Does no science make statements about sensa? Some, for instance, would distinguish '*a priori*' sciences from 'empirical' sciences: and hold that the 'truth' of the former is *not* correspondence, while the statements of the latter *are* about sensa. Of course, too, the assumption that the sciences are true is a large one.[1] But all this cannot be entered into.

What it is important to notice for our purposes is that here too the argument is *transcendental*. The 'universal' is an x, which is to solve our problem for us: we know only that it is nonsensible, and in addition must possess certain characters, the lack of which prohibits sensa from corresponding to the statements of the scientist. But we do not stumble across these 'universals': though, needless to say, philosophers soon take to talking as though they did.

Now it must be asked: what conceivable ground have we for *identifying* the 'universals' of our original argument with the 'universals' of this second argument? Except that both are

[1] Even Plato once decided that he ought not to make it. It has been suggested to me that the argument should be formulated in terms of 'having meaning' rather than of 'being true'. I doubt if this would be any improvement.

non-sensible, nothing more is known in which they are alike. Is it not odd to suppose that *any two* distinct transcendental arguments could possibly be known each to prove the existence of the *same* kind of thing? Hence the oddity of speaking of 'arguments for the existence of universals': in the first place, no two of these arguments are known to be arguments for the existence of the same thing: and in the second place, the phrase is misleading because it suggests that we know what a 'universal' is quite apart from the argument for its existence—whereas, in fact, 'universal' *means*, in each case, simply 'the entity which this argument proves to exist'.

As a matter of fact we can, indirectly, show that the objects 'proved' to exist by the two arguments so far mentioned are *not* the same. For firstly, the variety of 'universals' proved to exist in the case of the first argument is strangely greater than in the case of the second argument: the former proves a 'universal' to exist corresponding to every general name, the latter only does so when the name is that of an object studied by the scientist.[1] But it might still be thought that the 'universals' proved to exist by the second argument do, nevertheless, form part of the class of 'universals' proved to exist by the first argument: e.g. 'circularity' or 'straightness' could be proved to exist by either argument. Yet, in fact, no clearer cases could be chosen for demonstrating that the two kinds of 'universals' are distinct: for if 'circularity' is to be proved to exist by the first argument, then I must be able to say truly of certain sensa 'this is circular': whereas, the 'circularity' which is to be proved to exist by the second argument must be such that it cannot be truly predicated of *any* sensa.[2]

---

[1] It is to be remembered that, if we are to argue that 'science' is not about sensa, very little can be recognized as 'science'.

[2] It cannot be sense to say that sensible circles are more or less 'like' the universal 'circularity': a particular can be like nothing but another particular. Nor can I agree with Mr. Maclagan that, on his account, the 'sensible figure' could be an approximation to the 'geometrical figure': for what is sensed can be like nothing but something else which is sensed. But I must allow that 'non-sensuous perception', 'intuitive acquaintance' and so on seem to me to be

The purpose of this digression is to point out that, apart altogether from questions as to whether the 'arguments for the existence of universals' are good and as to whether they permit us to talk further about universals, an immeasurable confusion arises from the fact that 'universal' may mean at any moment any one of a number of different things. For example, if 'universal' is being used in the sense of the second argument, it is good enough sense to ask 'How are universals related to particulars?' though any answer would be difficult to find. (The answer that particulars are 'approximations' to universals not only implies that the two are the *same* in kind whereas they were said to be different, but also again exposes the difference between this argument and the other; since it would be absurd to say, of some non-scientific object like a bed, that there was no sensible bed which was *really* a bed, but all sensible beds were only more or less remote 'approximations' to beds.) Again, to ask 'Are there universals without instances?' is now absurd for the reason that a 'universal', in the sense of the second argument, is not the sort of thing which 'has instances' at all (indeed, someone will certainly be found to *apply* the first argument *to* the objects 'proved' to exist by the second argument).

2. So far, we have not investigated the validity of our argument.

(i) It is to be observed that if the argument holds in its first part (*a*), it certainly also holds in its second part (*b*). If there 'are universals', then they are not sensed: the whole point of the argument is that there must exist something of a kind quite

---

contradictions in terms, attempts to have things both ways. I find confirmation of this when Mr. Maclagan says a sensible circle might be *more* than an 'approximation' to a geometrical circle: i.e. as I understand him, it would *be* a geometrical circle, although we did not know it. Thus he is making the objects of intuition the same in kind as the objects of sense—indeed interchangeable. I wonder if Mr. Maclagan's non-sensuous intuition is such that we can say on occasion, '*This is* a (geometrical) circle'? For whatever reason, we do not ever, I think, speak so. Yet, surely, if we are 'acquainted' with geometrical circles we ought to be able to do this.

different from sensa. Nevertheless, a fatal mistake has been made by many philosophers: they accept the *first* part of the argument ('there are universals') which, as we shall shortly see, is wrong, and they *reject* the second part, which is a necessary corollary of the first. Of course, the talk is at first still to the effect that universals are 'thought': but theories are soon formed as to how we 'abstract universals from particulars' and then 'see universals in particulars'.[1] Undoubtedly, there are 'reasons' of a kind for constructing these theories and rejecting the 'separation' of universals, of which the following will be the most pleasing to self-refuting nominalists: if we accept both (*a*) and (*b*), it becomes difficult to give any account of how I come to classify together the various things called 'grey'; true, if and when I am correct in classifying a certain sensum as 'grey', then the universal must be 'in' it: but it is not *sensed* 'in' it: how then am I to decide whether it is or is not there, or even guess it?[2] Hence we depart from the argument in its pristine form, and embark on mythologies: and by the time we have finished, we may well have reached the position of so many philosophers, and hold that what I *do* sense are 'universals', what I do *not* sense are 'particulars';[3] which, considering the meanings of the words, comprises two self-contradictions.

(ii) Finally, it must be pointed out that the first part of the argument (*a*), is wrong. Indeed, it is so artless that it is difficult to state it plausibly. Clearly it depends on a suppressed premiss which there is no reason whatever to accept, namely, that words are essentially 'proper names', *unum nomen unum nominatum*. But why, if 'one identical' word is used, *must* there be 'one identical' object present which it denotes? Why should it not be the whole function of a word to denote many things?[4] Why should not words be by nature 'general'? However, it is in any case simply false that we use the *same* name for different

[1] Do we taste universals in particulars too?

[2] In *this* sense of 'giving an explanation of naming', the theory gives none.

[3] Other theories: that the particular *is* just a cluster of universals: that the universal *is* a particular of a special sort (an image).

[4] Many *similar* things, on a plausible view: but other views might be held.

things: 'grey' and 'grey' are *not* the same, they are two similar symbols (tokens), just as the things denoted by 'this' and by 'that' are similar things. In this matter, the 'words' are in a position precisely analogous to that of the objects denoted by them.[1]

But, it may be objected, by the 'same single' word it was never meant that it is *numerically* identical. In what sense, then, was it meant? If it meant 'qualitatively identical', then it is clear that the sense in which there is an identical 'type' of the tokens is just like the sense in which the sensa share in an identical common character: hence the former cannot be taken as self-explanatory while the latter is admitted obscure. If it meant that all these tokens 'have the same meaning', then we cannot *assume* that it is the business of similar tokens to 'mean' something which is numerically self-identical, without begging our whole question in the manner already pointed out.

But, it will be further said, I do *sense* something identical in different sensa. How this could be I do not understand; but if it is true, it is clear that this identical something is not an entity different in kind from sensa.

I conclude that this argument does not prove 'the existence of universals'; and that, if it did, nothing more could be said about them than is said in the course of the argument itself, except that they are certainly quite different from 'universals' in other senses of that word, i.e. as 'proved' to exist by other transcendental arguments.

In a certain sense it perhaps is *sometimes* not harmful to talk about 'universals' or 'concepts'; just as it is *sometimes* convenient to talk about 'propositions', and as it is very often convenient to use 'material object language'. To say something about 'concepts' is sometimes a convenient way of saying something complicated about sensa (or even about other objects of acquaintance, if there are any), including symbols and images,

[1] There are ways, of course, in which they are not so analogous: for instance, that one token is of the same type as another, is determined by convention as well as by similarity.

and about our use of them:[1] though very different methods of translation will have to be employed on different occasions. But on the whole there is remarkably little to be said in favour of 'universals', even as an admitted logical construction: the plain man did not use it until he acquired the habit from philosophers, and the errors into which that habit leads are very common and numerous. For example, in addition to those already noted, the error of taking a single *word* or *term*, instead of a sentence, as that which 'has meaning'; hence, given some word like 'resemblance', we search for what *it* denotes (cf. III). Or again, we confuse the view that all sentences are about sensa, with the view that every word or term denotes a sensum. Or again, and this most concerns us, we think of the 'abstracted' universal as a solid piece of property of ours, and inquire into its 'origin'.

I should like, then, to learn from Mr. Mackinnon and Mr. Maclagan, 'what a concept is'.

II

In criticizing Mr. Mackinnon, and elsewhere, Mr. Maclagan mentions two questions which, he says, it is important to ask and to distinguish. They are formulated in different ways, but a typical formulation is the following:

   (i) *Do we* (actually) *possess* such-and-such a concept?
   (ii) *How do we come to possess* such-and-such a concept?

I recognize that these two questions have been distinguished and asked, by philosophers of reputation: Descartes, for example, asks both questions, severally, about 'the idea of God'. Nevertheless, it may be doubted whether these really are distinct and answerable types of question.

As for the first question it would have been helpful to me if

---

[1] But we must 'be careful'. We must not say, for example, 'a universal is an image': Berkeley probably did not make this mistake, but Hume probably did: hence Hume is led, whereas Berkeley is not, into a theory about 'the origin' of our ideas.

Mr. Maclagan had volunteered to argue it, at least in some one case: for then I might have learned what it means, or how it may be decided.[1] As for the second question, it is, I think, quite clear that Mr. Maclagan, like Professor Broad, regards the distinction between '*a priori*' and 'empirical' concepts as a matter of 'the manner in which we come to acquire' them. This I notice as a preliminary, because, in the opening paragraph of his section II, he does not define 'empirical' in this way. That he really does mean what I claim is shown by a great many remarks throughout his paper, but more particularly by the opening paragraph of his concluding section, and by the nature of the ensuing conclusions.

The principal objection which I have to bring against both questions is the general one; that they are examples of the nonsense into which we are led through the facile use of the word 'concept'. A concept is treated, by Mr. Maclagan as by Professor Broad, as an *article of property*, a pretty straightforward piece of goods, which comes into my 'possession', if at all, in some definite enough manner and at some definite enough moment:[2] whether I do possess it or not is, apparently, ascertained simply by making an inventory of the 'furniture' of my mind.

Let us consider first the first question: when we ask 'Do we possess the concept?' what are we asking? If we are asking about some individual, or about some group of individuals, whether *he* or *they* 'possess the concept of redness', some meanings can well be attached to this expression. It might be supposed to mean, for example, 'Does he, or do they, understand the word "red"?' But that again needs further explanation; we shall almost certainly find that it is still ambiguous, and that, at least on many interpretations, no precise

---

[1] Perhaps he does intend to argue it—though, if so, he does not clearly enough distinguish it from the second question—in the case of 'the causal continuant': but there the issue is further obscured by our 'having' a concept, the elements of which do not combine into a 'single' concept, and the content of which is 'dim'.

[2] Can I 'lose' a concept, as well as acquire it?

answer can be given as to whether the individual does or does not 'understand' the 'word'. Does the word 'red' matter? Would it not do if he used 'rouge' and understood that? Or even 'green' if he meant by that what most Englishmen mean by 'red'? And so on. Perhaps we should say he 'possesses the concept of redness' if he has paid attention to certain features in that with which he is acquainted, to call attention to which most Englishmen would use the words 'red', 'redness', &c., and has adopted some symbolism to call attention to them, and has not 'forgotten' either the features or the symbolism. This is still only one of the things which might be meant, and is still not precise enough: and all the difficulties arise with which we are even more familiar in the puzzles about material objects—surely he might do all you say and yet *still not* possess the concept?

But we do not need to pursue this question. For it appears that this is anyhow not the question being asked by Mr. Maclagan as his first question. In asking 'Do *we* possess, &c.?' the 'we' does not mean *us* as contrasted with others; it means any and everybody at once. It means, as he elsewhere puts it, '*Is there* such-and-such a concept?' And now what does *that* mean, if anything? It looks as though it had a meaning, because it seems easy to proceed from the question 'Does Socrates possess, &c.?' to the question 'Does *any* man possess, &c.?' But although verbally like the first, the second question is really very different. Similarly, although meaning may be attached to the question, 'Does *he*, or do *they*, understand this word?', it is not obvious that the question 'Does *anyone* understand this word?' has a meaning at all. For, in the former of these questions, to 'understand' means, speaking roughly, to use as we, or as most Englishmen, or as some other assignable persons use: or again, the features of *his* experience,[1] about which it is asked whether he has or has not paid attention to them, require to be indicated by referring to certain definite experiences of *other* persons. Clearly nothing of the kind is possible in the case of

[1] I use this as equivalent to 'that with which he is acquainted'.

the second question. Yet it seems to me that its verbal similarity to the first has led people to pose it—together of course, with a belief in 'concepts' as palpable objects: if they were such, the second question *would* be rather like the first. Whereas it is not.

It seems clear, then, that to ask 'whether we possess a certain concept?' is the same as to ask whether a certain word—or rather, sentences in which it occurs—has any meaning. Whether *that* is a sensible question to ask, and if so how it is to be answered, I do not know: in any case, it is likely to be ambiguous.

What it is here of interest to observe is, how our question (1) is liable to become confused with (2). Since it is going to be awkward, to say the least, to prove that a certain concept simply is not, it is tempting to try another way. Instead of maintaining that it *does* not exist, we maintain that it *cannot* exist. For instance, in certain cases we may hope to show that an 'idea' is 'self-contradictory', as Leibniz thought he could show of the 'infinite number' or Berkeley[1] of 'matter'. This

---

[1] Since Mr. Mackinnon makes much of this, a note may be excused. Berkeley, I think, maintains exactly the same position with regard to 'matter' as with regard to 'universals': these two are chosen as typical of the two most popular kinds of entities alleged to differ in kind from sensa. He expresses himself much more clearly about 'matter' than about 'universals', (though always suffering from a lack of technical terms). He holds (1) that the plain man's ordinary statements about 'ideas' or about 'material objects' are translatable into other statements which are solely about sensa (including symbols), (2) that the plain philosopher's theories about the 'nature' of matter (inert, &c.) and of universals (formed by abstraction, &c.) are nonsense: partly his descriptions of these entities are self-contradictory (e.g. in the way mentioned by Mr. Maclagan at the end of his section V), partly he can be shown simply to have misunderstood the nature of a 'logical construction'. In one sense 'there are' both universals and material objects, in another sense there is no such thing as either: statements about each can usually be analysed, but not always, nor always without remainder.

Mr. Mackinnon seems to me to underrate the second line of attack. I do not think that Berkeley would have been by any means content simply to propound the view that matter is a 'logical construction' and then to abandon the plain man still asking for more: he patiently asks '*What* more do you want?', and laboriously shows that either what is asked for is nonsensical or else he has granted it already. And this, if we will not be content to let plain men work out their own damnation, is perhaps all that can be done. Nor do I think that

particular method, however, is not suitable in some of the most crucial cases, namely those of *simple* 'ideas' like that of 'necessity'. So here another method is tried: we claim to show that it is *causally* impossible for anyone to possess such a concept. We construct a theory about the condition or conditions under which alone we can 'acquire' concepts: and then we claim that, in the case of certain alleged concepts, these conditions are not satisfied in the case of any man: therefore *no one* possesses them, i.e. they do not exist.

Thus Hume rapidly deploys a theory that we can never come by any idea unless we have previously experienced an impression similar to it: and argues that we cannot possess an idea of power-in-objects such as we commonly think ourselves to possess, because there is no antecedent impression of it.

But this roundabout method of showing that I do not, because I cannot, possess certain concepts, will not do. For how is Hume's conclusion, that we possess no ideas not derived from antecedent impressions, established? Presumably by induction. But not merely is his survey of the evidence inadequate: if he is to make an induction, he must first consider all cases where I do possess an 'idea', and discover the antecedent conditions in each case. He must, therefore, consider whether we do or do not have the idea of power-in-objects before making his induction: and he must also, and this is more important, have some means of establishing in particular cases whether we do or do not 'possess' a certain idea which is quite distinct from the, as yet unformulated, theory of how we

Berkeley would say 'There *are* universals' quite so handsomely as Mr. Mackinnon makes him do: he would not maintain that there *are* universals in any sense in which he would *deny* that there is matter: Berkeley says that 'there are general ideas' meaning that statements like 'all demonstration is about general ideas' have a meaning—but also, he says that '*abstract* general ideas' i.e. general ideas as entities of a kind different from sensa, do *not* exist. (This does not mean 'general ideas are sensa'.) Mr. Mackinnon gives me the impression, perhaps wrongly, that he thinks 'abstract' general ideas to be a limited *class* of general ideas, which Berkeley denies to exist: but it is rather a *theory about the nature* of general ideas in general that Berkeley means to deny. (I omit the supplementary theory of 'notions'.)

'come to' possess them. Now what is that means? In Hume's case, if the 'idea' were really an *image*, then direct introspection might do, though it would then be surprising that he has to go such a roundabout way to prove we have no idea of power-in-objects: but this will scarcely do on some other theories of what concepts are. I should very much like to know what Mr. Maclagan's method is.

It is also often very hard to gather how philosophers are *claiming* to establish their theories of 'how we come to acquire concepts'. Professor Broad, for instance, in the passage referred to by Mr. Maclagan, says: 'It is quite certain that many, if not all, simple intuitive dispositional ideas are formed in the following way', and then proceeds to a theory about 'comparing', 'abstracting', and so on. How is this proved? If it is known, then I must confess myself bad at knowing. Or again, discussing the question as to whether we do or do not 'have' a certain idea, in connexion with Hume's problem about the shade of blue which I have never actually sensed, Professor Broad says: '(*a*) If by an "idea of the missing shade" you mean an image which is characterized by the missing shade, the question is purely a question for empirical psychology. (*b*) If by "idea" you mean "intuitive idea", the answer is in the negative'. It is satisfactory to have the answer: but it would be pleasant also to learn how it is reached, and by whom.

It seems to me that it is seriously questionable whether Mr. Maclagan's second question can be kept distinct from his first question. The latter seemed to amount to the question: whether a certain word has a meaning? But now does the question about 'origins' really not amount to this, that we want to know: how do words mean? Hume's theory about the 'derivation of our ideas' really amounts to the theory that a word, *x*, can only have meaning provided that I can know, on at least one occasion, that 'this is an *x*', where 'this' denotes something *sensible*. And most other theories about this subject, are really theories of a very similar sort: Mr. Maclagan himself inclines to such a view, though he would not, of course, add that the 'this' must be sensible. The 'origin of a concept' is commonly admitted to be found, when an occasion is found on which I can say, with knowledge, 'this is an *x*'. Mr. Maclagan almost formulates the problem himself in this way in the opening of his section II. The question of 'innate ideas' seems very commonly to be simply the question: whether a word can have a meaning even though I can never know 'this is an *x*'?[1] But surely it will be very difficult indeed to keep the two questions: 'Has *x* a meaning?' and 'How do words mean?' apart. It would appear that to ask the latter is to ask 'What is meant by "having a meaning"?'[2] Now, *if* either of these questions can be treated independently of the other, it seems clear that it is this latter (which would be contrary to Mr. Maclagan's view); unless the question, whether a certain word has a meaning, is to be taken as absolutely unanalysable, and to be answered by means of some sort of direct inspection.

Nevertheless, it is certain that much discussion is devoted *seriously* to the questions of 'origin' and 'acquisition' and 'formation' of concepts. And where this is so I suspect that we are always told either nothing or nonsense. For instance, Kant speaks with emphasis on this subject, saying that the whole

---

[1] We may distinguish several questions: Do I know the meaning of the word *x*? Do I know that there are *x*'s? Do I know that there is an *x here*? Do I know that *this* is the *x* which is here? But the theory that a word only has meaning if I can know sometimes that 'this is an *x*' is so engrained in us that we confuse these questions together: for, if it is true, I cannot answer *any* of the questions in the affirmative unless I sometimes answer the *last*, and therefore *all* of them, in the affirmative. Even Kant, it seems to me, who has every interest in distinguishing these questions with regard to such words as 'duty' and 'cause', since, as against Hume's verification theory, he is claiming that the first three questions can be answered in the affirmative though the last must be answered in the negative, fails to keep them always apart: just as he fails sufficiently to distinguish the question, 'How are synthetic *a priori* propositions meaningful?' from, 'How are they known to be true?' *Perhaps* they cannot be distinguished. I should say that Mr. Maclagan, in putting to me the question he does about his classes (4) and (5), is posing the really difficult question: can *x* have a meaning when I can never know that 'this is an *x*'? I wish I could answer it.

[2] This, if true, explains why theories about the 'origins' of our ideas are far from being as inductive as they apparently should be.

point of Hume's theories, and the whole point of his own transcendental deduction, is about the *origin* of *a priori* concepts: it will be remembered how the wretched Beattie is slated for not understanding this. With trepidation, I confess I do not understand it either. Beyond that the 'origin' of these concepts is 'in the nature of the mind itself', I cannot see that we are given any information about it. Is the Metaphysical Deduction intended to show that this 'origin' lies in the forms of judgement? A strange sense of 'origin'. And yet even so, it seems to me that no account is given of the 'origin' of our concept of 'necessity'.

The fact is that words like 'origin' or 'source' and phrases like 'how we acquire' are very vague, and may mean many things. Unless we carefully distinguish them we shall fall into confusions. For example, Descartes' division of 'ideas' into innate, adventitious, and factitious, seems, if we attempt to eliminate the metaphor from the ways of acquiring property, to rest on no single *fundamentum divisionis*. I suppose that really these expressions are intended to embrace *all* conditions antecedent to our 'possession' of a concept: but plainly these conditions are of very various kinds, for example, we may be given:

(a) Theories about the *agents* (spiritual or material) responsible for my possession of concepts, e.g. myself, God, material objects.

(b) Theories about the *operations*, which lead to the 'formation' of concepts, e.g. the honest spadework of 'abstraction'.

(c) Theories about the *materials* on which those operations must be conducted, e.g. non-sensuous intuitions, sensa.

(d) Theories about the *sources* from which concepts are somehow drawn, e.g. the mind.

(e) Theories about the times or *occasions* on which concepts are acquired, e.g. at birth, before birth, on the occasion of sensing x.

Probably this list could be extended. I do not see that these questions are anything but confusing, if taken seriously: (*c*) and perhaps (*d*) might be interpreted to make sense. It is strange that we should continue to ask about 'concepts' much the same questions about 'origins' as were for so long and so fruitlessly asked about sensa.

I should like, then, to ask Mr. Mackinnon and Mr. Maclagan what they are asking when they ask about 'the formation' of concepts, or about their 'acquisition': and also what is meant by our 'having a concept'.

III

The case of 'resemblance', which Mr. Maclagan introduces as one where we are obviously not acquainted in sensation with the object of a concept, is of course a special and difficult case in many ways. Yet it seems to me true to say that I do sense resemblance, though what that means needs explanation.

1. Mr. Maclagan asks 'What is given in sensation?'—an unfortunate way of putting a very easy question, to which the answer must and can only be 'Sensa'. What is unfortunate is the word 'given' (cf. 'sense-*data*', 'the data of sense'). For this suggests (*a*) that something is here 'given' us *by* somebody; (*b*) that sensa are called 'given' in contrast with something which is rather 'made' or 'taken', namely, my thoughts: but it is dubious whether there is any sense in which my thoughts *are* in my own control but my sensa *not* so; (*c*) that some *proposition* is 'given' to us in sensation as incorrigible, as premisses are 'given' in sciences or 'data' to the detective: but sensa are *dumb*, and nothing is more surely fatal than to confuse sensing with thinking.

2. Owing to his 'concept' language, Mr. Maclagan seems to try, when presented with any substantive, to find some isolable part of the sensefield which is an instance of it but not of anything else. That is, I admit, vague. Given the sentence 'A resembles B', it seems that Mr. Maclagan says to himself: That means there should be three things to sense, A and B and a

resemblance: now we do sense the colours, but we do not sense the resemblance. But surely, speaking carefully, we do not sense 'red' and 'blue' any more than 'resemblance' (or 'qualities' any more than 'relations'): we sense something of which we might say, if we wished to talk about it, that 'this is red': and so we sense something of which we might say, if we wished to talk about it, that 'this is similar to that' or 'that this red is similar to that red'. If we insist on trying to *say* what we *sense* (which is impossible), we might try saying that 'I sense A-resembling-B': and see if that helps.

3. There are, I willingly admit, special difficulties about resemblance: but it seems to me that they are not before us— for Mr. Maclagan would, as is shown by his commendation of Locke and others,[1] say about other 'relations', and apparently about *all* of them, precisely what he says about resemblance. 'Relations are not sensed'. This dogma, held by a very great number and variety of philosophers,[2] seems to me so odd that, like Mr. Maclagan, I find it difficult to discover arguments. If I say 'this dot is to the right of that dot', is it not quaint to say that I am sensing the two dots but not sensing the to the right of? It is true that I cannot say I *do* sense the to the right of: that is not good English—but then nor is it good English to say that I do not sense it, or that I intuite it. I sense what in English is described by means of two demonstrative pronouns and an adverbial phrase. To look for an isolable entity corresponding to the latter is a bad habit encouraged by talk about 'concepts'. What, I wonder, does Mr. Maclagan say about verbs? If 'he

---

[1] Does Hume really not allow that *any* 'relations' are sensed: for instance, 'contiguity'?

[2] Even by Berkeley, who jeopardized his whole theory by doing so. A pretty anthology might be compiled of the phrases found by philosophers to express their distrust and contempt for relations: 'entia semi-mentalia' and what not. I suppose it goes back to Aristotle, who assumes, with the plain man, that 'what is real is things', and then adds, grudgingly, 'also their qualities', these being somehow inseparable from the things: but he draws the line at relations, which are really too flimsy. I doubt if there is much more behind the prejudice against relations than this: there was not in Leibniz's case, and few have hammered relations so hard as he.

is batting the cat', do I sense him and the cat, and intuite relations of batting and of being batted? But perhaps this is unfair: for verbs are only used in this way in unanalysed material-object language.

4. There are those who hold that 'relations' do not have 'instances' at all: but Mr. Maclagan, like Mr. Joseph, takes the less extreme view that they do have instances, but not 'sensible' ones. For this he has, as he candidly admits, no arguments whatever to adduce. But the difficulty is not so much to argue for the view as to understand it at all. 'The colours' I sense, I do not intuite them: I intuite 'the resemblance'—or 'their resemblance'? Or 'the resemblance between the two colours'? Or what exactly? This 'intuition' is a form of acquaintance: and if we can be acquainted with relations *thus*, it seems difficult to see why we should not be acquainted with them in sensation. And there seems the absurdity that we have now separated off 'the resemblance' from 'the colours': we have a sensing and simultaneously an intuiting, as we might feel a stab of jealousy while tasting porridge. Even if one is never found without the other, what has the one to do with the other?

5. Mr. Maclagan, recognizing that there are arguments which tell against him, advances a 'purely defensive' argument, based on considerations about 'If A then B, if B then C'. Now in the first place there seems to be some muddle about the symbolism here. In any ordinary sense of 'if . . . then', I do not think that the premiss given above will help us at all to answer the question which is asked, viz. 'What is required if we are to have C?' For the premiss tells us about certain *sufficient* conditions for C, whereas the question is about *necessary* conditions for C. Which does Mr. Maclagan mean to talk about?

Apparently A is to be 'the sensing of the colours', B 'the intuiting of the resemblance', and C 'the knowing that the colours resemble'. Now if we interpret 'if . . . then' to mean that A is a *sufficient* condition of B, and B of C, it seems impossible to suppose that the 'intuiting' (alone) is a *sufficient* condition of the knowing. Surely the sensing is also necessary?

(As a matter of fact, it seems to me quite untrue that even the sensing and the intuiting would necessitate the knowing: in order to *know*, I must also *think about* the objects of acquaintance.[1] However, Mr. Maclagan is not called upon to point this out, since the plain man, against whom he is arguing, overlooks it.) On the other hand, in the case of the sensing and intuiting, Mr. Maclagan must mean that the former does necessitate, i.e. is a *sufficient* condition of, the latter: for he is arguing that the plain man is able to say that 'sensing is the sole necessary condition of knowing', because, though as a matter of fact the intuiting is *also* a necessary condition, the sensing does of itself necessitate the intuiting.

It seems to me, therefore, that the symbolism here is merely confusing: 'if . . . then' cannot mean the same in the case of A and B as in the case of B and C. Moreover, I am very much in the dark as to what really are the relations between the sensing and the intuiting, the intuiting and the knowing. 'Condition' and 'necessitation' are words which may refer to entailment, or again to natural causation: is it in either of these senses that the sensing necessitates the intuiting, or that the intuiting is necessary to the knowing? I should doubt whether in either case 'necessary' is being used in either of these familiar senses; and further, whether it is being used in the same sense in each case.

Clearly, what we are most concerned with is the sense in which the sensing necessitates the intuiting. Mr. Maclagan distinguishes the case of 'resemblance' from that of 'straightness', in that in the former the intuiting is 'logically inseparable' from the sensing, whereas in the latter the intuiting is 'psychologically conditioned' by the sensing. These *look*, from the words used, rather like 'entailment' and 'natural causation' respectively: but whatever may be true in the case of 'straightness', I do not

---

[1] Mr. Maclagan permits himself to wonder whether the intuiting (? sensing + intuiting) can really be distinguished from the knowing. But, if it cannot, not merely does Mr. Maclagan abandon one of his original premisses, as he recognizes, but also, in our present problem, 'B' cannot be distinguished from 'C'; which is frustrating.

see, in the case of resemblance, how one event can *entail* another, so that 'logically inseparable' entirely eludes me. If Mr. Maclagan says it is obscure, we may remember how obscure the 'intuiting' itself is, and be content to note one more example of the high differential fertility of obscurities.

Further, Mr. Maclagan holds that other relations are in the same case as 'resemblance': if so, then other relations between our two colours will also be intuited, and these intuitings will also be necessitated by the sensing of the 'colours'. What I wonder about, is: do I, as soon as I 'sense the colours', *eo ipso* intuite *all* these relations (and know them)? For example, suppose I do know that these two colours are similar: then I must have 'sensed the colours', for I have had the intuition of resemblance. Now if I have 'sensed the colours', I have presumably *already had* 'intuitions' about which is the lighter, &c., those being inseparable from the sensing. Yet it seems clear to me I may very well know the two colours are similar and yet, if asked which is lighter, have to look back at them again. Why so, on Mr. Maclagan's theory?

Mr. Maclagan notices, but does not attempt to defend himself against, other arguments drawn from the plain man, viz. that he says he 'sees' or 'hears' resemblances, and says things are 'sensibly' alike or different. These facts seem to me important, and I think the plain man would quite rightly persevere in these assertions. I have heard it said that it is odd to talk of '*smelling* a resemblance': and certainly it is well to consider other senses than that of sight. But it is not odd to talk of smelling two similar smells, or two smells which are sensibly alike (though, the plain man might well ask, how could they be alike *except* sensibly?). And if I were forced to say either 'I smell the resemblance' or 'I intuite it', I know which I should choose. The plain dog would, I am sure, say it smelled resemblances: but no doubt your philosophical dog would persuade itself that it 'inhaled' them.

Similar considerations hold also in the case of other 'relations': plain men say 'this *tastes* sweeter than that' or 'this *sounds* louder than that'.[1] In the case of such 'relations' as these, indeed, I can scarcely conjecture what it is that Mr. Maclagan would try to persuade me I really mean. Later on, Mr. Maclagan comes to discuss 'louder'[2] and says it is a 'comparative word': I wonder whether 'louder than' is a 'relation' which has to be intuited? Surely, in such cases as these, it is evident that sentences containing 'relation' words describe what we sense in precisely the same way as sentences containing 'quality' words? For it is difficult to decide which sort of word 'loud' is.

6. I agree with Mr. Maclagan that, on his view of 'resemblance', a non-sensuous acquaintance with the particular instance would occur, to which nothing similar would occur in the case of 'redness'. But he seems to hold that, even if I am to say 'this is red', *some* non-sensuous acquaintance (or 'awareness') must occur: apparently because, in order to name this colour red, I must institute a certain 'comparison'. I am not sure what this means. I agree that, in many cases, where I say, for example, 'this is puce', I have compared the present sensum with some 'pattern', perhaps a memory-image of the insect, but in any case an entity of the same kind as the sensum itself. Now this seems to me to require no non-sensuous acquaintance with anything: but I realize that Mr. Maclagan may think it does, because, when I compare the present image with the pattern, I must notice that they *resemble*. Is it, then, that he thinks an intuition *of resemblance* is needed even if I am to say 'this is red'? At least this rather qualifies his original statement that 'I sense the colours'. However, I am not sure he does mean this: he does not state *with what* I 'compare' the sensum, and perhaps he is thinking that I compare the sensum *with* something which is the object of a non-sensuous awareness, e.g., the universal 'redness' (though it would be surprising to find

[1] Very plain men will say 'I hear this louder than that'.

[2] Professor W. G. Maclagan, whose paper is here referred to, has suggested in a private letter that 'loud' must be meant here, not 'louder', though it is the latter that appears in the printed text of 1939. It seems clear that 'loud' is what the sense requires.—Eds.

ourselves 'acquainted' with universals, Mr. Maclagan is prepared to allow the possibility for the sake of argument). I
should like, then, to know what non-sensuous acquaintance
Mr. Maclagan has here in mind.

3

THE MEANING OF A WORD

SPECIMENS OF SENSE

1. 1.   What-is-the-meaning-of (the word) 'rat'?
1. 11.   What-is-the-meaning-of (the word) 'word'?
1. 21.   What is a 'rat'?
1. 211. What is a 'word'?
1. 22.   What is the 'muzzle' of a rat?
2. 1.   What-is-the-meaning-of (the phrase) 'What-is-the-meaning-of'?
2. 11.   What-is-the-meaning-of (the sentence) 'What-is-the-meaning-of (the word) "x"'?'?

SPECIMENS OF NONSENSE

1. 1.   What-is-the-meaning-of a word?
1. 11.   What-is-the-meaning-of any word?
1. 12.   What-is-the-meaning-of a word in general?
1. 21.   What is the-meaning-of-a-word?
1. 211. What is the-meaning-of-(the-word)-'rat'?
1. 22.   What is the 'meaning' of a word?
1. 221. What is the 'meaning' of (the word) 'rat'?
2. 1.   What-is-the-meaning-of (the phrase) 'the-meaning-of-a word'?
2. 11.   What-is-the-meaning-of (the sentence) 'What is the-meaning-of-(the-word)-"x"'?'?
2. 12.   What-is-the-meaning-of (the sentence) 'What is the "meaning" of "the word" "x"'?'?

THIS paper is about the phrase 'the meaning of a word'. It is divided into three parts, of which the first is the most trite and the second the most muddled: all are too long. In the first, I try to make it clear that the phrase 'the meaning of a word' is, in general, if not always, a dangerous nonsense-phrase. In the other two parts I consider in turn two questions, often asked in philosophy, which clearly need new and careful scrutiny if that facile phrase 'the meaning of a word' is no longer to be permitted to impose upon us.

I

I begin, then, with some remarks about 'the meaning of a word'. I think many persons now see all or part of what I shall say: but not all do, and there is a tendency to forget it, or to get it slightly wrong. In so far as I am merely flogging the converted, I apologize to them.

A preliminary remark. It may justly be urged that, properly speaking, what alone has meaning is a *sentence*. Of course, we can speak quite properly of, for example, 'looking up the meaning of a word' in a dictionary. Nevertheless, it appears that the sense in which a word or a phrase 'has a meaning' is derivative from the sense in which a sentence 'has a meaning': to say a word or a phrase 'has a meaning' is to say that there are sentences in which it occurs which 'have meanings': and to know the meaning which the word or phrase has, is to know the meanings of sentences in which it occurs. All the dictionary can do when we 'look up the meaning of a word' is to suggest aids to the understanding of sentences in which it occurs. Hence it appears correct to say that what 'has meaning' in the primary sense is the sentence. And older philosophers who discussed the problem of 'the meaning of words' tend to fall into *special* errors, avoided by more recent philosophers, who discuss rather the parallel problem of 'the meaning of sentences'. Nevertheless, if we are on our guard, we perhaps need not fall into these special errors, and I propose to overlook them at present.

There are many sorts of sentence in which the words 'the meaning of the word so-and-so' are found, e.g. 'He does not know, or understand, the meaning of the word *handsaw*': 'I shall have to explain to her the meaning of the word *pikestaff*': and so on. I intend to consider primarily the common question, 'What is the meaning of *so-and-so*?' or 'What is the meaning of *the word so-and-so*?'

Suppose that in ordinary life I am asked: 'What is the meaning of the word *racy*?' There are two sorts of thing I may do in response: I may reply *in words*, trying to describe what raciness is and what it is not, to give examples of sentences in which one might use the word *racy*, and of others in which one should not. Let us call this *sort* of thing 'explaining the syntactics' of the word 'racy' in the English language. On the other hand, I might do what we may call 'demonstrating the semantics' of the word, by getting the questioner to *imagine*, or even actually to *experience*, situations which we should describe correctly by means of sentences containing the words 'racy' 'raciness', &c., and again other situations where we should *not* use these words. This is, of course, a simple case: but perhaps the same two *sorts* of procedure would be gone through in the case of at least most ordinary words. And in the same way, if I wished to find out 'whether he understands the meaning of the word *racy*', I should test him at some length in these two ways (which perhaps could not be entirely divorced from each other).

Having asked in this way, and answered, 'What is the meaning of (the word) "rat"?', 'What is the meaning of (the word) "cat"?', 'What is the meaning of (the word) "mat"?', and so on, we then try, being philosophers, to ask the further *general* question, 'What is the meaning of a word?' But there is something spurious about this question. We do not intend to mean by it a certain question which would be perfectly all right, namely, 'What is the meaning of (the word) "word"?': *that* would be no more general than is asking the meaning of the word 'rat', and would be answered in a precisely similar way.

No: we want to ask rather, 'What is the meaning of a-word-in-general?' or 'of *any* word'—not meaning 'any' word *you like to choose*, but rather *no particular* word *at all*, just 'any word'. Now if we pause even for a moment to reflect, this is a perfectly absurd question to be trying to ask. I can only answer a question of the form 'What is the meaning of "*x*"?' if "*x*" is some *particular* word you are asking about. This supposed *general* question is really just a spurious question of a type which commonly arises in philosophy. We may call it the fallacy of asking about 'Nothing-in-particular' which is a practice decried by the plain man, but by the philosopher called 'generalizing' and regarded with some complacency. Many other examples of the fallacy can be found: take, for example, the case of 'reality'—we try to pass from such questions as 'How would you distinguish a real rat from an imaginary rat?' to 'What is a real thing?', a question which merely gives rise to nonsense.

We may expose the error in our present case thus. Instead of asking 'What is the meaning of (the word) "rat"?' we might clearly have asked 'What is a "rat"?' and so on. But if our questions have been put in *that* form, it becomes very difficult to formulate any *general* question which could impose on us for a moment. Perhaps 'What is anything?'? Few philosophers, if perhaps not none, have been foolhardy enough to pose such a question. In the same way, we should not perhaps be tempted to generalize such a question as 'Does he know the meaning of (the word) "rat"?' 'Does he know the meaning of a word?' would be silly.

Faced with the nonsense question 'What is the meaning of a word?', and perhaps dimly recognizing it to be nonsense, we are nevertheless not inclined to give it up. Instead, we transform it in a curious and noteworthy manner. Up to now, we had been asking '*What-is-the-meaning-of* (the word) "rat"?', &c.; and ultimately '*What-is-the-meaning-of* a word?' But now, being baffled, we change so to speak, the hyphenation, and ask 'What is *the-meaning-of-a-word*?' or sometimes, 'What is the "meaning" of a word?' (1. 22): I shall refer, for brevity's sake, only to the other (1. 21). It is easy to see how very different this question is from the other. At once a crowd of traditional and reassuring answers present themselves: 'a concept', 'an idea', 'an image', 'a class of similar sensa', &c. All of which are equally spurious answers to a pseudo-question. Plunging ahead, however, or rather retracing our steps, we now proceed to ask such questions as 'What is the-meaning-of-(the-word) "rat"?' which is as spurious as 'What-is-the-meaning-of (the word) "rat"?' was genuine. And again we answer 'the idea of a rat' and so forth. How quaint this procedure is, may be seen in the following way. Supposing a plain man puzzled, were to ask me 'What is the meaning of (the word) "muggy"?', and I were to answer, 'The idea or concept of "mugginess" ' or 'The class of sensa of which it is correct to say "This is muggy" ': the man would stare at me as at an imbecile. And that is sufficiently unusual for me to conclude that that was not at all the sort of answer he expected: nor, in plain English, *can* that question *ever* require that sort of answer.

To show up this pseudo-question, let us take a parallel case, where perhaps no one has yet been deluded, though they well might be. Suppose that I ask 'What is the point of doing so-and-so?' For example, I ask Old Father William 'What is the point of standing on one's head?' He replies in the way we know. Then I follow this up with 'What is the point of balancing an eel on the end of one's nose?' And he explains. Now suppose I ask as my third question 'What is the point of doing *anything*—not anything *in particular*, but just *anything*?' Old Father William would no doubt kick me downstairs without the option. But lesser men, raising this same question and finding no answer, would very likely commit suicide or join the Church. (Luckily, in the case of 'What is the meaning of a word?' the effects are less serious, amounting only to the writing of books.) On the other hand, more adventurous intellects would no doubt take to asking 'What is the-point-of-doing-a-thing?' or 'What is the "point" of doing a thing?':

and then later 'What is the-point-of-eating-suet?' and so on. Thus we should discover a whole new universe of a kind of entity called 'points', not previously suspected of existence.

To make the matter clearer, let us consider another case which is precisely *unlike* the case of 'What is the meaning of?' I can ask not only the question, 'What is the square root of 4?', of 8, and so on, but also 'What is the square root of a number?': which is either nonsense or equivalent to 'What is the "square root" of a number?' I then give a definition of the 'square root' of a number, such that, for any given number x, 'the square root of x' is a definite description of another number y. This differs from our case in that 'the meaning of p' is not a definite description of any entity.

The general questions which we want to ask about 'meaning' are best phrased as, 'What-is-the-meaning-of (the phrase) "what-is-the-meaning-of (the word) 'x'?"?' The *sort* of answer we should get to these quite sensible questions is that with which I began this discussion: viz. that when I am asked 'What-is-the-meaning-of (the word) "x"?', I naturally reply by explaining its syntactics and demonstrating its semantics.

All this must seem very obvious, but I wish to point out that it is fatally easy to forget it: no doubt I shall do so myself many times in the course of this paper. Even those who see pretty clearly that 'concepts', 'abstract ideas', and so on are fictitious entities, which we owe in part to asking questions about 'the meaning of a word', nevertheless themselves think that there *is something* which is 'the meaning of a word'. Thus Mr. Hampshire[1] attacks to some purpose the theory that there is such a thing as '*the* meaning of a word': what *he* thinks is wrong is the belief that there is a *single* thing called *the* meaning: 'concepts' are nonsense, and no single particular 'image' can be *the* meaning of a general word. So, he goes on to say, the meaning of a word must really be 'a *class* of similar particular ideas'. 'If we are asked "What does this mean?" we point to (!) a class of

[1] 'Ideas, Propositions and Signs', in the *Proceedings of the Aristotelian Society*, 1939–40.

particular ideas.' But a 'class of particular ideas' is every bit as fictitious an entity as a 'concept' or 'abstract idea'. In the same way Mr. C. W. Morris (in the *Encyclopaedia of Unified Science*) attacks, to some purpose, those who think of 'a meaning' as a definite something which is 'simply located' somewhere: what *he* thinks is wrong is that people think of 'a meaning' as a kind of·entity which can be described wholly without reference to the total activity of 'semiosis'. Well and good. Yet he himself makes some of the crudest possible remarks about 'the designatum' of a word: every sign has a designatum, which is not a particular thing but a *kind* of object or *class* of object. Now this is quite as fictitious an entity as any 'Platonic idea': and is due to precisely the same fallacy of looking for 'the meaning (or designatum) of a word'.

Why are we tempted to slip back in this way? Perhaps there are two main reasons. First, there is the curious belief that all words are *names*, i.e. in effect *proper* names, and therefore stand for something or designate it in the way that a proper name does. But this view that general names 'have denotation' in the same way that proper names do, is quite as odd as the view that proper names 'have connotation' in the same way that general names do, which is commonly recognized to lead to error. Secondly, we are afflicted by a more common malady, which is this. When we have given an analysis of a certain sentence, containing a word or phrase '*x*', we often feel inclined to ask, of our analysis, 'What *in it, is "x"*?' For example, we give an analysis of 'The State owns this land', in sentences about individual men, their relations and transactions: and then at last we feel inclined to ask: well now, *what*, in all that, *is* the State? And we might answer: the State *is* a collection of individual men united in a certain manner. Or again, when we have analysed the statement 'trees can exist unperceived' into statements about sensing sensa, we still tend to feel uneasy unless we can say *something* 'really does' 'exist unperceived': hence theories about 'sensibilia' and what not. So in our present case, having given all that is required, viz. an account of

'What-is-the-meaning-of "What is-the-meaning-of (the word) 'x'?"' we *still* feel tempted, wrongly supposing our original sentence to contain a constituent 'the-meaning-of (the-word)-"x"', to ask 'Well now, as it turns out, what *is* the meaning of the word "x", after all?' And we answer, 'a class of similar particular ideas' and what not.

Of course, all my account of our motives in this matter may be only a convenient didactic schema: I do not think it is—but I recognize that one should not impute motives, least of all rational motives. Anyhow, what I claim is clear, is that there is *no* simple and handy appendage of a word called 'the meaning of (the word) "x"'.

II

I now pass on to the first of the two points which need now a careful scrutiny if we are no longer to be imposed upon by that convenient phrase 'the meaning of a word'. What I shall say here is, I know, not as clear as it should be.

Constantly we ask the question, 'Is y the meaning, or *part of* the meaning, or *contained* in the meaning, of x?—or is it *not*?' A favourite way of putting the question is to ask, 'Is the judgement "x is y" analytic or synthetic?' Clearly, we suppose, y *must* be *either* a part of the meaning of x, *or* not any part of it. And, if y *is* a part of the meaning of x, to say 'x is not y' will be self-contradictory: while if it is *not* a part of the meaning of x, to say 'x is not y' will present no difficulty—such a state of affairs will be readily 'conceivable'. This seems to be the merest common sense. And no doubt it *would* be the merest common sense *if* 'meanings' were things in some ordinary sense which contained parts in some ordinary sense. But they are *not*. Unfortunately, many philosophers who know they are not, still speak as though y must either be or not be 'part of the meaning' of x. But this is the point: *if* 'explaining the meaning of a word' is really the complicated sort of affair that we have seen it to be, and *if* there is really nothing to call 'the meaning of a word'—*then* phrases like 'part of the meaning of the word *x*' are completely undefined; it is left hanging in the air, we do not know what it means at all. *We are using a working-model which fails to fit the facts that we really wish to talk about.* When we consider what we really do want to talk about, and not the working-model, what would really be meant at all by a judgement being 'analytic or synthetic'? We simply do not know. Of course, we feel inclined to say 'I can easily produce examples of analytic and synthetic judgements; for instance, I should confidently say "Being a professor is *not* part of the meaning of being a man" and so forth.' 'A is A is analytic.' Yes, but it is when we are required to give a *general definition* of what we mean by 'analytic' or 'synthetic', and when we are required to justify our dogma that *every* judgement is either analytic or synthetic, that we find we have, in fact, nothing to fall back upon *except our working-model*. From the start, it is clear that our working-model fails to do justice, for example, to the distinction between syntactics and semantics: for instance, talking about the contradictory of every sentence having to be either self-contradictory or not so, is to talk as though all sentences which we are prohibited from saying were sentences which offended against *syntactical* rules, and could be formally reduced to verbal self-contradictions. But this overlooks all semantical considerations, which philosophers are sadly prone to do. Let us consider two cases of some things which we simply *cannot say*: although they are *not* 'self-contradictory' and although—and this of course is where many will have axes to grind—we cannot possibly be tempted to say that we have 'synthetic *a priori*' knowledge of their contradictions.

Let us begin with a case which, being about *sentences* rather than *words*, is not quite in point, but which may encourage us. Take the well-known sentence 'The cat is on the mat, and I do not believe it'. That seems absurd. On the other hand 'The cat is on the mat, and I believe it' seems trivial. If we were to adopt a customary dichotomy, and to say *either* a proposition *p* implies another proposition *r*, *or p* is perfectly compatible with not-*r*, we should at once in our present case be tempted to say that 'The cat is on the mat' *implies* 'I believe it': hence both the triviality of adding 'and I believe it' and the absurdity of adding 'and I do not believe it'. But of course 'the cat is on the mat' does *not* imply 'Austin believes the cat is on the mat': nor even 'the speaker believes the cat is on the mat'—for the speaker may be lying. The doctrine which is produced in this case is, that not *p* indeed, but *asserting p* implies 'I (who assert *p*) believe *p*'. And here 'implies' must be given a special sense: for of course it is not that 'I assert *p*' implies (in the ordinary sense) 'I believe *p*', for I may be lying. It is the sort of sense in which by asking a question I 'imply' that I do not know the answer to it. By asserting *p* I *give it to be understood* that I believe *p*.

Now the reason why I cannot say 'The cat is on the mat and I do not believe it' is not that it offends against syntactics in the sense of being in some way 'self-contradictory'. What prevents my saying it, is rather some semantic convention (implicit, of course), about the way we use words *in situations*. What precisely is the account to be given in this case we need not ask. Let us rather notice one significant feature of it. Whereas '*p* and I believe it' is somehow trivial, and '*p* and I do not believe it' is somehow nonsense, a third sentence '*p* and *I might not have* believed it' makes perfectly good sense. Let us call these three sentences Q, not Q, and 'might not Q'. Now what prohibits us from saying '*p*' implies 'I believe *p*' in the ordinary sense of 'implies', is precisely shown by this fact: that although not-Q is (*somehow*) absurd, 'might not Q' is not at all absurd. For in ordinary cases of implications, not merely is not Q absurd, but 'might not Q' is *also* absurd: e.g. 'triangles are figures and triangles have no shape' is no more absurd than 'triangles are figures and triangles might have had no shape'. Consideration of the sentence 'might not Q' will afford a rough test as to whether *p* 'implies' *r* in the *ordinary* sense, or in the special sense, of 'implies'.

Bearing this in mind, let us now consider a sentence which, as I claim, cannot possibly be classified as *either* 'analytic' *or* 'synthetic'. I refer to the sentence, 'This x exists', where x is a sensum, e.g. 'This noise exists'. In endeavouring to classify it, one party would point to the triviality of 'This noise exists', and to the absurdity of 'This noise does not exist'. They would say, therefore, that *existence* is 'part of the meaning of' *this*. But another party would point out, that 'This noise might not have existed' makes perfectly good sense. *They* would say, therefore, that *existence* cannot be 'part of the meaning of' *this*.

Both parties, as we are now in a position to see, would be correct in their *arguments*, but incorrect in their *conclusions*. What seems to be true is that *using the word 'this'* (not: the word 'this') *gives it to be understood that* the sensum referred to 'exists'.

Perhaps, historically, this fact about the sentence-trio, 'This noise exists', 'This noise does not exist', and 'This noise might not have existed', was pointed out before any philosopher had had time to pronounce that 'This noise exists' is analytic, or is synthetic. But such a pronouncement might well have been made: and *to this day*, even when the fact has been pointed out, many philosophers *worry* about the case, supposing the sentence *must* be one or the other but painfully aware of the difficulties in choosing either. I wish to point out that consideration of the analogy between this case and the other, should cure us once and for all of this bogy, and of insisting on classifying sentences as *either* analytic *or* synthetic. It may encourage us to consider again what the facts in their actual complexity really are. (One thing it suggests is a reconsideration of 'Caesar is bald' and similar propositions: but I cannot go into that.)

So far, however, we have scarcely begun in earnest: we have merely felt that initial trepidation, experienced when the firm ground of prejudice begins to slip away beneath the feet. Perhaps there are other cases, or other sorts of cases, where it will not be possible to say either that y is a 'part of the meaning' of x or that it is not, without being misleading.

Suppose we take the case of 'being thought good by me' and 'being approved of by me'. Are we to rush at this with the dichotomy: *either* 'being approved of by me' *is* part of the meaning of 'being thought good by me' *or* it is *not*? Is it *obvious* that 'I think *x* good but I do not approve of it' is self-contradictory? Of course it is not *verbally* self-contradictory. That it either is or is not 'really' self-contradictory would seem to be difficult to establish. Of course, we think, it must be one or the other—only 'it's difficult to decide *which*': or 'it depends on how you use the words'. But are those really the difficulties which baffle us? Of course, *if* it were certain that every sentence *must* be either analytic or synthetic, those *must* be the difficulties. But then, it is not certain: no account even of what the distinction means, is given except by reference to our shabby working-model. I suggest that 'I think *x* good but I do not approve of it' may very well be neither self-contradictory nor yet 'perfectly good sense' in the way in which 'I think *x* exciting but I do not approve of it' *is* 'perfectly good sense'.

Perhaps this example does not strike you as awkward. It cannot be expected that all examples will appeal equally to all hearers. Let us take some others. Is 'What is good ought to exist' analytic or synthetic? According to Moore's theory, this must be 'synthetic': yet he constantly in *Principia Ethica* takes its truth for granted. And that illustrates one of the main drawbacks of insisting on saying that a sentence *must* be either analytic or synthetic: you are almost certain to have left on your hands some general sentences which are certainly not analytic but which you find it difficult to conceive being false: i.e. you are landed with 'synthetic *a priori* knowledge'. Take that sentence of ill fame 'Pink is more like red than black'. It is rash to pronounce this 'synthetic *a priori* knowledge' on the ground that 'being more like red than black' is not 'part of the meaning' or 'part of the definition' of 'pink' and that it is not 'conceivable' that pink should be more like black than red: I dare say, so far as those phrases have any clear meaning, that it *is not*: but the question is: *is* the thing therefore 'synthetic' *a priori* knowledge?

Or, again, take some examples from Berkeley: is *extended* 'part of the meaning' of *coloured* or of *shaped*, or *shaped* 'part of the meaning' of *extended*? Is 'est sed non percipitur' self-contradictory (when said of a sensum), or is it not? When we worry thus, is it not worth considering the possibility that we are oversimplifying?

What we are to say in these cases, what even the possibilities are, I do not at present clearly see. (1) Evidently, we must throw away the old working-model as soon as we take account even of the existence of a distinction between syntactics and semantics. (2) But evidently also, our *new* working-model, the supposed 'ideal' language, is in many ways a most inadequate model of any *actual* language: its careful separation of syntactics from semantics, its lists of explicitly formulated rules and conventions, and its careful delimitation of their spheres of operation—all are misleading. An *actual* language has few, if any, explicit conventions, no sharp limits to the spheres of operation of rules, no rigid separation of what is syntactical and what semantical. (3) Finally, I think I can see that there are difficulties about our powers of imagination, and about the curious way in which it is enslaved by words.

To encourage ourselves in the belief that this sort of consideration may play havoc with the distinction 'analytic or synthetic', let us consider a similar and more familiar case. It seems, does it not, perfectly obvious that every proposition must have a contradictory? Yet it does not turn out so. Suppose that I live in harmony and friendship for four years with a cat: and then it delivers a philippic. We ask ourselves, perhaps, 'Is it a real cat? or is it *not* a real cat?' 'Either it *is*, or it *is not*, but we cannot be sure which.' Now actually, that is not so: *neither* 'It is a real cat' *nor* 'it is not a real cat' fits the facts semantically: each is designed for other situations than this one: you could not say the former of something which delivers philippics, nor yet the latter of something which has behaved as this has for four years. There are similar difficulties about choosing between 'This *is* a hallucination' and 'This is *not* a hallucination'. With sound instinct, the plain man turns in such cases to Watson and says 'Well now, *what would you* say?' 'How would you *describe* it? The difficulty is just that: there is *no* short description which is not misleading: the only thing to do, and that can easily be done, is to set out the description of the facts at length. Ordinary language breaks down in extraordinary cases. (In such cases, the cause of the breakdown is semantical.) Now no doubt an *ideal* language would *not* break down, whatever happened. In doing physics, for example, where our language is tightened up in order precisely to describe complicated and unusual cases concisely, we *prepare linguistically for the worst*. In ordinary language we do not: *words fail us*. If we talk as though an ordinary must be like an ideal language, we shall misrepresent the facts.

Consider now 'being extended' and 'being shaped'. In ordinary life we never get into a situation where we learn to say that anything is extended but not shaped nor conversely. We have all learned to use, and have used, the words only in cases where it is correct to use both. Supposing now someone says '*x* is extended but has no shape'. Somehow we cannot see what this 'could mean'—there are no semantic conventions, explicit or implicit, to cover this case: yet it is not prohibited in any way— there are no limiting rules about what we might or might not say *in extraordinary cases*. It is not *merely* the difficulty of imagining or experiencing extraordinary cases, either, which causes worry. There is this too: we can only describe what it is we are trying to imagine, by means of words which precisely describe and evoke the *ordinary* case, which we are trying to think away. Ordinary language *blinkers* the already feeble imagination. It would be difficult, in this way, if I were to say 'Can I think of a case where a man would be neither at home nor not at home?' This is inhibiting, because I think of the *ordinary* case where I ask 'Is he at home?' and get the answer, 'No': when certainly he is not at home. But supposing I happen *first* to think of the situation when I call on him just after he has died: then I see at once it would be wrong to say either. So in our case, the only thing to do is to imagine or experience all kinds of odd situations, and then suddenly round on oneself and ask: there, *now* would I say that, being extended it must be shaped? A new idiom might in odd cases be demanded.

I should like to say, in concluding this section, that in the course of stressing that we must pay attention to the facts of *actual* language, what we can and cannot say, and *precisely* why, another and converse point takes shape. Although it will not do to force actual language to accord with some preconceived model: it *equally* will not do, having discovered the facts about 'ordinary usage' *to rest content* with that, as though there were nothing more to be discussed and discovered. There may be plenty that might happen and does happen which would need new and better language to describe it in. Very often philosophers are only engaged on this task, when they seem to be perversely using words in a way which makes no sense according to 'ordinary usage'. There may be extraordinary facts, even about our everyday experience, which plain men and plain language overlook.

III

The last, and perhaps least unimportant point I have to make is the following: it seems to me that far more *detailed* attention ought to be given to that celebrated question, the posing of which has given birth to, and still keeps alive, so many erroneous theories, namely: why do we call different things by the same name? In reply to this, the philoprogenitive invent theories of 'universals' and what not: some entity or other to be that of which the 'name' is the name. And in reply to *them*, the more cautious (the 'nominalists') have usually been content to reply simply that: the reason why we call different things by the same name is simply that the things are *similar*: there is nothing *identical* present in them. This reply is inadequate in many respects: it does not, for example, attack the misleading form in which the question is posed, nor sufficiently go into the peculiarities of the word 'similar'. But what I wish to object to in it tonight is rather this: that *it is not in the least true* that all the things which I 'call by the same (general) name' *are* in general 'similar', in any ordinary sense of that much abused word.

It is a most strange thing that 'nominalists' should rest content with this answer. Not merely is it untrue to the facts; but further, if they had examined the facts, which are, in themselves, interesting enough, they could have produced with little trouble a far more formidable case against their opponents. So long as they say the things *are similar*, it will always be open to someone to say: 'Ah yes, similar *in a certain respect*: and that can only be explained by means of universals' (or whatever the name may be that they prefer for that well-tried nostrum): or again to maintain that similarity is only 'intelligible' as partial *identity*: and so on. And even those who are not persuaded entirely, may yet go so far as to allow that the 'similarity' and 'identity' languages are *alternatives*, the choice between which is indifferent. But surely, if it were made evident that we often 'call different things by the same name', and for perfectly 'good reasons',[1] when the things are not even in any ordinary sense 'similar', it will become excessively difficult to maintain that there is something 'identical' present in each—and after all, it is in *refuting* that position that the nominalist is really interested. Not, of course, that we can really *refute* it, or hope to cure those incurables who have long since reached the tertiary stage of universals.

Leaving historical disputes aside, it is a matter of urgency that a doctrine should be developed about the various kinds of good reasons for which we 'call different things[2] by the same name'. This is an absorbing question, but habitually neglected, so far as I know, by philologists as well as by philosophers. Lying in the no man's land between them, it falls between two schools, to develop such a doctrine fully would be very complicated and perhaps tedious: but also very useful in many ways. It demands the study of *actual* languages, *not* ideal ones. That the Polish semanticists have discussed such questions I neither know nor believe. Aristotle did to a quite considerable extent, but scrappily and inexactly.

[1] We are not interested in mere equivocation, of course.
[2] Strictly, *sorts* of things rather than *particular* things.

I shall proceed forthwith simply to give some of the more obvious cases where the reasons for 'calling different sorts of things by the same name' are not to be dismissed lightly as 'similarity'. And show how consideration of these facts may warn us against errors which are constant in philosophy.

1. A very simple case indeed is one often mentioned by Aristotle: the adjective 'healthy': when I talk of a healthy body and again of a healthy complexion, of healthy exercise: the word is *not* just being used *equivocally*. Aristotle would say it is being used 'paronymously'.[1] In this case there is what we may call a *primary nuclear* sense of 'healthy': the sense in which 'healthy' is used of a healthy body: I call this *nuclear* because it is 'contained as a part' in the other two senses which may be set out as 'productive of healthy bodies' and 'resulting from a healthy body'.

This is a simple case, easily understood. Yet constantly it is forgotten when we start disputing as to whether a certain word *has* 'two senses' or has *not* two senses. I remember myself disputing as to whether 'exist' has two senses (as used of material objects and again of sensa), or only one: actually we were agreed that 'exist' is used paronymously, only he called that 'having two senses', and I did not. Prichard's paper[2] on ἀγαθόν (in Aristotle) contains a classic instance of misunderstanding about paronymity, and so worrying about whether a word really 'has always the same meaning' or 'has several different meanings'.

Now are we to be content to say that the exercise, the complexion, and the body are all called 'healthy' 'because they are similar'? Such a remark cannot fail to be misleading. Why make it? And why not direct attention to the important and actual facts?

2. The next case I shall take is what Aristotle calls 'analogous' terms. When A : B :: X : Y then A and X are often called by

---

[1] But there are other varieties of paronymity of course.

[2] 'The Meaning of ΑΓΑΘΟΝ in the *Ethics* of Aristotle', by H. A. Prichard. Reprinted in his *Moral Obligation*, Oxford, 1949.

the same name, e.g. the foot of a mountain and the foot of a list. Here there is a good reason for calling the things both 'feet' but are we to say they are 'similar'? Not in any ordinary sense. We may say that the relations in which they stand to B and Y respectively are similar relations. Well and good: but A and X are not the relations in which they stand: and any-one simply told that, in calling A and X both 'feet' I was calling attention to a 'similarity' in them, would probably be misled. Anyhow, it is most necessary to remember that 'similarity' covers such possibilities if it is to do so. (An especially severe case of 'analogy' arises when a term is used, as Aristotle says 'in different categories': e.g. when I talk about 'change' as qualitative change, change of position, place, &c., how far is it true to say these 'changes' are 'similar'?)

3. Another case is where I call B by the same name as A, because it resembles A, C by the same name because it resembles B, D . . . and so on. But ultimately A and, say, D do not resemble each other in any recognizable sense at all. This is a very common case: and the dangers are obvious, when we search for something 'identical' in all of them!

4. Another case which is commonly found is this. Take a word like 'fascist': this originally connotes, say, a great many characteristics at once: say x, y, and z. Now we will use 'fascist' subsequently of things which possess only *one* of these striking characteristics. So that things called 'fascist' in these senses, which we may call 'incomplete' senses, need not be similar at all to each other. This often puzzles us most of all when the original 'complete' sense has been forgotten: com-pare the various meanings of 'cynicism': we should be puzzled to find the 'similarity' there! Sometimes the 'incompleteness' of the resemblance is coupled with a positive lack of resem-blance, so that we invent a phrase to mark it as a warning, e.g. 'cupboard love'.

5. Another better-known case is that of a so-called deter-minable and its determinates: colour and red, green, blue, &c., or rather 'absolutely specific' reds, greens, blues, &c. Because

this is better known, I shall not discuss it, though I am as a matter of fact rather sceptical about the accounts usually given. Instead, it should be pointed out how common this sort of relationship is and that it should be suspected in cases where we are prone to overlook it. A striking example is the case of 'pleasure': pleasures we may say not merely resemble each other in being pleasant, but also *differ* precisely in the way in which they are pleasant.[1] No greater mistake could be made than the hedonistic mistake (copied by non-hedonists) of thinking that pleasure is always a single similar feeling, somehow isolable from the various activities which 'give rise' to it.

6. Another case which often provides puzzles, is that of words like 'youth' and 'love': which sometimes mean the object loved, or the thing which is youthful, sometimes the passion 'Love' or the quality (?) 'youth'. These cases are of course easy (rather *like* 'healthy'?). But suppose we take the noun 'truth': here is a case where the disagreements between different theorists have largely turned on whether they interpreted this as a name of a substance, of a quality, or of a relation.

7. Lastly, I want to take a specially interesting sort of case, which is perhaps commoner and at the bottom of more muddles than we are aware of. Take the sense in which I talk of a cricket bat and a cricket ball and a cricket umpire. The reason that all are called by the same name is perhaps that each has its part—its *own special* part—to play in the activity called cricketing: it is no good to say that cricket *simply* means 'used in cricket': for we cannot explain what we mean by 'cricket' *except* by explaining the special parts played in cricketing by the bat, ball, &c. Aristotle's suggestion was that the word 'good' might be used in such a way: in which case it is obvious how far astray we should go if we look for a 'definition' of the word 'good' in any ordinary simple sense: or look for the way in which 'good' things are 'similar' to each other, in any ordinary sense. If we tried to find out by such methods what

---

[1] If we say that they are all called 'pleasures' 'because they are similar', we shall overlook this fact.

'cricket' meant, we should very likely conclude that it too was a simple unanalysable supersensible quality.

Another thing that becomes plain from such examples is that the apparently common-sense distinction between 'What is the meaning of the word x' and 'What particular things *are* x and to what degrees?' is not of universal application by any means. The questions cannot be distinguished in such cases. Or a similar case would be some word like 'golfing': it is not sense to ask 'What is the meaning of golfing?' 'What things are golfing?' Though it *is* sense to ask what component activities go to constitute golfing, what implements are used in golfing ('golf' clubs, &c.) and in what ways. Aristotle suggests 'happiness' is a word of this kind: in which case it is evident how far astray we shall go if we treat it as though it were a word like 'whiteness'.

These summarily treated examples are enough to show how essential it is to have a thorough knowledge of the different reasons for which we call different things by the same name, before we can embark confidently on an inquiry. If we rush up with a demand for a definition in the simple manner of Plato or many other philosophers, if we use the rigid dichotomy 'same meaning, different meaning', or 'What x means', as distinguished from 'the things which are x', we shall simply make hashes of things. Perhaps some people are now discussing such questions seriously. All that is to be found in traditional Logics is the mention that there are, besides univocal and equivocal words, 'also analogous words': which, without further explanation, is used to lump together all cases where a word has not always absolutely the same meaning, nor several absolutely different meanings. All that 'similarity' theorists manage is to say that all things called by some one name are similar to some one pattern, or are all more similar to each other than any of them is to anything else; which is *obviously* untrue. Anyone who wishes to see the complexity of the problem, has only got to look in a (good) dictionary under such a word as 'head': the different meanings of the word 'head' will be related to each other in all sorts of different ways at once.

To summarize the contentions of this paper then. Firstly, the phrase 'the meaning of a word' is a spurious phrase. Secondly and consequently, a re-examination is needed of phrases like the two which I discuss, 'being a part of the meaning of' and 'having the same meaning'. On these matters, dogmatists require prodding: although history indeed suggests that it may sometimes be better to let sleeping dogmatists lie.

4

OTHER MINDS[1]

I FEEL that I agree with much, and especially with the more important parts, of what Mr. Wisdom has written, both in his present paper and in his beneficial series of articles on 'Other Minds' and other matters. I feel ruefully sure, also, that one must be at least one sort of fool to rush in over ground so well trodden by the angels. At best I can hope only to make a contribution to one part of the problem, where it seems that a little more industry still might be of service. I could only wish it was a more central part. In fact, however, I did find myself unable to approach the centre while still bogged down on the periphery. And Mr. Wisdom himself may perhaps be sympathetic towards a policy of splitting hairs to save starting them.

Mr. Wisdom, no doubt correctly, takes the 'Predicament' to be brought on by such questions as 'How do we know that another man is angry?' He also cites other forms of the question—'Do we (ever) know?', 'Can we know?', 'How can we know?' the thoughts, feelings, sensations, mind, &c., of another creature, and so forth. But it seems likely that each of these further questions is rather different from the first, which alone has been enough to keep me preoccupied, and to which I shall stick.

Mr. Wisdom's method is to go on to ask: *Is it like the way in which we know* that a kettle is boiling, or that there is a tea-party next door, or the weight of thistledown? But it seemed to me that perhaps, as he went on, he was not giving an altogether accurate account (perhaps only because too cursory a

[1] Reprinted from *Proceedings of the Aristotelian Society*, Supplementary Volume xx (1946), by courtesy of the editor.

one) of what we should say if asked 'How do you know?'
these things. For example, in the case of the tea-party, to say
we knew of it 'by analogy' would at best be a very sophisticated answer (and one to which some sophisticates might prefer
the phrase 'by induction'), while in addition it seems incorrect
because we don't, I think, claim to *know* by analogy, but only
to *argue* by analogy. Hence I was led on to consider what sort
of thing does actually happen when ordinary people are asked
'How do you know?'

Much depends, obviously, on the sort of item it is about
which we are being asked 'How do you know?' and there are
bound to be many kinds of case that I shall not cover at all, or
not in detail. The sort of statement which seems simplest, and
at the same time not, on the face of it, unlike 'He is angry', is
such a statement as 'That is a goldfinch' ('The kettle is boiling')
—a statement of particular, current, empirical fact. This is the
sort of statement on making which we are liable to be asked
'How do you know?' and the sort that, at least sometimes, we
say we don't know, but only believe. It may serve for a stalking-
horse as well as another.

When we make an assertion such as 'There is a goldfinch
in the garden' or 'He is angry', there is a sense in which we
imply that we are sure of it or know it ('But I took it you
knew', said reproachfully), though what we imply, in a similar
sense and more strictly, is only that we *believe* it. On making
such an assertion, therefore, we are directly exposed to the
questions (1) 'Do you *know* there is?' 'Do you *know* he is?' and
(2) '*How* do you know?' If in answer to the first question we
reply 'Yes', we may then be asked the second question, and
even the first question alone is commonly taken as an invitation
to state not merely *whether* but also *how* we know. But on the
other hand, we may well reply 'No' in answer to the first
question: we may say 'No, but I think there is', 'No, but I
believe he is'. For the implication that I know or am sure
is not strict: we are not all (terribly or sufficiently) strictly
brought up. If we do this, then we are exposed to the question,

which might also have been put to us without preliminaries, 'Why do you believe that?' (or 'What makes you think so?', 'What induces you to suppose so?', &c.).

There is a singular difference between the two forms of challenge: '*How* do you know?' and '*Why* do you believe?' We seem never to ask '*Why* do you know?' or '*How* do you believe?' And in this, as well as in other respects to be noticed later, not merely such other words as 'suppose' 'assume', &c., but also the expressions 'be sure' and 'be certain', follow the example of 'believe', not that of 'know'.

Either question, 'How do you know?' or 'Why do you believe?', may well be asked only out of respectful curiosity, from a genuine desire to learn. But again, they may both be asked as *pointed* questions, and, when they are so, a further difference comes out. 'How do you know?' suggests that perhaps you *don't* know it at all, whereas 'Why do you believe?' suggests that perhaps you *oughtn't* to believe it. There is no suggestion[1] that you *ought* not to know or that you *don't* believe it. If the answer to 'How do you know?' or to 'Why do you believe?' is considered unsatisfactory by the challenger, he proceeds rather differently in the two cases. His next riposte will be, on the one hand, something such as 'Then you *don't* know any such thing', or 'But that doesn't prove it: in that case you don't really know it at all', and on the other hand, something such as 'That's very poor evidence to go on: you oughtn't to believe it on the strength of that alone'.[2]

The 'existence' of your alleged belief is not challenged, but the 'existence' of your alleged knowledge *is* challenged. If we like to say that 'I believe', and likewise 'I am sure' and 'I am certain', are descriptions of subjective mental or cognitive states

---

[1] But in special senses and cases, there is—for example, if someone has announced some top secret information, we can ask, 'How do *you* know?', nastily.

[2] An interesting variant in the case of knowing would be 'You *oughtn't to say* (you've no business to say) you know it at all'. But of course this is only superficially similar to 'You oughtn't to believe it': you ought *to say* you believe it, if you do believe it, however poor the evidence.

or attitudes, or what not, then 'I know' is not that, or at least not merely that: it functions differently in talking.

'But of course', it will be said, ' "I know" is obviously more than that, more than a description of my own state. If I *know*, I *can't be wrong*. You can always show I don't know by showing I am wrong, or may be wrong, or that I didn't know by showing that I might have been wrong. *That's* the way in which knowing differs even from being as certain as can be.' This must be considered in due course, but first we should consider the types of answer that may be given in answer to the question 'How do you know?'

Suppose I have said 'There's a bittern at the bottom of the garden', and you ask 'How do you know?' my reply may take very different forms:

(*a*) I was brought up in the fens
(*b*) I heard it
(*c*) The keeper reported it
(*d*) By its booming
(*e*) From the booming noise
(*f*) Because it is booming.

We may say, roughly, that the first three are answers to the questions 'How do you come to know?', 'How are you in a position to know?', or 'How do *you* know?' understood in different ways: while the other three are answers to 'How can you tell?' understood in different ways. That is, I may take you to have been asking:

(1) How do I come to be in a position to know about bitterns?
(2) How do I come to be in a position to say there's a bittern here and now?
(3) How do (can) I tell bitterns?
(4) How do (can) I tell the thing here and now as a bittern?

The implication is that in order to know this is a bittern, I must have:

   (1) been trained in an environment where I could become
       familiar with bitterns
   (2) had a certain opportunity in the current case
   (3) learned to recognize or tell bitterns
   (4) succeeded in recognizing or telling this as a bittern.

(1) and (2) mean that my experiences must have been of
certain kinds, that I must have had certain opportunities: (3)
and (4) mean that I must have exerted a certain kind and
amount of acumen.[1]

The questions raised in (1) and (3) concern our *past* experiences, our opportunities and our activities in learning to
discriminate or discern, and, bound up with both, the correctness or otherwise of the linguistic usages we have acquired.
Upon these earlier experiences depends how *well* we know
things, just as, in different but cognate cases of 'knowing', it is
upon earlier experience that it depends how *thoroughly* or how
intimately we know: we know a person by sight or intimately,
a town inside out, a proof backwards, a job in every detail, a
poem word for word, a Frenchman when we see one. 'He
doesn't know what love (real hunger) is' means he hasn't
had enough experience to be able to recognize it and to
distinguish it from other things slightly like it. According to
how well I know an item, and according to the kind of item
it is, I can recognize it, describe it, reproduce it, draw it, recite
it, apply it, and so forth. Statements like 'I know *very well* he
isn't angry' or 'You know *very well* that isn't calico', though of
course about the current case, ascribe the excellence of the
knowledge to past experience, as does the general expression
'You are old enough to know better'.[2]

---

  [1] 'I know, I *know*, I've seen it a hundred times, don't keep on telling me'
complains of a superabundance of opportunity: 'knowing a hawk from a
handsaw' lays down a minimum of acumen in recognition or classification.
'As well as I know my own name' is said to typify something I *must* have
experienced and *must* have learned to discriminate.
  [2] The adverbs that can be inserted in 'How . . . do you know?' are few in
number and fall into still fewer classes. There is practically no overlap with

By contrast, the questions raised in (2) and (4) concern the circumstances of the current case. Here we can ask 'How *definitely* do you know?' You may know it for certain, quite positively, officially, on his own authority, from unimpeachable sources, only indirectly, and so forth.

Some of the answers to the question 'How do you know?' are, oddly enough, described as 'reasons for knowing' or 'reasons to know', or even sometimes as 'reasons why I know', despite the fact that we do not ask 'Why do you know?' But now surely, according to the Dictionary, 'reasons' should be given in answer to the question 'Why?' just as we do in fact give reasons for believing in answer to the question 'Why do you believe?' However there is a distinction to be drawn here. 'How do you know that IG Farben worked for war?' 'I have every reason to know: I served on the investigating commission': here, giving my reasons for knowing is stating how I come to be in a position to know. In the same way we use the expressions 'I know *because* I saw him do it' or 'I know *because* I looked it up only ten minutes ago': these are similar to 'So it is: it *is* plutonium. How did you know?' 'I did quite a bit of physics at school before I took up philology', or to 'I ought to know: I was standing only a couple of yards away'. Reasons for *believing* on the other hand are normally quite a different affair (a recital of symptoms, arguments in support, and so forth), though there are cases where we do give as reasons for believing our having been in a position in which we could get good evidence: 'Why do you believe he was lying?' 'I was watching him very closely.'

Among the cases where we give our reasons for knowing things, a special and important class is formed by those where we cite authorities. If asked 'How do you know the election is today?', I am apt to reply 'I read it in *The Times*', and if asked 'How do you know the Persians were defeated at Marathon?' I am apt to reply 'Herodotus expressly states that they

those that can be inserted in 'How . . . do you believe?' (firmly, sincerely, genuinely, &c.).

were'. In these cases 'know' is correctly used: we know 'at second hand' when we can cite an authority who was in a position to know (possibly himself also only at second hand).[1] The statement of an authority makes me aware of something, enables me to know something, which I shouldn't otherwise have known. It is a source of knowledge. In many cases, we contrast such reasons for knowing with other reasons for believing the very same thing: 'Even if we didn't know it, even if he hadn't confessed, the evidence against him would be enough to hang him'.

It is evident, of course, that this sort of 'knowledge' is 'liable to be wrong', owing to the unreliability of human testimony (bias, mistake, lying, exaggeration, &c.). Nevertheless, the occurrence of a piece of human testimony radically alters the situation. We say 'We shall never know what Caesar's feelings were on the field of the battle of Philippi', because he did not pen an account of them: *if* he *had*, then to say 'We shall never know' won't do in the same way, even though we may still perhaps find reason to say 'It doesn't read very plausibly: we shall never *really* know the *truth*' and so on. Naturally, we are judicious: we don't say we know (at second hand) if there is any special reason to doubt the testimony: but there has to be *some* reason. It is fundamental in talking (as in other matters) that we are entitled to trust others, except in so far as there is some concrete reason to distrust them. Believing persons, accepting testimony, is the, or one main, point of talking. We don't play (competitive) games except in the faith that our opponent is trying to win: if he isn't, it isn't a game, but something different. So we don't talk with people

---

[1] Knowing at second hand, or on authority, is not the same as 'knowing indirectly', whatever precisely that difficult and perhaps artificial expression may mean. If a murderer 'confesses', then, whatever our opinion of the worth of the 'confession', we cannot say that 'we (only) know indirectly that he did it', nor can we so speak when a witness, reliable or unreliable, has stated that he saw the man do it. Consequently, it is not correct, either, to say that the murderer himself knows 'directly' that he did it, whatever precisely 'knowing directly' may mean.

(descriptively) except in the faith that they are trying to convey information.[1]

It is now time to turn to the question 'How can you tell?', i.e. to senses (2) and (4) of the question 'How do you know?' If you have asked 'How do you know it's a goldfinch?' then I may reply 'From its behaviour', 'By its markings', or, in more detail, 'By its red head', 'From its eating thistles'. That is, I indicate, or to some extent set out with some degree of precision, those features of the situation which enable me to recognize it as one to be described in the way I did describe it. Thereupon you may still object in several ways to my saying it's a goldfinch, without in the least 'disputing my facts', which is a further stage to be dealt with later. You may object:

(1) But goldfinches *don't* have red heads

(1a) But that's not a *goldfinch*. From your own description I can recognize it as a gold*crest*

(2) But that's not enough: plenty of other birds have red heads. What you say doesn't prove it. For all you know, it may be a woodpecker.

Objections (1) and (1a) claim that, in one way or another, I am evidently unable to recognize goldfinches. It may be (1a)—that I have not learned the right (customary, popular, official) name to apply to the creature ('Who taught you to use the word "goldfinch"?'):[2] or it may be that my powers of discernment, and consequently of classification, have never been brought sharply to bear in these matters, so that I remain

---

[1] Reliance on the authority of others is fundamental, too, in various special matters, for example, for corroboration and for the correctness of our own use of words, which we learn from others.

[2] Misnaming is not a trivial or laughing matter. If I misname I shall mislead others, and I shall also misunderstand information given by others to me. 'Of course I knew all about his condition perfectly, but I never realized that was *diabetes*: I thought it was cancer, and all the books agree that's incurable: if I'd only known it was diabetes, I should have thought of insulin at once'. Knowing *what a thing is* is, to an important extent, knowing what the name for it, and the right name for it, is.

confused as to how to tell the various species of small British bird. Or, of course, it may be a bit of both. In making this sort of accusation, you would perhaps tend not so much to use the expression 'You don't know' or 'You oughtn't to say you know' as, rather, 'But that *isn't* a goldfinch (*goldfinch*)', or 'Then you're wrong to call it a goldfinch'. But still, if asked, you would of course deny the statement that I do know it is a goldfinch.

It is in the case of objection (2) that you would be more inclined to say right out 'Then you don't know'. Because it doesn't prove it, it's not enough to prove it. Several important points come out here:

(*a*) If you say 'That's not enough', then you must have in mind some more or less definite lack. 'To be a goldfinch, besides having a red head it must also have the characteristic eye-markings': or 'How do you know it isn't a woodpecker? Woodpeckers have red heads too'. If there is no definite lack, which you are at least prepared to specify on being pressed, then it's silly (outrageous) just to go on saying 'That's not enough'.

(*b*) Enough is enough: it doesn't mean everything. Enough means enough to show that (within reason, and for present intents and purposes) it 'can't' be anything else, there is no room for an alternative, competing, description of it. It does *not* mean, for example, enough to show it isn't a *stuffed* goldfinch.

(*c*) '*From* its red head', given as an answer to 'How do you know?' requires careful consideration: in particular it differs very materially from '*Because* it has a red head', which is also sometimes given as an answer to 'How do you know?', and is commonly given as an answer to 'Why do you believe?' It is much more akin to such obviously 'vague' replies as 'From its markings' or 'From its behaviour' than at first appears. Our claim, in saying we know (i.e. that we can tell) is to *recognize*: and recognizing, at least in this sort of case, consists in seeing, or otherwise sensing, a feature or features which we are sure are similar to something noted (and usually named) before, on some earlier occasion in our experience. But, this that we see, or otherwise sense, is not necessarily *describable in words*, still less describable in detail, and in non-committal words, and by anybody you please. Nearly everybody can recognize a surly look or the smell of tar, but few can describe them non-committally, i.e. otherwise than as 'surly' or 'of tar': many can recognize, and 'with certainty', ports of different vintages, models by different fashion houses, shades of green, motor-car makes from behind, and so forth, without being able to say '*how* they recognize them', i.e. without being able to 'be more specific about it'—they can only say they can tell 'by the taste', 'from the cut', and so on. So, when I say I can tell the bird 'from its red head', or that I know a friend 'by his nose', I imply that there is something *peculiar* about the red head or the nose, something peculiar to goldfinches or to him, by which you can (always) tell them or him. In view of the fewness and crudeness of the classificatory words in any language compared with the infinite number of features which are recognized, or which could be picked out and recognized, in our experience, it is small wonder that we often and often fall back on the phrases beginning with 'from' and 'by', and that we are not able to *say*, further and precisely, *how* we can tell. Often we know things quite well, while scarcely able at all to say 'from' what we know them, let alone what there is so very special about them. Any answer beginning 'From' or 'By' has, intentionally, this saving 'vagueness'. But on the contrary, an answer beginning 'Because' is dangerously definite. When I say I know it's a goldfinch 'Because it has a red head', that implies that all I have noted, or needed to note, about it is that its head is red (nothing special or peculiar about the shade, shape, &c. of the patch): so that I imply that there is no other small British bird that has any sort of red head except the goldfinch.

(*d*) Whenever I say I know, I am always liable to be taken to claim that, in a certain sense appropriate to the kind of statement (and to present intents and purposes), I am able to *prove* it. In the present, very common, type of case, 'proving' seems to mean stating what are the features of the current case which are enough to constitute it one which is correctly describable in the way we have described it, and not in any other way relevantly variant. Generally speaking, cases where I can 'prove' are cases where we use the 'because' formula: cases where we 'know but can't prove' are cases where we take refuge in the 'from' or 'by' formula.

I believe that the points so far raised are those most genuinely and normally raised by the question 'How do you know?' But there are other, further, questions sometimes raised under the same rubric, and especially by philosophers, which may be thought more important. These are the worries about 'reality' and about being 'sure and certain'.

Up to now, in challenging me with the question 'How do you know?', you are not taken to have *queried my credentials as stated*, though you have asked what they were: nor have you *disputed my facts* (the facts on which I am relying to prove it is a goldfinch), though you have asked me to detail them. It is this further sort of challenge that may now be made, a challenge as to the *reliability* of our alleged 'credentials' and our alleged 'facts'. You may ask:

(1) But do you know it's a *real* goldfinch? How do you know you're not dreaming? Or after all, mightn't it be a stuffed one? And is the head really red? Couldn't it have been dyed, or isn't there perhaps an odd light reflected on it?

(2) But are you certain it's the *right* red for a goldfinch? Are you quite sure it isn't too orange? Isn't it perhaps rather too strident a note for a bittern?

These two sorts of worry are distinct, though very probably they can be combined or confused, or may run into one another: e.g. 'Are you sure it's really red?' may mean 'Are you sure it isn't orange?' or again 'Are you sure it isn't just the peculiar light?'

1. *Reality*

If you ask me, 'How do you know it's a real stick?' 'How do you know it's really bent?' ('Are you sure he's really angry?'), then you are querying my credentials or my facts (it's often uncertain which) in a certain special way. In various *special*, *recognized* ways, depending essentially upon the nature of the matter which I have announced myself to know, either my current experiencing or the item currently under consideration (or uncertain which) may be abnormal, *phoney*. Either I myself may be dreaming, or in delirium, or under the influence of mescal, &c.: or else the item may be stuffed, painted, dummy, artificial, trick, freak, toy, assumed, feigned, &c.: or else again there's an uncertainty (it's left open) whether *I* am to blame or *it* is—mirages, mirror images, odd lighting effects, &c.

These doubts are all to be allayed by means of recognized procedures (more or less roughly recognized, of course), appropriate to the particular type of case. There are recognized ways of distinguishing between dreaming and waking (how otherwise should we know how to use and to contrast the words?), and of deciding whether a thing is stuffed or live, and so forth. The doubt or question 'But is it a *real* one?' has always (*must* have) a special basis, there must be some 'reason for suggesting' that it isn't real, in the sense of some specific way, or limited number of specific ways, in which it is suggested that this experience or item may be phoney. Sometimes (usually) the context makes it clear what the suggestion is: the goldfinch might be stuffed but there's no suggestion that it's a mirage, the oasis might be a mirage but there's no suggestion it might be stuffed. If the context doesn't make it clear, then I am entitled to ask 'How do you mean? Do you mean it may be stuffed or what? *What are you suggesting*?' The wile of the metaphysician consists in asking 'Is it a real table?' (a kind of object which has no obvious way of being phoney) and not specifying or limiting what may be wrong with it, so that I feel at a loss 'how to prove' it *is* a real one.[1] It is the use of the word 'real' in this

---

[1] Conjurers, too, trade on this. 'Will some gentleman kindly satisfy himself that this is a perfectly ordinary hat?' This leaves us baffled and uneasy: sheepishly we agree that it seems all right, while conscious that we have not the least idea what to guard against.

manner that leads us on to the supposition that 'real' has a single meaning ('the real world' 'material objects'), and that a highly profound and puzzling one. Instead, we should insist always on specifying with what 'real' is being contrasted—'not what' I shall have to show it is, in order to show it is 'real': and then usually we shall find some specific, less fatal, word, appropriate to the particular case, to substitute for 'real'.

Knowing it's a 'real' goldfinch isn't in question in the ordinary case when I say I know it's a goldfinch: reasonable precautions only are taken. But when it *is* called in question, in *special* cases, then I make sure it's a real goldfinch in ways essentially similar to those in which I made sure it was a goldfinch, though corroboration by other witnesses plays a specially important part in some cases. Once again the precautions cannot be more than reasonable, relative to current intents and purposes. And once again, in the special cases just as in the ordinary cases, two further conditions hold good:

(*a*) I don't by any means *always* know whether it's one or not. It may fly away before I have a chance of testing it, or of inspecting it thoroughly enough. This is simple enough: yet some are prone to argue that because I *sometimes* don't know or can't discover, I *never* can.

(*b*) 'Being sure it's real' is no more proof against miracles or outrages of nature than anything else is or, *sub specie humanitatis*, can be. If we have made sure it's a goldfinch, and a real goldfinch, and then in the future it does something outrageous (explodes, quotes Mrs. Woolf, or what not), we don't say we were wrong to say it was a goldfinch, *we don't know what to say*. Words literally fail us: 'What would you have said?' 'What are we to say now?' 'What would *you* say?' When I have made sure it's a real goldfinch (not stuffed, corroborated by the disinterested, &c.) then I am *not* 'predicting' in saying it's a real goldfinch, and in a very good sense I can't be proved wrong whatever happens. It seems a serious mistake to suppose that language (or most language, language about real things) is 'predictive' in such a way that the future can always prove it wrong. What the future *can* always do, is to make us *revise our ideas* about goldfinches or real goldfinches or anything else.

Perhaps the normal procedure of language could be schematized as follows. First, it is arranged that, on experiencing a complex of features C, then we are to say 'This is C' or 'This is a C'. Then subsequently, the occurrence either of the whole of C or of a significant and characteristic part of it is, on one or many occasions, accompanied or followed in definite circumstances by another special and distinctive feature or complex of features, which makes it seem desirable to revise our ideas: so that we draw a distinction between 'This looks like a C, but in fact is only a dummy, &c.' and 'This is a real C (live, genuine, &c.)'. *Henceforward*, we can only ascertain that it's a *real* C by ascertaining that the special feature or complex of features is present in the appropriate circumstances. The old expression 'This is a C' will tend as heretofore to fail to draw any distinction between 'real, live, &c.' and 'dummy, stuffed, &c.' If the special distinctive feature is one which does not have to manifest itself in *any* definite circumstances (on application of some specific test, after some limited lapse of time, &c.) then it is not a suitable feature on which to base a distinction between 'real' and 'dummy, imaginary, &c.' All we can then do is to say 'Some Cs are and some aren't, some do and some don't: and it may be very interesting or important whether they are or aren't, whether they do or don't, but they're all Cs, real Cs, just the same'.[1] Now if the special feature is one which must appear in (more or less) definite circumstances, then 'This is a real C' is not necessarily predictive: we can, in favourable cases, make sure of it.[2]

[1] The awkwardness about some snarks being boojums.

[2] Sometimes, on the basis of the new special feature, we distinguish, not between 'Cs' and 'real Cs', but rather between Cs and Ds. There is a reason for choosing the one procedure rather than the other: all cases where we use the 'real' formula exhibit (complicated and serpentine) likenesses, as do all cases where we use 'proper', a word which behaves in many ways like 'real', and is no less nor more profound.

2. *Sureness and Certainty*

The other way of querying my credentials and proofs ('Are you sure it's the *right* red?') is quite different. Here we come up against Mr. Wisdom's views on 'the peculiarity of a man's knowledge of his own sensations', for which he refers us to 'Other Minds VII' (*Mind*, vol. lii, N.S., no. 207), a passage with which I find I disagree.

Mr. Wisdom there says that, excluding from consideration cases like 'being in love' and other cases which 'involve prediction', and considering statements like 'I am in pain' which, in the requisite sense, do *not* involve prediction, then a man *cannot* 'be wrong' in making them, in the most favoured sense of being wrong: that is, though it is of course possible for him to *lie* (so that 'I am in pain' may be false), and though it is also possible for him to *misname*, i.e. to use the word 'pawn', say, instead of 'pain', which would be liable to mislead others but would not mislead himself, either because he regularly uses 'pawn' for 'pain' or because the use was a momentary aberration, as when I call John 'Albert' while knowing him quite well to be John—though it is possible for him to be 'wrong' in these two senses, it is not possible for him to be wrong in the most favoured sense. He says again that, with this class of statement (elsewhere called 'sense-statements'), to know directly that one is in pain is 'to say that one is, and to say it on the basis of being in pain': and again, that the peculiarity of sense-statements lies in the fact that 'when they are correct and made by X, then X knows they are correct'.

This seems to me mistaken, though it is a view that, in more or less subtle forms, has been the basis of a very great deal of philosophy. It is perhaps the original sin (Berkeley's apple, the tree in the quad) by which the philosopher casts himself out from the garden of the world we live in.

Very clearly detailed, this is the view that, at least and only in a certain favoured type of case, I can 'say what I see (or otherwise sense)' almost quite literally. On this view, if I were to say 'Here is something red', then I might be held to imply or to state that it is really a red thing, a thing which would appear red in a standard light, or to other people, or tomorrow too, and perhaps even more besides: all of which 'involves prediction' (if not also a metaphysical substratum). Even if I were to say 'Here is something which looks red', I might still be held to imply or to state that it looks red to others also, and so forth. If, however, I confine myself to stating 'Here is something that looks red to me now', then at last I can't be wrong (in the most favoured sense).

However, there is an ambiguity in 'something that looks red to me now'. Perhaps this can be brought out by italics, though it is not really so much a matter of emphasis as of tone and expression, of confidence and hesitancy. Contrast 'Here is something that (definitely) *looks to me* (anyhow) red' with 'Here is something that looks to me (something like) *red* (I should say)'. In the former case I am quite confident that, however it may look to others, whatever it may 'really be', &c., it certainly does look red to me at the moment. In the other case I'm not confident at all: it looks reddish, but I've never seen anything quite like it before, I can't quite describe it— or, I'm not very good at recognizing colours, I never feel quite happy about them, I've constantly been caught out about them. Of course, this sounds silly in the case of 'red': red is so *very* obvious, we all know red when we see it, it's *unmistakable*.[1] Cases where we should not feel happy about red are not easy (though not impossible) to find. But take 'magenta': 'It looks rather like magenta to me—but then I wouldn't be too sure about distinguishing magenta from mauve or from heliotrope. Of course I know in a way it's purplish, but I don't really know whether to say it's magenta or not: I just can't be sure.' Here, I am not interested in ruling out consideration of how it looks to others (looks *to me*) or considerations about what its *real* colour is (*looks*): what I am ruling out is *my being sure or certain* what it looks to me. Take tastes, or take sounds:

[1] And yet she always *thought* his shirt was white until she saw it against Tommy's Persil-washed one.

these are so much better as examples than colours, because we never feel so happy with our other senses as with our eyesight. Any description of a taste or sound or smell (or colour) or of a feeling, involves (is) saying that it is like one or some that we have experienced before: any descriptive word is classificatory, involves recognition and in that sense memory, and only when we use such words (or names or descriptions, which come down to the same) are we knowing anything, or believing anything. But memory and recognition are often uncertain and unreliable.

Two rather different ways of being hesitant may be distinguished.

(a) Let us take the case where we are tasting a certain taste. We may say 'I simply don't know what it is: I've never tasted anything remotely like it before. . . . No, it's no use: the more I think about it the more confused I get: it's perfectly distinct and perfectly distinctive, quite unique in my experience'. This illustrates the case where I can find nothing in my past experience with which to compare the current case: I'm certain it's not appreciably like anything I ever tasted before, not sufficiently like anything I know to merit the same description. This case, though distinguishable enough, shades off into the more common type of case where I'm not quite certain, or only fairly certain, or practically certain, that it's the taste of, say, laurel. In all such cases, I am endeavouring to recognize the current item by searching in my past experience for something like it, some likeness in virtue of which it deserves, more or less positively, to be described by the same descriptive word:[1] and I am meeting with varying degrees of success.

(b) The other case is different, though it very naturally combines itself with the first. Here, what I try to do is to *savour* the current experience, to *peer* at it, to sense it vividly. I'm not sure it *is* the taste of pineapple: isn't there perhaps just *some-*

---

[1] Or, of course, related to it in some other way than by 'similarity' (in any ordinary sense of 'similarity'), which is yet sufficient reason for describing it by the same word.

thing about it, a tang, a bite, a lack of bite, a cloying sensation, which isn't *quite* right for pineapple? Isn't there perhaps just a peculiar hint of green, which would rule out mauve and would hardly do for heliotrope? Or perhaps it is faintly odd: I must look more intently, scan it over and over: maybe just possibly there is a suggestion of an unnatural shimmer, so that it doesn't look quite like ordinary water. There is a lack of sharpness in what we actually sense, which is to be cured not, or not merely, by thinking, but by acuter discernment, by sensory discrimination (though it is of course true that thinking of other, and more pronounced, cases in our past experience can and does assist our powers of discrimination).[1]

Cases (*a*) and (*b*) alike, and perhaps usually together, lead to our being not quite sure or certain what it is, what to say, how to describe it: what our feelings really are, whether the tickling is painful exactly, whether I'm really what you'd call angry with him or only something rather like it. The hesitation is of course, in a sense, over misnaming: but I am not so much or merely worried about possibly misleading others as about misleading myself (the most favoured sense of being wrong). I should suggest that the two expressions 'being certain' and 'being sure', though from the nature of the case they are often used indiscriminately, have a tendency to refer to cases (*a*) and (*b*) respectively. 'Being certain' tends to indicate confidence in our memories and our past discernment, 'being sure' to indicate confidence in the current perception. Perhaps this comes out in our use of the concessives 'to be sure' and 'certainly', and in our use of such phrases as 'certainly not 'and 'surely not'. But it may be unwise to chivvy language beyond the coarser nuances.

It may be said that, even when I don't know exactly how to describe it, I nevertheless *know* that I *think* (and roughly how confidently I think) it is mauve. So I do know *something*. But

[1] This appears to cover cases of dull or careless or uninstructed perception, as opposed to cases of diseased or drugged perception.

this is irrelevant: I *don't* know it's mauve, that it definitely looks to me now mauve. Besides, there are cases where I really don't know what I think: I'm completely baffled by it.

Of course, there are any number of 'sense-statements' about which I can be, and am, completely sure. In ordinary cases ordinary men are nearly always certain when a thing looks red (or reddish, or anyhow reddish rather than greenish), or when they're in pain (except when that's rather difficult to say, as when they're being tickled): in ordinary cases an expert, a dyer or a dress designer, will be quite sure when something looks (to him in the present light) reseda green or nigger brown, though those who are not experts will not be so sure. Nearly always, if not quite always, we can be quite, or pretty, sure if we take refuge in a sufficiently *rough* description of the sensation: roughness and sureness tend to vary inversely. But the less rough descriptions, just as much as the rough, are all 'sense-statements'.

It is, I think, the problems of sureness and certainty, which philosophers tend (if I am not mistaken) to neglect, that have considerably exercised scientists, while the problem of 'reality', which philosophers have cultivated, does not exercise them. The whole apparatus of measures and standards seems designed to combat unsureness and uncertainty, and concomitantly to increase the possible precision of language, which, in science, pays. But for the words 'real' and 'unreal' the scientist tends to substitute, wisely, their cash-value substitutes, of which he invents and defines an increasing number, to cover an increasing variety of cases: he doesn't ask 'Is it real?' but rather 'Is it denatured?' or 'Is it an allotropic form?' and so on.

It is not clear to me what the class of sense-statements is, nor what its 'peculiarity' is. Some who talk of sense-statements (or sense data) appear to draw a distinction between talking about simple things like red or pain, and talking about complicated things like love or tables. But apparently Mr. Wisdom does not, because he treats 'This looks to me now like a man eating poppies' as in the same case with 'This looks to me now red'.

In this he is surely right: a man eating poppies may be more 'complex' to recognize, but it is often not appreciably more difficult than the other. But if, again, we say that non-sense-statements are those which involve 'prediction', why so? True, if I say, 'This is a (real) oasis' without first ascertaining that it's not a mirage, then I do chance my hand: but if I *have* ascertained that it's not, and can recognize for sure that it isn't (as when I am drinking its waters), then surely I'm not chancing my hand any longer. I believe, of course, that it will continue to perform as (real) oases normally do: but if there's a *lusus naturae*, a miracle, and it doesn't, that wouldn't mean I was wrong, previously, to call it a real oasis.

With regard to Mr. Wisdom's own chosen formulae, we have seen already that it can't be right to say that the peculiarity of sense-statements is that 'when they are correct, and made by X, then X knows they are correct': for X may *think*, without much confidence, that it tastes to him like Lapsang, and yet be far from certain, and then subsequently become certain, or more certain, that it did or didn't. The other two formulae were: 'To know that one is in pain is to say that one is and to say it on the basis of being in pain' and that the only mistake possible with sense-statements is typified by the case where 'knowing him to be Jack I call him "Alfred", thinking his name is Alfred or not caring a damn what his name is'. The snag in both these lies in the phrases 'on the basis of being in pain' and 'knowing him to be Jack'. 'Knowing him to be Jack' means that I have recognized him as Jack, a matter over which I may well be hesitant and/or mistaken: it is true that I needn't recognize him *by name* as 'Jack' (and hence I may call him 'Alfred'), but at least I must be recognizing him correctly as, for instance, the man I last saw in Jerusalem, or else I *shall* be misleading *myself*. Similarly, if 'on the basis of being in pain' only means 'when I am (what would be correctly described as) in pain', then something more than merely *saying* 'I'm in pain' is necessary for knowing I'm in pain: and this something more, as it involves recognition, may be hesitant and/or mistaken, though it is of course unlikely to be so in a case so comparatively obvious as that of pain.

Possibly the tendency to overlook the problems of recognition is fostered by the tendency to use a direct object after the word *know*. Mr. Wisdom, for example, confidently uses such expressions as 'knowing the feelings of another (his mind, his sensations, his anger, his pain) in the way that *he* knows them'. But, although we do correctly use the expressions 'I know your feelings on the matter' or 'He knows his own mind' or (archaically) 'May I know your mind?', these are rather special expressions, which do not justify any general usage. 'Feelings' here has the sense it has in 'very strong feelings' in favour of or against something: perhaps it means 'views' or 'opinions' ('very decided opinions'), just as 'mind' in this usage is given by the Dictionary as equivalent to 'intention' or 'wish'. To extend the usage uncritically is somewhat as though, on the strength of the legitimate phrase 'knowing someone's tastes', we were to proceed to talk of 'knowing someone's sounds' or 'knowing someone's taste of pineapple'. If, for example, it is a case of *physical* feelings such as fatigue, we do not use the expression 'I know your feelings'.

When, therefore, Mr. Wisdom speaks generally of 'knowing his sensations', he presumably means this to be equivalent to 'knowing *what* he is seeing, smelling, &c.', just as 'knowing the winner of the Derby' means 'knowing *what won* the Derby'. But here again, the expression 'know what' seems sometimes to be taken, unconsciously and erroneously, to lend support to the practice of putting a direct object after *know*: for 'what' is liable to be understood as a relative, = 'that which'. This is a grammatical mistake: 'what' *can* of course be a relative, but in 'know what you feel' and 'know what won' it is an interrogative (Latin *quid*, not *quod*). In this respect, 'I can smell what he is smelling' differs from 'I can know what he is smelling'. 'I know what he is feeling' is not 'There is an x which both I know and he is feeling', but 'I know the answer to the question "What is he feeling?"' And similarly with 'I know what I am feeling': this does *not* mean that there is something which I am *both knowing and feeling*.

Expressions such as 'We don't know another man's anger in the way he knows it' or 'He knows his pain in a way we can't' seem barbarous. The man doesn't 'know his pain': he feels (not knows) what he recognizes as, or what he knows to be, anger (not his anger), and he knows that he is feeling angry. Always assuming that he does recognize the feeling, which in fact, though feeling it acutely, he may not: 'Now I know what it was, it was jealousy (or gooseflesh or angina). At the time I did not know at all what it was, I had never felt anything quite like it before: but since then I've got to know it quite well'.[1]

Uncritical use of the direct object after *know* seems to be one thing that leads to the view that (or to talking as though) sensa, that is things, colours, noises, and the rest, speak or are labelled by nature, so that I can literally *say* what (that which) I *see*: it pipes up, or I read it off. It is as if sensa were *literally* to 'announce themselves' or to 'identify themselves', in the way we indicate when we say 'It presently identified itself as a particularly fine white rhinoceros'. But surely this is only a manner of speaking, a reflexive idiom in which the French, for example, indulge more freely than the English: sensa are dumb, and only previous experience enables *us* to identify them. If we choose to say that they 'identify themselves' (and certainly 'recognizing' is not a highly voluntary activity of ours), then it must be admitted that they share the birthright of all speakers, that of speaking unclearly and untruly.

If I know I can't be wrong

One final point about 'How do you know?', the challenge to the user of the expression 'I know', requires still to be brought

---

[1] There are, of course, legitimate uses of the direct object after *know*, and of the possessive pronoun before words for feelings. 'He knows the town well', 'He has known much suffering', 'My old vanity, how well I know it!'—even the pleonastic 'Where does he feel his (= the) pain?' and the educative tautology '*He* feels *his* pain'. But none of these really lends support to the metaphysical 'He knows his pain (in a way we can't)'.

out by consideration of the saying that 'If you know you can't
be wrong'. Surely, if what has so far been said is correct, then
we are often right to say we *know* even in cases where we turn
out subsequently to have been mistaken—and indeed we seem
always, or practically always, liable to be mistaken.

Now, we are perfectly, and should be candidly, aware of
this liability, which does not, however, transpire to be so very
onerous in practice. The human intellect and senses are, indeed,
inherently fallible and delusive, but not by any means *inveterately*
so. Machines are inherently liable to break down, but good
machines don't (often). It is futile to embark on a 'theory of
knowledge' which denies this liability: such theories constantly
end up by admitting the liability after all, and denying the
existence of 'knowledge'.

'When you know you can't be wrong' is perfectly good
sense. You are prohibited from saying 'I know it is so, but
I may be wrong', just as you are prohibited from saying
'I promise I will, but I may fail'. If you are aware you may be
mistaken, you ought not to say you know, just as, if you are
aware you may break your word, you have no business to
promise. But of course, being aware that you may be mistaken
doesn't mean merely being aware that you are a fallible
human being: it means that you have some concrete reason to
suppose that you may be mistaken in this case. Just as 'but I may
fail' does not mean merely 'but I am a weak human being' (in
which case it would be no more exciting than adding 'D.V.'):
it means that there is some concrete reason for me to suppose
that I shall break my word. It is naturally *always* possible
('humanly' possible) that I may be mistaken or may break my
word, but that by itself is no bar against using the expressions
'I know' and 'I promise' as we do in fact use them.

At the risk (long since incurred) of being tedious, the
parallel between saying 'I know' and saying 'I promise' may
be elaborated.[1]

---

[1] It is the use of the expressions 'I know' and 'I promise' (first person
singular, present indicative tense) alone that is being considered. 'If I knew,

When I say 'S is P', I imply at least that I believe it, and, if I have been strictly brought up, that I am (quite) sure of it: when I say 'I shall do A', I imply at least that I hope to do it, and, if I have been strictly brought up that I (fully) intend to. If I only believe that S is P, I can add 'But of course I may (very well) be wrong:' if I only hope to do A, I can add 'But of course I may (very well) not'. When I only believe or only hope, it is recognized that further evidence or further circumstances are liable to make me change my mind. If I say 'S is P' when I don't even believe it, I am lying: if I say it when I believe it but am not sure of it, I may be misleading but I am not exactly lying. If I say 'I shall do A' when I have not even any hope, not the slightest intention, of doing it, then I am deliberately deceiving: if I say it when I do not fully intend to, I am misleading but I am not deliberately deceiving in the same way.

But now, when I say 'I promise', a new plunge is taken: I have not merely announced my intention, but, by using this formula (performing this ritual), I have bound myself to others, and staked my reputation, in a new way. Similarly, saying 'I know' is taking a new plunge. But it is *not* saying 'I have performed a specially striking feat of cognition, superior, in the same scale as believing and being sure, even to being merely quite sure': for there *is* nothing in that scale superior to being quite sure. Just as promising is not something superior, in the same scale as hoping and intending, even to merely fully intending: for there *is* nothing in that scale superior to fully intending. When I say 'I know', I *give others my word*: I *give others my authority for saying* that 'S is P'.

I can't have been wrong' or 'If she knows she can't be wrong' are not worrying in the way that 'If I ("you") know I ("you") can't be wrong' is worrying. Or again, 'I promise' is quite different from 'he promises': if I say 'I promise', I don't say I *say* I promise, I *promise*, just as if he says he promises, he doesn't say he says he promises, he promises: whereas if I say 'he promises', I do (only) say he *says* he promises—in the other 'sense' of 'promise', the 'sense' in which *I* say *I* promise, only *he* can say he promises. I *describe* his promising, but I *do* my own promising and he must do *his* own.

When I have said only that I am sure, and prove to have been mistaken, I am not liable to be rounded on by others in the same way as when I have said 'I know'. I am sure *for my part*, you can take it or leave it: accept it if you think I'm an acute and careful person, that's your responsibility. But I don't know 'for my part', and when I say 'I know' I don't mean you can take it or leave it (though of course you *can* take it or leave it). In the same way, when I say I fully intend to, I do so for my part, and, according as you think highly or poorly of my resolution and chances, you will elect to act on it or not to act on it: but if I say I promise, you are *entitled* to act on it, whether or not you choose to do so. If I have said I know or I promise, you insult me in a special way by refusing to accept it. We all *feel* the very great difference between saying even 'I'm *absolutely* sure' and saying 'I know': it is like the difference between saying even 'I firmly and irrevocably intend' and 'I promise'. If someone has promised me to do A, then I am entitled to rely on it, and can myself make promises on the strength of it: and so, where someone has said to me 'I know', I am entitled to say *I* know too, at second hand. The right to say 'I know' is transmissible, in the sort of way that other authority is transmissible. Hence, if I say it lightly, I may be *responsible* for getting *you* into trouble.

If you say you *know* something, the most immediate challenge takes the form of asking 'Are you in a position to know?': that is, you must undertake to show, not merely that you are sure of it, but that it is within your cognisance. There is a similar form of challenge in the case of promising: fully intending is not enough—you must also undertake to show that 'you are in a position to promise', that is, that it is within your power. Over these points in the two cases parallel series of doubts are apt to infect philosophers, on the ground that I cannot foresee the future. Some begin to hold that I should never, or practically never, say I know anything—perhaps only what I am sensing at this moment: others, that I should never, or practically never, say I promise—perhaps only what is actually within my power at this moment. In both cases there is an obsession: if I know *I can't be wrong*, so I can't have the right to say I know, and if I promise *I can't fail*, so I can't have the right to say I promise. And in both cases this obsession fastens on my inability to make *predictions* as the root of the matter, meaning by predictions claims to know the future. But this is doubly mistaken in both cases. As has been seen, we may be perfectly justified in saying we know or we promise, in spite of the fact that things 'may' turn out badly, and it's a more or less serious matter for us if they do. And further, it is overlooked that the conditions which must be satisfied if I am to show that a thing is within my cognisance or within my power are conditions, not about the future, but about *the present and the past*: it is not demanded that I do more than *believe* about the future.[1]

We feel, however, an objection to saying that 'I know' performs the same sort of function as 'I promise'. It is this. Supposing that things turn out badly, then we say, on the one hand 'You're proved wrong, so you *didn't* know', but on the other hand 'You've failed to perform, although you *did* promise'. I believe that this contrast is more apparent than real. The sense in which you 'did promise' is that you did *say* you promised (did say 'I promise'): and you did *say* you knew. That is the gravamen of the charge against you when you let us down, after we have taken your word. But it may well transpire that you never fully intended to do it, or that you had concrete reason to suppose that you wouldn't be able to do it (it might even be manifestly impossible), and in another 'sense' of promise you *can't* then have promised to do it, so that you *didn't* promise.

Consider the use of other phrases analogous to 'I know' and 'I promise'. Suppose, instead of 'I know', I had said 'I swear': in that case, upon the opposite appearing, we should say, exactly as in the promising case, 'You *did* swear, but you were

---

[1] If 'Figs never grow on thistles' is taken to mean 'None ever have and none ever will', then it is implied that I *know* that none ever have, but only that I *believe* that none ever will.

wrong'. Suppose again that, instead of 'I promise', I had said 'I guarantee' (e.g. to protect you from attack): in that case, upon my letting you down, you can say, exactly as in the knowing case 'You *said* you guaranteed it, but you *didn't* guarantee it'.[1] Can the situation perhaps be summed up as follows? In these 'ritual' cases, the approved case is one where *in the appropriate circumstances*, I say a certain formula: e.g. 'I do' when standing, unmarried or a widower, beside woman, unmarried or a widow and not within the prohibited degrees of relationship, before a clergyman, registrar, &c., or 'I give' when it is mine to give, &c., or 'I order' when I have the authority to, &c. But now, if the situation transpires to have been in some way not orthodox (I was already married: it wasn't mine to give: I had no authority to order), then we tend to be rather hesitant about how to put it, as heaven was when the saint blessed the penguins. We call the man a bigamist, but his second marriage was not a marriage, is null and void (a useful formula in many cases for avoiding saying either 'he did' or 'he didn't'): he did 'order' me to do it, but, having no authority over me, he *couldn't* 'order' me: he did warn me it was going to charge, but it wasn't or anyway I knew much more about it than he did, so in a way he couldn't warn me, didn't warn me.[2] We hesitate between 'He didn't order me', 'He had no right to order me', 'He oughtn't to have said he ordered me', just as we do between 'You didn't know', 'You can't have known', 'You had no right to say you knew' (these perhaps having slightly different nuances, according to what precisely it is that has gone wrong). But the essential factors

---

[1] 'Swear', 'guarantee', 'give my word', 'promise', all these and similar words cover cases both of 'knowing' and of 'promising', thus suggesting the two are analogous. Of course they differ subtly from each other; for example, *know* and *promise* are in a certain sense 'unlimited' expressions, while when I swear I swear *upon* something, and when I guarantee I guarantee that, upon some adverse and more or less to be expected circumstance arising, I will take *some more or less definite action* to nullify it.

[2] 'You can't warn someone of something that isn't going to happen' parallels 'You can't know what isn't true'.

are (a) You said you knew: you said you promised (b) You were mistaken: you didn't perform. The hesitancy concerns only the precise way in which we are to round on the original 'I know' or 'I promise'.

To suppose that 'I know' is a descriptive phrase, is only one example of the *descriptive fallacy*, so common in philosophy. Even if some language is now purely descriptive, language was not in origin so, and much of it is still not so. Utterance of obvious ritual phrases, in the appropriate circumstances, is not *describing* the action we are doing, but *doing* it ('I do'): in other cases it functions, like tone and expression, or again like punctuation and mood, as an intimation that we are employing language in some special way ('I warn', 'I ask', 'I define'). Such phrases cannot, strictly, *be* lies, though they can 'imply' lies, as 'I promise' implies that I fully intend, which may be untrue.

If these are the main and multifarious points that arise in familiar cases where we ask 'How do you know that this is a case of so-and-so?', they may be expected to arise likewise in cases where we say 'I know he is angry'. And if there are, as no doubt there are, special difficulties in this case, at least we can clear the ground a little of things which are not special difficulties, and get the matter in better perspective.

As a preliminary, it must be said that I shall only discuss the question of feelings and emotions, with special reference to anger. It seems likely that the cases where we know that another man thinks that 2 and 2 make 4, or that he is seeing a rat, and so on, are different in important respects from, though no doubt also similar to, the case of knowing that he is angry or hungry.

In the first place, we certainly do say sometimes that we know another man is angry, and we also distinguish these occasions from others on which we say only that we *believe* he is angry. For of course, we do not for a moment suppose that we *always* know, of *all* men, whether they are angry or not, or that we could discover it. There are many occasions when I realize that I can't possibly tell what he's feeling: and there are many *types* of people, and many individuals too, with whom I (they being what they are, and I being what I am) never can tell. The feelings of royalty, for example, or fakirs or bushmen or Wykehamists or simple eccentrics—these may be very hard to divine: unless you have had a prolonged acquaintance with such persons, and some intimacy with them, you are not in any sort of position to know what their feelings are, especially if, for one reason or another, they can't or don't tell you. Or again, the feelings of some individual whom you have never met before—they might be almost anything: you don't know his character at all or his tastes, you have had no experience of his mannerisms, and so on. His feelings are elusive and personal: people differ so much. It is this sort of thing that leads to the situation where we say 'You never know' or 'You never can tell'.

In short, here even more than in the case of the goldfinch, a great deal depends on how familiar we have been in our past experience with this type of person, and indeed with this individual, in this type of situation. If we have no great familiarity, then we hesitate to say we know: indeed, we can't be expected to say (tell). On the other hand, if we *have* had the necessary experience, then we can, in favourable current circumstances, say we know: we certainly can recognize when some near relative of ours is angrier than we have ever seen him.

Further, we must have had experience also of the emotion or feeling concerned, in this case anger. In order to know what you are feeling, I must also apparently be able to imagine (guess, understand, appreciate) what you're feeling. It seems that more is demanded than that I shall have learned to discriminate displays of anger in others: I must also have been angry myself.[1] Or at any rate, if I have never felt a certain

---

[1] We say we don't know what it must feel like to be a king, whereas we do know what one of our friends must have felt when mortified. In this ordinary (imprecise and evidently not whole-hog) sense of 'knowing what it

emotion, say ambition, then I certainly feel an *extra* hesitation in saying that his motive is ambition. And this seems to be due to the very special nature (grammar, logic) of feelings, to the special way in which they are related to their occasions and manifestations, which requires further elucidation.

At first sight it may be tempting to follow Mr. Wisdom, and to draw a distinction between (1) the physical symptoms and (2) the feeling. So that when, in the current case, I am asked 'How can you tell he's angry?' I should answer 'From the physical symptoms', while if *he* is asked how *he* can tell he's angry, he should answer 'From the feeling'. But this seems to be a dangerous over-simplification.

In the first place, 'symptoms' (and also 'physical') is being used in a way different from ordinary usage, and one which proves to be misleading.

'Symptoms', a term transferred from medical usage,[1] tends to be used only, or primarily, in cases where that of which there are symptoms is something undesirable (of incipient disease rather than of returning health, of despair rather than of hope, of grief rather than of joy): and hence it is more colourful than 'signs' or 'indications'. This, however, is comparatively trivial. What is important is the fact that we never talk of 'symptoms' or 'signs' except *by way of implied contrast with inspection of the item itself*. No doubt it would often be awkward to have to say exactly where the signs or symptoms end and the item itself begins to appear: but such a division is always implied to exist. And hence the words 'symptom' and 'sign' have no use except in cases where the item, as in the case

---

would be like' we do often know what it would be like to be our neighbour drawing his sword, whereas we don't know (can't even guess or imagine), really, what it would feel like to be a cat or a cockroach. But of course we don't ever 'know' what in our neighbour accompanies the drawing of his sword in Mr. Wisdom's peculiar sense of 'know what' as equivalent to 'directly experience that which'.

[1] Doctors nowadays draw a distinction of their own between 'symptoms' and '(physical) signs': but the distinction is not here relevant, and perhaps not very clear.

of disease, is liable to be *hidden*, whether it be in the future, in the past, under the skin, or in some other more or less notorious casket: and when the item is itself before us, we no longer talk of signs and symptoms. When we talk of 'signs of a storm', we mean signs of an impending storm, or of a past storm, or of a storm beyond the horizon: we do *not* mean a storm on top of us.[1]

The words function like such words as 'traces' or 'clues'. Once you know the murderer, you don't get any more clues, only what were or would have been clues: nor is a confession, or an eye-witness's view of the crime, a particularly good clue— these are something different altogether. When the cheese is not to be found or seen, then there may be traces of it: but not when it's there in front of us (though of course, there aren't, then, 'no traces' of it either).

For this reason, it seems misleading to lump together, as a general practice, all the characteristic features of any casual item as 'signs' or 'symptoms' of it: though it is of course some-times the case that some things which could in appropriate circumstances be called characteristics or effects or manifesta-tions or parts or sequelae or what not of certain items may *also* be called signs or symptoms of those items in the appropriate circumstances. It seems to be this which is really wrong with Mr. Wisdom's paradox (Other Minds III) about looking in the larder and finding 'all the signs' of bread, when we see the loaf, touch it, taste it and so on. Doing these things is not find-ing (some) signs of bread at all: the taste or feel of bread is not a sign or symptom of bread at all. What I might be taken to mean if I announced that I had found signs of bread in the larder seems rather doubtful, since bread is not normally

[1] There are some, more complicated, cases like that of inflation, where the signs of incipient inflation are of the same nature as inflation itself, but of a less intensity or at a slower tempo. Here, especially, it is a matter for decision where the signs or 'tendencies' end and where the state itself sets in: moreover, with inflation, as with some diseases, we can in some contexts go on talking of signs or symptoms even when the item itself is quite fairly decidedly present, because it is such as not to be patent to simple observation.

casketed (or if in the bin, leaves no traces), and not being a transeunt event (impending bread, &c.), does not have any normally accepted 'signs': and signs, peculiar to the item, have to be more or less normally accepted. I might be taken to mean that I had found traces of bread, such as crumbs, or signs that bread had at one time been stored there, or something of the kind: but what I could *not* be taken to mean is that I had seen, tasted, or touched (something like) bread.

The sort of thing we do actually say, if the look is all right but we haven't yet tasted it, is 'Here is something that looks like bread'. If it turns out not to be bread after all, we might say 'It tasted like bread, but actually it was only bread-substitute', or 'It exhibited many of the characteristic features of bread, but differed in important respects: it was only a synthetic imitation'. That is, we don't use the words 'sign' or 'symptom' at all.

Now, if 'signs' and 'symptoms' have this restricted usage, it is evident that to say that we only get at the 'signs' or 'symptoms' of anything is to imply that we never get at *it* (and this goes for '*all* the signs' too). So that, if we say that I only get at the *symptoms* of his anger, that carries an important implication. But *is* this the way we do talk? Surely we do not consider that we are never aware of more than *symptoms* of anger in another man?

'Symptoms' or 'signs' of anger tend to mean signs of *rising* or of *suppressed* anger. Once the man has exploded, we talk of something different—of an expression or manifestation or display of anger, of an exhibition of temper, and so forth. A twitch of the eyebrow, pallor, a tremor in the voice, all these may be symptoms of anger: but a violent tirade or a blow in the face are not, they are the acts in which the anger is vented. 'Symptoms' of anger are not, at least normally, contrasted with the man's own inner personal feeling of anger, but rather with the actual display of anger. Normally at least, where we have only symptoms to go upon, we should say only that we *believe* that the man is angry or getting angry: whereas when he has given himself away we say that we *know*.[1]

The word 'physical' also, as used by Mr. Wisdom in contrast to 'mental', seems to me abused, though I am not confident as to whether this abuse is misleading in the current case. He evidently does not wish to call a man's feelings, which he cites as a typical example of a 'mental' event, *physical*. Yet this is what we ordinarily often do. There are many physical feelings, such as giddiness, hunger or fatigue: and these are included by some doctors among the physical signs of various complaints. Most feelings we do not speak of as either mental or physical, especially emotions, such as jealousy or anger itself: we do not assign them to the *mind* but to the *heart*. Where we do describe a feeling as mental, it is because we are using a word normally used to describe a physical feeling in a special transferred sense, as when we talk about 'mental' discomfort or fatigue.

It is then, clear, that more is involved in being, for example, angry than simply showing the symptoms and feeling the feeling. For there is also the display or manifestation. And it is to be noted that the feeling is related in a unique sort of way to the display. When we are angry, we have an impulse, felt and/or acted on, to do actions of particular kinds, and, unless we suppress the anger, we do actually proceed to do them. There is a peculiar and intimate relationship between the emotion and the natural manner of venting it, with which, having been angry ourselves, we are acquainted. The ways in which anger is normally manifested are *natural* to anger just

---

[1] Sometimes, it is said, we use 'I know' where we should be prepared to substitute 'I believe', as when we say 'I know he's in, because his hat is in the hall': thus 'know' is used loosely for 'believe', so why should we suppose there is a fundamental difference between them? But the question is, what exactly do we mean by 'prepared to substitute' and 'loosely'? We are 'prepared to substitute' *believe* for *know* not as an *equivalent* expression but as a weaker and therefore preferable expression, in view of the seriousness with which, as has become apparent, the matter is to be treated: the presence of the hat, which would serve as a proof of it's owner's presence in many circumstances, could only through laxity be adduced as a proof in a court of law.

as there are tones *naturally* expressive of various emotions (indignation, &c.). There is not normally taken to be[1] such a thing as 'being angry' apart from any impulse, however vague, to vent the anger in the natural way.

Moreover, besides the natural expressions of anger, there are also the natural *occasions* of anger, of which we have also had experience, which are similarly connected in an intimate way with the 'being angry'. It would be as nonsensical to class these as 'causes' in some supposedly obvious and 'external' sense, as it would be to class the venting of anger as the 'effect' of the emotion in a supposedly obvious and 'external' sense. Equally it would be nonsensical to say that there are three wholly distinct phenomena, (1) cause or occasion, (2) feeling or emotion, and (3) effect or manifestation, which are related together 'by definition' as all necessary to anger, though this would perhaps be less misleading than the other.

It seems fair to say that 'being angry' is in many respects like 'having mumps'. It is a description of a whole pattern of events, including occasion, symptoms, feeling and manifestation, and possibly other factors besides. It is as silly to ask 'What, really, *is* the anger *itself*?' as to attempt to fine down 'the disease' to some one chosen item ('the functional disorder'). That the man himself feels something which we don't (in the sense that he feels angry and we don't) is, in the absence of Mr. Wisdom's variety of telepathy,[2] evident enough, and incidentally nothing to complain about as a 'predicament': but there is no call to say that 'that' ('the feeling')[3] *is* the *anger*. The pattern of events

---

[1] A new language is naturally necessary if we are to admit unconscious feelings, and feelings which express themselves in paradoxical manners, such as the psycho-analysts describe.

[2] There is, it seems to me, something which does actually happen, rather different from Mr. Wisdom's telepathy, which does sometimes contribute towards our knowledge of other people's feelings. We do talk, for example, of 'feeling another person's displeasure', and say, for example, 'his anger could be felt', and there seems to be something genuine about this. But the feeling we feel, though a genuine 'feeling', is *not*, in these cases, displeasure or anger, but a special *counterpart* feeling.

[3] The 'feelings', i.e. sensations, we can observe in ourselves when angry are

whatever its precise form, is, fairly clearly, peculiar to the case
of 'feelings' (emotions)—it is not by any means exactly like
the case of diseases: and it seems to be this peculiarity which
makes us prone to say that, unless we have had experience of
a feeling ourselves, we cannot know when someone else is
experiencing it. Moreover, it is our confidence in the general
pattern that makes us apt to say we 'know' another man is
angry when we have only observed parts of the pattern: for
the parts of the pattern are related to each other very much
more intimately than, for example, newspapermen scurrying
in Brighton are related to a fire in Fleet Street.[1]

The man himself, such is the overriding power of the
pattern, will sometimes accept corrections from outsiders about
his own emotions, i.e. about the correct description of them.
He may be got to agree that he was not really angry so much
as, rather, indignant or jealous, and even that he was not in
pain, but only fancied he was. And this is not surprising,
especially in view of the fact that he, like all of us, has primarily
learnt to use the expression 'I am angry' of himself by (a)
noting the occasion, symptoms, manifestation, &c., in cases
where other persons say 'I am angry' of *themselves* (b) being
told by others, who have noted all that can be observed about
him on certain occasions, that 'You are angry', i.e. that he
should say 'I am angry'. On the whole, 'mere' feelings or
emotions, if there are such things genuinely detectable, are
certainly very hard to be sure about, even harder than, say,
tastes, which we already choose to describe, normally, only by
their occasions (the taste 'of tar', 'of pineapple', &c.).

All words for emotions are, besides, on the vague side, in
two ways, leading to further hesitations about whether we
'know' when he's angry. They tend to cover a rather wide
and ill-defined variety of situations: and the patterns they cover

---

such things as a pounding of the heart or tensing of the muscles, which cannot
in themselves be justifiably called 'the feeling of anger'.

[1] It is therefore misleading to ask 'How do I get from the scowl to the
anger?'

tend to be, each of them, rather complex (though common and so not difficult to recognize, very often), so that it is easy for one of the more or less necessary features to be omitted, and thus to give rise to hesitation about what exactly we should say in such an unorthodox case. We realize, well enough, that the challenge to which we are exposed if we say we *know* is to *prove* it, and in this respect vagueness of terminology is a crippling handicap.

So far, enough has perhaps been said to show that most of the difficulties which stand in the way of our saying we know a thing is a goldfinch arise in rather greater strength in the case where we want to say we know another man is angry. But there is still a feeling, and I think a justified feeling, that there is a further and quite *special* difficulty in the latter case.

This difficulty seems to be of the sort that Mr. Wisdom raises at the very outset of his series of articles on 'Other Minds'. It is asked, might the man not exhibit all the symptoms (and display and everything else) of anger, even ad infinitum, and yet still *not* (*really*) *be* angry? It will be remembered that he there treats it, no doubt provisionally, as a difficulty similar to that which can arise concerning the reality of any 'material object'. But in fact, it has special features of its own.

There seem to be three distinguishable doubts which may arise:

1. When to all appearances angry, might he not really be labouring under some other emotion, in that, though he normally feels the same emotion as we should on occasions when we, in his position, should feel anger and in making displays such as we make when angry, in this particular case he is acting abnormally?

2. When to all appearances angry, might he not really be labouring under some other emotion, in that he normally feels, on occasions when we in his position should feel anger and when acting as we should act if we felt anger, some feeling which we, if we experienced it, should distinguish from anger?

3. When to all appearances angry, might he not really be feeling no emotion at all?

In everyday life, all these problems arise in special cases, and occasion genuine worry. We may worry (1) as to whether someone is *deceiving* us, by suppressing his emotions, or by feigning emotions which he does not feel: we may worry (2) as to whether we are *misunderstanding* someone (or he us), in wrongly supposing that he does 'feel like us', that he does share emotions like ours: or we may worry (3) as to whether some action of another person is really deliberate, or perhaps only involuntary or inadvertent in some manner or other. All three varieties of worry may arise, and often do, in connexion with the actions of persons whom we know very well.[1] Any or all of them may be at the bottom of the passage from Mrs. Woolf:[2] all work together in the feeling of loneliness which affects everybody at times.

None of these three special difficulties about 'reality' arises in connexion with goldfinches or bread, any more than the special difficulties about, for example, the oasis arise in connexion with the reality of another person's emotions. The goldfinch cannot be assumed, nor the bread suppressed: we may be deceived by the appearance of an oasis, or misinterpret the signs of the weather, but the oasis cannot lie to us and we cannot misunderstand the storm in the way we misunderstand the man.

Though the difficulties are special, the ways of dealing with them are, initially, similar to those employed in the case of the goldfinch. There are (more or less roughly) established procedures for dealing with suspected cases of deception or of misunderstanding or of inadvertence. By these means we do very often establish (though we do not expect *always* to establish) that someone is acting, or that we were misunder-

---

[1] There is, too, a special way in which we can doubt the 'reality' of our own emotions, can doubt whether we are not 'acting to ourselves'. Professional actors may reach a state where they never really know what their genuine feelings are.

[2] [Quoted by Wisdom in his contribution to this Symposium. Ed.]

standing him, or that he is simply impervious to a certain emotion, or that he was not acting voluntarily. These special cases where doubts arise and require resolving, are contrasted with the normal cases which hold the field[1] *unless* there is some special suggestion that deceit, &c., is involved, and deceit, moreover, of an intelligible kind in the circumstances, that is, of a kind that can be looked into because motive, &c., is specially suggested. There is no suggestion that I *never* know what other people's emotions are, nor yet that in particular cases I might be wrong for no special reason or in no special way.

Extraordinary cases of deceit, misunderstanding, &c. (which are themselves not the normal), do not, *ex vi termini*, ordinarily occur: we have a working knowledge of the occasions for, the temptations to, the practical limits of, and the normal types of deceit and misunderstanding. Nevertheless, they *may* occur, and there may be varieties which are common without our yet having become aware of the fact. If this happens, we are in a certain sense wrong, because our terminology is inadequate to the facts, and we shall have thenceforward to be more wary about saying we know, or shall have to revise our ideas and terminology. This we are constantly ready to do in a field so complex and baffling as that of the emotions.

There remains, however, one further special feature of the case, which also differentiates it radically from the goldfinch case. The goldfinch, the material object, is, as we insisted above, uninscribed and *mute*: but the man *speaks*. In the complex of occurrences which induces us to say we know another man is angry, the complex of symptoms, occasion, display, and the rest, a peculiar place is occupied by the man's own statement as to what his feelings are. In the usual case, we accept this statement without question, and we then say that we know (as it were 'at second-hand') what his feelings are: though of course 'at second-hand' here could not be used to imply that anybody but he could know 'at first-hand', and hence perhaps it is not

[1] 'You cannot fool all of the people all of the time' is 'analytic'.

in fact used. In unusual cases, where his statement conflicts with the description we should otherwise have been inclined to give of the case, we do not feel bound to accept it, though we always feel some uneasiness in rejecting it. If the man is an habitual liar or self-deceiver, or if there are patent reasons why he should be lying or deceiving himself on this occasion, then we feel reasonably happy: but if such a case occurred as the imagined one where a man, having given throughout life every appearance of holding a certain pointless belief, leaves behind a remark in his private diary to the effect that he never did believe it, then we probably should not know what to say.

I should like to make in conclusion some further remarks about this crucial matter of our believing what the man says about his own feelings. Although I know very well that I do not see my way clearly in this, I cannot help feeling sure that it is fundamental to the whole Predicament, and that it has not been given the attention it deserves, possibly just because it is so obvious.

The man's own statement is not (is not treated primarily as) a sign or symptom, although it can, secondarily and artificially, be treated as such. A unique place is reserved for it in the summary of the facts of the case. The question then is: 'Why believe him?'

There are answers that we can give to this question, which is here to be taken in the general sense of 'Why believe him ever?' not simply as 'Why believe him this time?' We may say that the man's statements on matters other than his own feelings have constantly been before us in the past, and have been regularly verified by our own observations of the facts he reported: so that we have in fact some basis for an induction about his general reliability. Or we may say that his behaviour is most simply 'explained' on the view that he does feel emotions like ours, just as psycho-analysts 'explain' erratic behaviour by analogy with normal behaviour when they use the terminology of 'unconscious desires'.

These answers are, however, dangerous and unhelpful. They are so obvious that they please nobody: while on the other hand they encourage the questioner to push his question to 'profounder' depths, encouraging us, in turn, to exaggerate these answers until they become distortions.

The question, pushed further, becomes a challenge to the very possibility of 'believing another man', in its ordinarily accepted sense, at all. What 'justification' is there for supposing that there is another mind communicating with you at all? How can you know what it would be like for another mind to feel anything, and so how can you understand it? It is then that we are tempted to say that we only mean by 'believing him' that we take certain vocal noises as signs of certain impending behaviour, and that 'other minds' are no more really real than unconscious desires.

This, however, is distortion. It seems, rather, that believing in other persons, in authority and testimony, is an essential part of the act of communicating, an act which we all constantly perform. It is as much an irreducible part of our experience as, say, giving promises, or playing competitive games, or even sensing coloured patches. We can state certain advantages of such performances, and we can elaborate rules of a kind for their 'rational' conduct (as the Law Courts and historians and psychologists work out the rules for accepting testimony). But there is no 'justification' for our doing them as such.

Final Note

One speaker at Manchester said roundly that the real crux of the matter remains still that 'I ought not to say that I know Tom is angry, because I don't introspect his feelings': and this no doubt is just what many people do boggle at. The gist of what I have been trying to bring out is simply:

1. *Of course* I *don't* introspect Tom's feelings (we should be in a pretty predicament if I did).
2. *Of course* I *do* sometimes know Tom is angry.

Hence

3. to suppose that the question 'How do I know that Tom is angry?' is meant to mean 'How do I introspect Tom's feelings?' (because, as we know, that's the sort of thing that knowing is or ought to be), is simply barking our way up the wrong gum tree.

5

TRUTH[1]

1. 'WHAT is truth?' said jesting Pilate, and would not stay for an answer. Pilate was in advance of his time. For 'truth' itself is an abstract noun, a camel, that is, of a logical construction, which cannot get past the eye even of a grammarian. We approach it cap and categories in hand: we ask ourselves whether Truth is a substance (the Truth, the Body of Knowledge), or a quality (something like the colour red, inhering in truths), or a relation ('correspondence').[2] But philosophers should take something more nearly their own size to strain at. What needs discussing rather is the use, or certain uses, of the word 'true'. *In vino*, possibly, '*veritas*', but in a sober symposium '*verum*'.

2. What is it that we say is true or is false? Or, how does the phrase 'is true' occur in English sentences? The answers appear at first multifarious. We say (or are said to say) that beliefs are true, that descriptions or accounts are true, that propositions or assertions or statements are true, and that words or sentences are true: and this is to mention only a selection of the more obvious candidates. Again, we say (or are said to say) 'It is true that the cat is on the mat', or 'It is true to say that the cat is on the mat', or ' "The cat is on the mat" is true'. We also remark on occasion, when someone else has said something, 'Very true' or 'That's true' or 'True enough'.

Most (though not all) of these expressions, and others besides,

---

[1] Reprinted from *Proceedings of the Aristotelian Society*, Supplementary Volume xxiv (1950), by courtesy of the editor.

[2] It is sufficiently obvious that 'truth' is a substantive, 'true' an adjective and 'of' in 'true of' a preposition.

certainly do occur naturally enough. But it seems reasonable to ask whether there is not some use of 'is true' that is primary, or some generic name for that which at bottom we are always saying 'is true'. Which, if any, of these expressions is to be taken *au pied de la lettre*? To answer this will not take us long, nor, perhaps, far: but in philosophy the foot of the letter is the foot of the ladder.

I suggest that the following are the primary forms of expression:

> It is true (to say) that the cat is on the mat.
>
> That statement (of his, &c.) is true.
>
> The statement that the cat is on the mat is true.

But first for the rival candidates.

(a) Some say that 'truth is primarily a property of beliefs'. But it may be doubted whether the expression 'a true belief' is at all common outside philosophy and theology: and it seems clear that a man is said to hold a true belief when and in the sense that he believes (in) *something which* is true, or believes that *something which* is true is true. Moreover if, as some also say, a belief is 'of the nature of a picture', then it is of the nature of what cannot be true, though it may be, for example, faithful.[1]

(b) True descriptions and true accounts are simply varieties of true statements or of collections of true statements, as are true answers and the like. The same applies to propositions too, in so far as they are genuinely said to be true (and not, as more commonly, sound, tenable and so on).[2] A proposition in law or in geometry is something portentous, usually a generalization, that we are invited to accept and that has to be recommended by argument: it cannot be a direct report on current observation—if you look and inform me that the cat is on the mat, that

---

[1] A likeness is true *to* life, but not true *of* it. A *word* picture can be true, just because it is *not* a picture.

[2] Predicates applicable also to 'arguments', which we likewise do not say are true, but, for example, valid.

is not a proposition though it is a statement. In philosophy, indeed, 'proposition' is sometimes used in a special way for 'the meaning or sense of a sentence or family of sentences': but whether we think a lot or little of this usage, a proposition in this sense cannot, at any rate, be what we say is true or false. For we never say 'The meaning (or sense) of this sentence (or of these words) is true': what we do say is what the judge or jury says, namely that 'The words taken in this sense, or if we assign to them such and such a meaning, or so interpreted or understood, are true'.

(c) Words and sentences are indeed said to be true, the former often, the latter rarely. But only in certain senses. Words as discussed by philologists, or by lexicographers, grammarians, linguists, phoneticians, printers, critics (stylistic or textual) and so on, are not true or false: they are wrongly formed, or ambiguous or defective or untranslatable or un-pronounceable or mis-spelled or archaistic or corrupt or what not.[1] Sentences in similar contexts are elliptic or involved or alliterative or ungrammatical. We may, however, genuinely say 'His closing words were very true' or 'The third sentence on page 5 of his speech is quite false': but here 'words' and 'sentence' refer, as is shown by the demonstratives (possessive pronouns, temporal verbs, definite descriptions, &c.), which in this usage consistently accompany them, to the words or sentence *as used by a certain person on a certain occasion*. That is, they refer (as does 'Many a true word spoken in jest') to *statements*.

A statement is made and its making is an historic event, the utterance by a certain speaker or writer of certain words (a

---

[1] Peirce made a beginning by pointing out that there are two (or three) different senses of the word 'word', and adumbrated a technique ('counting' words) for deciding what is a 'different sense'. But his two senses are not well defined, and there are many more—the 'vocable' sense, the philologist's sense in which 'grammar' is the same word as 'glamour', the textual critic's sense in which the 'the' in l. 254 has been written twice, and so on. With all his 66 divisions of signs, Peirce does not, I believe, distinguish between a sentence and a statement.

sentence) to an audience with reference to an historic situation, event or what not.[1]

A sentence is made *up of* words, a statement is made *in* words. A sentence is not English or not good English, a statement is not in English or not in good English. Statements are made, words or sentences are used. We talk of *my* statement, but of *the English* sentence (if a sentence is mine, I coined it, but I do not coin statements). The *same* sentence is used in making *different* statements (I say 'It is mine', you say 'It is mine'): it may also be used on two occasions or by two persons in making the *same* statement, but for this the utterance must be made with reference to the same situation or event.[2] We speak of 'the statement that S,' but of 'the sentence "S"', not of 'the sentence that S'.[3]

When I say that a statement is what is true, I have no wish to become wedded to one word. 'Assertion', for example, will in most contexts do just as well, though perhaps it is slightly wider. Both words share the weakness of being rather solemn (much more so than the more general 'what you said' or 'your words')—though perhaps we are generally being a little solemn when we discuss the truth of anything. Both have the merit

---

[1] 'Historic' does not, of course, mean that we cannot speak of future or possible statements. A 'certain' speaker need not be any definite speaker. 'Utterance' need not be public utterance—the audience may be the speaker himself.

[2] 'The same' does not always mean the same. In fact it has no meaning in the way that an 'ordinary' word like 'red' or 'horse' has a meaning: it is a (the typical) device for establishing and distinguishing the meanings of ordinary words. Like 'real', it is part of our apparatus *in* words for fixing and adjusting the semantics *of* words.

[3] Inverted commas show that the words, though uttered (in writing), are not to be taken as a statement by the utterer. This covers two possible cases, (i) where what is to be discussed is the sentence, (ii) where what is to be discussed is a statement made elsewhen in the words 'quoted'. Only in case (i) is it correct to say simply that the token is doing duty for the type (and even here it is quite incorrect to say that 'The cat is on the mat' is the *name* of an English sentence—though possibly *The Cat is on the Mat* might be the title of a novel, or a bull might be known as *Catta est in matta*). Only in case (ii) is there something true or false, *viz.* (not the quotation but) the statement made in the words quoted.

of clearly referring to the historic use of a sentence by an utterer, and of being therefore precisely not equivalent to 'sentence'. For it is a fashionable mistake to take as primary '(The sentence) "S" is true (in the English language)'. Here the addition of the words 'in the English language' serves to emphasize that 'sentence' is not being used as equivalent to 'statement', so that it precisely is not what can be true or false (and moreover, 'true in the English language' is a solecism, mismodelled presumably, and with deplorable effect, on expressions like 'true in geometry').

3. When is a statement true? The temptation is to answer (at least if we confine ourselves to 'straightforward' statements): 'When it corresponds to the facts'. And as a piece of standard English this can hardly be wrong. Indeed, I must confess I do not really think it is wrong at all: the theory of truth is a series of truisms. Still, it can at least be misleading.

If there is to be communication of the sort that we achieve by language at all, there must be a stock of symbols of some kind which a communicator ('the speaker') can produce 'at will' and which a communicatee ('the audience') can observe: these may be called the 'words', though, of course, they need not be anything very like what we should normally call words —they might be signal flags, &c. There must also be something other than the words, which the words are to be used to communicate about: this may be called the 'world'. There is no reason why the world should not include the words, in every sense except the sense of the actual statement itself which on any particular occasion is being made about the world. Further, the world must exhibit (we must observe) similarities and dissimilarities (there could not be the one without the other): if everything were either absolutely indistinguishable from anything else or completely unlike anything else, there would be nothing to say. And finally (for present purposes—of course there are other conditions to be satisfied too) there must be two sets of conventions:

Descriptive conventions correlating the words (= sentences) with the *types* of situation, thing, event, &c., to be found in the world.

Demonstrative conventions correlating the words (= statements) with the *historic* situations, &c., to be found in the world.[1]

A statement is said to be true when the historic state of affairs to which it is correlated by the demonstrative conventions (the one to which it 'refers') is of a type[2] with which the sentence used in making it is correlated by the descriptive conventions.[3]

3*a*. Troubles arise from the use of the word 'facts' for the historic situations, events, &c., and in general, for the world. For 'fact' is regularly used in conjunction with 'that' in the sentences 'The fact is that S' or 'It is a fact that S' and in the expression 'the fact that S', all of which imply that it would be true to say that S.[4]

---

[1] Both sets of conventions may be included together under 'semantics'. But they differ greatly.

[2] 'Is of a type with which' means 'is sufficiently like those standard states of affairs with which'. Thus, for a statement to be true one state of affairs must be *like* certain others, which is a natural relation, but also *sufficiently* like·to merit the same 'description', which is no longer a purely natural relation. To say 'This is red' is not the same as to say 'This is like those', nor even as to say 'This is like those which were called red'. That things are *similar*, or even 'exactly' similar, I may literally see, but that they are the *same* I cannot literally see—in calling them the same colour a convention is involved additional to the conventional choice of the name to be given to the colour which they are said to be.

[3] The trouble is that sentences contain words or verbal devices to serve both descriptive and demonstrative purposes (not to mention other purposes), often both at once. In philosophy we mistake the descriptive for the demonstrative (theory of universals) or the demonstrative for the descriptive (theory of monads). A sentence as normally distinguished from a mere word or phrase is characterized by its containing a minimum of verbal demonstrative devices (Aristotle's 'reference to time'); but many demonstrative conventions are non-verbal (pointing, &c.), and using these we can make a statement in a single word which is not a 'sentence'. Thus, 'languages' like that of (traffic, &c.) *signs* use quite distinct media for their descriptive and demonstrative elements (the sign on the post, the site of the post). And however many verbal demonstrative devices we use as auxiliaries, there must *always* be a non-verbal *origin* for these co-·ordinates, which is the point of utterance of the statement.

[For footnote 4 see p. 91.

This may lead us to suppose that

  (i) 'fact' is only an alternative expression for 'true statement'. We note that when a detective says 'Let's look at the facts' he does not crawl round the carpet, but proceeds to utter a string of statements: we even talk of 'stating the facts';

  (ii) for every true statement there exists 'one' and its own precisely corresponding fact—for every cap the head it fits.

It is (i) which leads to some of the mistakes in 'coherence' or formalist theories; (ii) to some of those in 'correspondence' theories. Either we suppose that there is nothing there but the true statement itself, nothing to which it corresponds, or else we populate the world with linguistic *Doppelgänger* (and grossly overpopulate it—every nugget of 'positive' fact overlaid by a massive concentration of 'negative' facts, every tiny detailed fact larded with generous general facts, and so on).

When a statement is true, there is, *of course*, a state of affairs which makes it true and which is *toto mundo* distinct from the true statement about it: but equally of course, we can only *describe* that state of affairs *in words* (either the same or, with luck, others). I can only describe the situation in which it is true to say that I am feeling sick by saying that it is one in which I am feeling sick (or experiencing sensations of nausea):[1]

---

⁴ I use the following *abbreviations*:

    S for the cat is on the mat.

    ST for it is true that the cat is on the mat.

    tst for the statement that.

I take tstS as my example throughout and not, say, tst Julius Caesar was bald or tst all mules are sterile, because these latter are apt in their different ways to make us overlook the distinction between sentence and statement: we have, apparently, in the one case a sentence capable of being used to refer to only one historic situation, in the other a statement without reference to at least (or to any particular) one.

If space permitted other types of statement (existential, general, hypothetical, &c.) should be dealt with: these raise problems rather of meaning than of truth, though I feel uneasiness about hypotheticals.

[1] If this is what was meant by ' "It is raining" is true if and only if it is raining', so far so good.

yet between stating, however truly, that I am feeling sick and feeling sick there is a great gulf fixed.[1]

'Fact that' is a phrase designed for use in situations where the distinction between a true statement and the state of affairs about which it is a truth is neglected; as it often is with advantage in ordinary life, though seldom in philosophy—above all in discussing truth, where it is precisely our business to prise the words off the world and keep them off it. To ask 'Is the fact that S the true statement that S or that which it is true of?' may beget absurd answers. To take an analogy: although we may sensibly ask 'Do we *ride* the word "elephant" or the animal?' and equally sensibly 'Do we *write* the word or the animal?' it is nonsense to ask 'Do we *define* the word or the animal?' For defining an elephant (supposing we ever do this) is a compendious description of an operation involving both word and animal (do we focus the image or the battleship?); and so speaking about 'the fact that' is a compendious way of speaking about a situation involving both words and world.[2]

3b. 'Corresponds' also gives trouble, because it is commonly given too restricted or too colourful a meaning, or one which in this context it cannot bear. The only essential point is this: that the correlation between the words (= sentences) and the type of situation, event, &c., which is to be such that when a statement in those words is made with reference to an historic situation of that type the statement is then true, is *absolutely and purely* conventional. We are absolutely free to appoint *any* symbol to describe *any* type of situation, so far as merely being true goes. In a small one-spade language tst nuts might be true in exactly the same circumstances as the statement in English

___

[1] It takes two to make a truth. Hence (obviously) there can be no criterion of truth in the sense of some feature detectable in the statement itself which will reveal whether it is true or false. Hence, too, a statement cannot without absurdity refer to itself.

[2] 'It is true that S' and 'It is a fact that S' are applicable in the same circumstances; the cap fits when there is a head it fits. Other words can fill the same role as 'fact': we say, e.g. 'The situation is that S'.

that the National Liberals are the people's choice.[1] There is no need whatsoever for the words used in making a true statement to 'mirror' in any way, however indirect, any feature whatsoever of the situation or event; a statement no more needs, in order to be true, to reproduce the 'multiplicity,' say, or the 'structure' or 'form' of the reality, than a word needs to be echoic or writing pictographic. To suppose that it does, is to fall once again into the error of reading back into the world the features of language.

The more rudimentary a language, the more, very often, it will tend to have a 'single' word for a highly 'complex' type of situation: this has such disadvantages as that the language becomes elaborate to learn and is incapable of dealing with situations which are non-standard, unforeseen, for which there may just be no word. When we go abroad equipped only with a phrase-book, we may spend long hours learning by heart—

A^l-moest-fa^{i}nd-^{e}tschâ^{r}woum^{e}n,
Ma^{i}hwîl-iz-wau^{r}pt (bènt),

and so on and so on, yet faced with the situation where we have the pen of our aunt, find ourselves quite unable to say so. The characteristics of a more developed language (articulation, morphology, syntax, abstractions, &c.), do not make statements in it any more capable of being true or capable of being any more true, they make it more adaptable, more learnable, more comprehensive, more precise, and so on; and *these* aims may no doubt be furthered by making the language (allowance made for the nature of the medium) 'mirror' in conventional ways features descried in the world.

Yet even when a language does 'mirror' such features very closely (and does it ever?) the truth of statements remains still a matter, as it was with the most rudimentary languages, of the words used being the ones *conventionally appointed* for

---

[1] We could use 'nuts' even now as a code-word: but a code, as a transformation of a language, is distinguished from a language, and a code-word dispatched is not (called) 'true'.

situations of the type to which that referred to belongs. A picture, a copy, a replica, a photograph—these are *never* true in so far as they are reproductions, produced by natural or mechanical means: a reproduction can be accurate or lifelike (true *to* the original), as a gramophone recording or a transcription may be, but not true (*of*) as a record of proceedings can be. In the same way a (natural) sign *of* something can be infallible or unreliable but only an (artificial) sign *for* something can be right or wrong.[1]

There are many intermediate cases between a true account and a faithful picture, as here somewhat forcibly contrasted, and it is from the study of these (a lengthy matter) that we can get the clearest insight into the contrast. For example, maps: these may be called pictures, yet they are highly conventionalized pictures. If a map can be clear or accurate or misleading, like a statement, why can it not be true or exaggerated? How do the 'symbols' used in map-making differ from those used in statement-making? On the other hand, if an air-mosaic is not a map, why is it not? And when does a map become a diagram? These are the really illuminating questions.

4. Some have said that—

To say that an assertion is true is not to make any further assertion at all.

In all sentences of the form '*p* is true' the phrase 'is true' is logically superfluous.

To say that a proposition is true is just to assert it, and to say that it is false is just to assert its contradictory.

But wrongly. TstS (except in paradoxical cases of forced and dubious manufacture) refers to the world or any part of it exclusive of tstS, i.e. of itself.[2] TstST refers to the world or

---

[1] Berkeley confuses these two. There will not be books in the running brooks until the dawn of hydro-semantics.

[2] A statement may refer to 'itself' in the sense, for example, of the sentence used or the utterance uttered in making it ('statement' is not exempt from all ambiguity). But paradox does result if a statement purports to refer to itself in a more full-blooded sense, purports, that is, to state that it itself is true, or to state what it itself refers to ('This statement is about Cato').

any part of it *inclusive* of tstS, though once again exclusive of itself, i.e. of tstST. That is, tstST refers to something to which tstS cannot refer. TstST does not, certainly, include any statement referring to the world exclusive of tstS which is not included already in tstS—more, it seems doubtful whether it does include that statement about the world exclusive of tstS which is made when we state that S. (If I state that tstS is true, should we really agree that I have stated that S? Only 'by implication'.)[1] But all this does not go any way to show that tstST is not a statement different from tstS. If Mr. Q writes on a notice-board 'Mr. W is a burglar', then a trial is held to decide whether Mr. Q's published statement that Mr. W is a burglar is a libel: finding 'Mr. Q's statement was true (in substance and in fact)'. Thereupon a second trial is held, to decide whether Mr. W is a burglar, in which Mr. Q's statement is no longer under consideration: verdict 'Mr. W is a burglar'. It is an arduous business to hold a second trial: why is it done if the verdict is the same as the previous finding?[2]

What is felt is that the evidence considered in arriving at the one verdict is the same as that considered in arriving at the other. This is not strictly correct. It is more nearly correct that whenever tstS is true then tstST is also true and conversely, and that whenever tstS is false tstST is also false and conversely.[3] And it is argued that the words 'is true' are logically superfluous because it is believed that generally if any two statements are always true together and always false together then they must mean the same. Now whether this is in general a sound view may be doubted: but even if it is, why should it not break down in the case of so obviously 'peculiar' a phrase as 'is true'? Mistakes in philosophy notoriously arise through thinking that

---

[1] And 'by implication' tstST asserts something about the making of a statement which tstS certainly does not assert.

[2] This is not quite fair: there are many legal and personal reasons for holding two trials—which, however, do not affect the point that the issue being tried is not the same.

[3] Not *quite* correct, because tstST is only in place at all when tstS is envisaged as made and has been verified.

what holds of 'ordinary' words like 'red' or 'growls' must also hold of extraordinary words like 'real' or 'exists'. But that 'true' is just such another extraordinary word is obvious.[1]

There is something peculiar about the 'fact' which is described by tstST, something which may make us hesitate to call it a 'fact' at all; namely, that the relation between tstS and the world which tstST asserts to obtain is a *purely conventional* relation (one which 'thinking makes so'). For we are aware that this relation is one which we could alter at will, whereas we like to restrict the word 'fact' to *hard* facts, facts which are natural and unalterable, or anyhow not alterable at will. Thus, to take an analogous case, we may not like calling it a fact that the word elephant means what it does, though we can be induced to call it a (soft) fact—and though, of course, we have no hesitation in calling it a fact that contemporary English speakers use the word as they do.

An important point about this view is that it confuses falsity with negation: for according to it, it is the same thing to say 'He is not at home' as to say 'It is false that he is at home'. (But what if no one has said that he *is* at home? What if he is lying upstairs dead?) Too many philosophers maintain, when anxious to explain away negation, that a negation is just a second order affirmation (to the effect that a certain first order affirmation is false), yet, when anxious to explain away falsity, maintain that to assert that a statement is false is just to assert its negation (contradictory). It is impossible to deal with so fundamental a matter here.[2] Let me assert the following merely. Affirmation

---

[1] *Unum, verum, bonum*—the old favourites deserve their celebrity. There *is* something odd about each of them. Theoretical theology is a form of onomatolatry.

[2] The following two sets of logical axioms are, as Aristotle (though not his successors) makes them, quite distinct:
  (*a*) No statement can be both true and false.
      No statement can be neither true nor false.
  (*b*) Of two contradictory statements—
      Both cannot be true.
      Both cannot be false.
The second set demands a definition of contradictories, and is usually joined

and negation are exactly on a level, in this sense, that no language can exist which does not contain conventions for both and that both refer to the world equally directly, not to statements about the world: whereas a language can quite well exist without any device to do the work of 'true' and 'false'. Any satisfactory theory of truth must be able to cope equally with falsity:[1] but 'is false' can only be maintained to be logically superfluous by making this fundamental confusion.

5. There is another way of coming to see that the phrase 'is true' is not logically superfluous, and to appreciate what sort of a statement it is to say that a certain statement is true. There are numerous other adjectives which are in the same class as 'true' and 'false', which are concerned, that is, with the relations between the words (as uttered with reference to an historic situation) and the world, and which nevertheless no one would dismiss as logically superfluous. We say, for example, that a certain statement is exaggerated or vague or bald, a description somewhat rough or misleading or not very good, an account rather general or too concise. In cases like these it is pointless to insist on deciding in simple terms whether the statement is

with an unconscious postulate that for every statement there is one and only one other statement such that the pair are contradictories. It is doubtful how far any language does or must contain contradictories, however defined, such as to satisfy both this postulate and the set of axioms (b).

Those of the so-called 'logical paradoxes' (hardly a genuine class) which concern 'true' and 'false' are *not* to be reduced to cases of self-contradiction, any more than 'S but I do not believe it' is. A statement to the effect that it is itself true is every bit as absurd as one to the effect that it is itself false. There are *other* types of sentence which offend against the fundamental conditions of all communication in ways *distinct from* the way in which 'This is red and is not red' offends—e.g. 'This does (I do) not exist', or equally absurd 'This exists (I exist)'. There are more deadly sins than one; nor does the way to salvation lie through any hierarchy.

[1] To be false is (not, of course, to correspond to a non-fact, but) to mis-correspond with a fact. Some have not seen how, then, since the statement which is false does not describe the fact with which it mis-corresponds (but mis-describes it), we know which fact to compare it with: this was because they thought of all linguistic conventions as descriptive—but it is the demonstrative conventions which fix which situation it is to which the statement refers. No statement can state what it itself refers to.

'true or false'. Is it true or false that Belfast is north of London?
That the galaxy is the shape of a fried egg? That Beethoven
was a drunkard? That Wellington won the battle of Waterloo?
There are various *degrees and dimensions* of success in making
statements: the statements fit the facts always more or less
loosely, in different ways on different occasions for different
intents and purposes. What may score full marks in a general
knowledge test may in other circumstances get a gamma. And
even the most adroit of languages may fail to 'work' in an
abnormal situation or to cope, or cope reasonably simply, with
novel discoveries: is it true or false that the dog goes round
the cow?[1] What, moreover, of the large class of cases where a
statement is not so much false (or true) as out of place, *inept*
('All the signs of bread' said when the bread is before us)?

We become obsessed with 'truth' when discussing statements, just as we become obsessed with 'freedom' when discussing conduct. So long as we think that what has always and
alone to be decided is whether a certain action was done freely
or was not, we get nowhere: but so soon as we turn instead
to the numerous other adverbs used in the same connexion
('accidentally', 'unwillingly', 'inadvertently', &c.), things become easier, and we come to see that no concluding inference
of the form 'Ergo, it was done freely (or not freely)' is required.
Like freedom, truth is a bare minimum or an illusory ideal (the
truth, the whole truth and nothing but the truth about, say, the
battle of Waterloo or the *Primavera*).

6. Not merely is it jejune to suppose that all a statement
aims to be is 'true', but it may further be questioned whether

---

[1] Here there is much sense in 'coherence' (and pragmatist) theories of truth,
despite their failure to appreciate the trite but central point that truth is a
matter of the relation between words and world, and despite their wrong-
headed *Gleichschaltung* of all varieties of statemental failure under the lone head
of 'partly true' (thereafter wrongly equated with 'part of the truth'). 'Correspondence' theorists too often talk as one would who held that every map is
either accurate or inaccurate; that accuracy is a single and the sole virtue of a
map; that every country can have but one accurate map; that a map on a
larger scale or showing different features must be a map of a different country;
and so on.

every 'statement' does aim to be true at all. The principle of
Logic, that 'Every proposition must be true or false', has too
long operated as the simplest, most persuasive and most per-
vasive form of the descriptive fallacy. Philosophers under its
influence have forcibly interpreted all 'propositions' on the
model of the statement that a certain thing is red, as made when
the thing concerned is currently under observation.

Recently, it has come to be realized that many utterances
which have been taken to be statements (merely because they
are not, on grounds of grammatical form, to be classed as
commands, questions, &c.) are not in fact descriptive, nor
susceptible of being true or false. When is a statement not a
statement? When it is a formula in a calculus: when it is a
performatory utterance: when it is a value-judgement: when it
is a definition: when it is part of a work of fiction—there are
many such suggested answers. It is simply not the business of such
utterances to 'correspond to the facts' (and even genuine statements have other businesses besides that of so corresponding).

It is a matter for decision how far we should continue to call
such masqueraders 'statements' at all, and how widely we
should be prepared to extend the uses of 'true' and 'false' in
'different senses'. My own feeling is that it is better, when once
a masquerader has been unmasked, *not* to call it a statement and
not to say it is true or false. In ordinary life we should not call
most of them statements at all, though philosophers and
grammarians may have come to do so (or rather, have lumped
them all together under the term of art 'proposition'). We make
a difference between 'You said you promised' and 'You stated
that you promised': the former can mean that you said 'I
promise', whereas the latter must mean that you said 'I
promised': the latter, which we say you 'stated', is something
which is true or false, whereas for the former, which is not true
or false, we use the wider verb to 'say'. Similarly, there is a
difference between 'You say this is (call this) a good picture'
and 'You state that this is a good picture'. Moreover, it was only
so long as the real nature of arithmetical formulae, say, or of

geometrical axioms remained unrecognized, and they were thought to record information about the world, that it was reasonable to call them 'true' (and perhaps even 'statements'—though were they ever so called?): but, once their nature has been recognized, we no longer feel tempted to call them 'true' or to dispute about their truth or falsity.

In the cases so far considered the model 'This is red' breaks down because the 'statements' assimilated to it are not of a nature to correspond to facts at all—the words are not descriptive words, and so on. But there is also another type of case where the words *are* descriptive words and the 'proposition' does in a way have to correspond to facts, but precisely not in the way that 'This is red' and similar statements setting up to be true have to do.

In the human predicament, for use in which our language is designed, we may wish to speak about states of affairs which have not been observed or are not currently under observation (the future, for example). And although we *can* state anything 'as a fact' (which statement will then be true or false[1]) we need not do so: we need only say 'The cat *may be* on the mat'. This utterance is quite different from tstS—it is not a statement at all (it is not true or false; it is compatible with 'The cat may *not* be on the mat'). In the same way, the situation in which we discuss whether and state that tstS is *true* is different from the situation in which we discuss whether it is *probable* that S. Tst it is probable that S is out of place, inept, in the situation where we can make tstST, and, I think, conversely. It is not our business here to discuss probability: but is worth observing that the phrases 'It is true that' and 'It is probable that' are in the same line of business,[2] and in so far incompatibles.

7. In a recent article in *Analysis* Mr. Strawson has propounded a view of truth which it will be clear I do not accept.

---

[1] Though it is not yet in place to call it either. For the same reason, one cannot lie or tell the truth about the future.

[2] Compare the odd behaviours of 'was' and 'will be' when attached to 'true' and to 'probable'.

He rejects the 'semantic' account of truth on the perfectly correct ground that the phrase 'is true' is not used in talking about *sentences*, supporting this with an ingenious hypothesis as to how meaning may have come to be confused with truth: but this will not suffice to show what he wants—that 'is true' is not used in talking about (or that 'truth is not a property of') *anything*. For it *is* used in talking about *statements* (which in his article he does not distinguish clearly from sentences). Further, he supports the 'logical superfluity' view to this extent, that he agrees that to say that ST is not to make any further assertion at all, beyond the assertion that S: but he disagrees with it in so far as he thinks that to say that ST *is* to *do* something more than just to assert that S—it is namely to *confirm* or to *grant* (or something of that kind) the assertion, made or taken as made already, that S. It will be clear that and why I do not accept the first part of this: but what of the second part? I agree that to say that ST 'is' very often, and according to the all-important linguistic occasion, to confirm tstS or to grant it or what not; but this cannot show that to say that ST is not also and at the same time to make an assertion about tstS. To say that I believe you 'is' on occasion to accept your statement; but it is also to make an assertion, which is not made by the strictly performatory utterance 'I accept your statement'. It is common for quite ordinary statements to have a performatory 'aspect': to say that you are a cuckold may be to insult you, but it is also and at the same time to make a statement which is true or false. Mr. Strawson, moreover, seems to confine himself to the case where I *say* 'Your statement is true' or something similar—but what of the case where you state that S and I *say* nothing but '*look and see*' that your statement is true? I do not see how this critical case, to which nothing analogous occurs with strictly performatory utterances, could be made to respond to Mr. Strawson's treatment.

One final point: if it is admitted (*if*) that the rather boring yet satisfactory relation between words and world which has here been discussed does genuinely occur, why should the phrase 'is true' not be our way of describing it? And if it is not, what else is?

6

HOW TO TALK[1]

SOME SIMPLE WAYS

CAN to describe X as Y really be the same as to call X Y? Or again the same as to state that X is Y? Have we, in using such a variety of terms for simple speech-acts, any clear and serious distinctions in mind? The presumption must surely be that we have: and what follows is an attempt to isolate and schematize some of them. But it is not contended that it contains an exact or full or final account of our ordinary uses of any one of the terms for speech-acts discussed. For one thing, this is a mere essay at one section of what must be a very large theme; for another, essential though it is as a preliminary to track down the detail of our ordinary uses of words, it seems that we shall in the end always be compelled to straighten them out to some extent.

We shall consider a simplified model of a situation in which we use language for talking about the world. This model we shall call by the name 'Speech-situation S_0'.

Possibly we never are actually in a situation exactly like S_0: more probably we sometimes are so, or, more strictly, regard ourselves for current intents and purposes as being so. But the purpose of considering the model is to elucidate some of our ordinary thought and language about the uses of speech: and it seems hardly deniable that in such thought and language we do, for better or worse and whether consciously or unconsciously, make use of such models (not, of course, necessarily only one such).

[1] Reprinted from *Proceedings of the Aristotelian Society*, 1952-3, by courtesy of the editor.

The world, then, in S_0 will consist of numerous individual *items*, each of one and only one definite *type*. Each type is totally and equally different from every other type: each item is totally and equally distinct from every other item. Numerous items may be of the same type, but no item is of more than one type. Item and type are (to speak with necessary roughness) apprehended by inspection merely. (Roughly, the world might consist of an orderless plurality of amorphous colour-patches, each of either the same pure red, or the same pure blue, or the same pure yellow. Then would not they be alike in being coloured, and possibly in other further general features? This must be ruled out—perhaps by the consideration that in these other respects every item in our world is identical with every other, so that nothing can be said about them: or perhaps by alterations and refinements—every item is *either* a colour-patch of the same pure red, *or* a noise of the same definite pitch, intensity, &c., *or* a smell, &c.: but anyway, by the ruling that our language is not going to be equipped to deal with any such further features.)

The language in S_0 will permit of the utterance only of sentences of one form, form S:

I is a T.

Besides the expression 'is a', which is used invariably in every sentence in the position shown above, our language may contain an indefinite number of other vocables to be inserted in the place of the 'I' or the 'T' in form S. Assuming that the conventions next to be mentioned have been established, each of these vocables will be either an I-word or a T-word in the language: and any utterance consisting of an I-word followed by 'is a' followed by a T-word will be a sentence in the language. Nothing else will be a sentence.

In order for this language to be used for talking about this world, two sets of (semantic) conventions will be needed. I-conventions, or conventions of *reference*, are needed in order to fix which item it is that the vocable which is to be an I-word is to refer to on each (and in our simple case, on *every*) occasion of the uttering (assertive) of a sentence containing it: we shall not concern ourselves here with the nature or genesis of these conventions, but simply take it that each item has had allotted to it its own I-word by which it is uniquely referred to, and each I-word similarly its own item. For I-words we shall use in what follows numerals, for example, '1227', and we shall speak of them in use not as '(proper) names', of which they are at most only a primitive variety, but as 'references'. T-conventions, or conventions of *sense*, are needed in order to associate the vocables which are to be T-words with the item-types, one to one: these conventions we may inaugurate by one or other of two procedures of linguistic legislation, viz.

1. Name-giving.
2. Sense-giving.

Name-giving ('naming' in one ordinary sense, but not, for example, in the sense of 'giving the name *of*' or of '*putting* a name to') consists in allotting a certain vocable to a certain item-type as its 'name'. Sense-giving ('defining' in the sense of 'ostensive definition', here in a simplified world) consists in allotting a certain item-type to a certain vocable as its 'sense'. These two procedures, at least in our simplified situation, produce the same upshot: when either has been gone through, the item-type, attached by nature to certain items, is attached by convention to a certain vocable, now a T-word and (as we shall call it) its 'name', as the 'sense' of that word.[1]

---

[1] The difference between name-giving and sense-giving is important in some connexions, though not here. If, not happily, we were to use, as we shall not, sentences of our form S for inaugurating T-conventions, there would be between '1227 is a *rhombus*' (name-giving) and '*1227* is a rhombus' (sense-giving) a difference in *direction* of allotment similar to that difference in direction of fit which is to be mentioned shortly. I say 'not happily' because, for example, if our interest were in linguistic legislation, we had better go back behind 'proper names' to 'that' and 'this'. But we are *not* here concerned with how these conventions are established, *nor* even to assert, for example, that the two types could be established independently of one another. All this is mere preliminary.

Every word in our language S_0 (except for 'is' and 'a') has either a reference fixed by I-conventions or a sense fixed by T-conventions, but not both, and is accordingly either an I-word or a T-word.

We shall not go into the 'metaphysical status' of types and senses (nor of items). If we went back to the rudiments of speech theory, both might appear as 'constructions'. Nevertheless, to talk of types and senses,[1] and, as we shall, of matching the one to the other, is not necessarily inexpedient in all contexts: and in particular it is expedient in our present context, where we are engaged to elucidate some of our ordinary language about speech-acts, since such ordinary language does embody a model like S_0. Conceive of our items here as, say, a number of *samples* or *specimens* of colours, or of (geometrical) shapes, each with a reference-numeral allotted to it: conceive of our senses as a number of standards or *patterns* of colours, or of (geo-metrical) shapes, each with a name allotted to it: think of name-giving or sense-giving as involving *the selection of a sample or specimen as a standard pattern*. This is not so far from the truth.

Let us now take the stage of linguistic legislation as over. We proceed to use our language in accordance with that legis-lation to talk about the world. Then a satisfactory utterance (assertive) on any particular occasion will be one where the item referred to by the I-word in accordance with the conven-tions of reference is of a (in S_0, the) type which matches the sense which is attached by the conventions of sense to the T-word. For the utterance to be satisfactory, we require the presence of

> *both* a *conventional* link between I-word and item, and another between T-word and sense,
> *and* a *natural* link (match)[2] between type and sense.

We shall call the expression 'is a' as uttered in the uttering

[1] Or ?: 'types' and 'senses'. 'Talk of' gives trouble with inverted commas, for reasons which can be understood.

[2] Here, in S_0, taken to be *purely* natural—apprehended by inspection without admixture of convention. This does not obtain in more complicated situations.

(assertive, of course: I shall omit this necessary qualification in future) of a sentence of form S by the name 'assertive link', and any utterance of form S an 'assertion'. Then the assertion is justified not *merely* by convention, nor *merely* by nature, but in a complex or roundabout way. Diagrammatically:

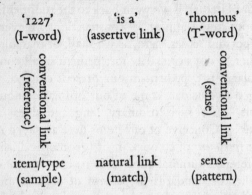

'1227' (I-word)	'is a' (assertive link)	'rhombus' (T-word)
conventional link (reference)		conventional link (sense)
item/type (sample)	natural link (match)	sense (pattern)

All this is, I hope, simple—and, it may be again emphasized, highly simplified. It is now time to get out of the way, as a preliminary, two very primitive ways in which I may on any occasion go wrong in my utterance. I may be guilty of

> 1. Misnaming.
> 2. Misreferring.

In both of these cases I match sample to pattern or pattern to sample it may be quite unexceptionably, but

> 1. I quote (give) the name wrongly.
> 2. I quote (give) the reference wrongly.

In either case alike I *mislead*, or more strictly *tend pro tanto* to mislead (not myself, at least at the time—if indeed that makes sense, but) my hearers who know the language. Misleading, at least as I use the term here, goes, it should be noted, to the *meaning* of the utterance, not to the *facts*: whether or not I create additionally in those hearers, or more strictly tend to create in them, a *misapprehension* as to the facts depends *additionally* on whether or not I have been correct in matching sample to pattern (or conversely), a quite distinct consideration. I mislead (as to meaning) when, through my use of the wrong I-word or T-word, my hearers are caused, in assessing or relying on the justifiability of my assertion, to advert to a different sample or a different pattern from that which I, in making the assertion, was adverting to.[1]

Misnaming and misreferring alike may be either *aberrational* or *idiosyncratic*. Aberrational misnaming or misreferring is a *sin against* my accepted linguistic legislation: my sample list is rightly numbered, my pattern stock is rightly labelled, but through aberration I quote or give the number or the name wrongly. Idiosyncratic misnaming or misreference is due to a *fault in* my accepted linguistic legislation: though I quote or give the number or the name rightly, my sample list is wrongly numbered or my pattern stock is wrongly labelled.[2]

Whenever in S_0 I utter an assertion, I am *eo ipso referring* and also *naming* (using these terms, as I shall here only do, in senses analogous to misnaming and misreferring as explained above). But in contrast with other varieties of speech-act, to be discussed next, which in uttering an assertion we may be said to be performing, 'referring' and 'naming' are terms for only *parts*, and we may say *ancillary* parts, of my performance on any occasion. By contrast, when we say, for example, that in uttering the assertion '1227 is a rhombus' I am *identifying* 1227 as a rhombus or *stating* that 1227 is a rhombus, then the *whole* issuing of the utterance is the making of the identification or the making of the statement, and the *whole* utterance is (in my use—not, of

[1] 'Misleading' is a speech-act of a totally distinct class from those speech-acts with which this paper is concerned. There are, of course, many such distinct classes.

[2] Clearly, in combination an aberration and an idiosyncrasy *may* cancel each other out, may not 'tend to mislead' on that occasion. Just as, similarly, a combination of misnaming with misreferring, or of either or both with mismatching, *may* not on a particular occasion tend to create a misapprehension. It is characteristic of ordinary language that it should not (bother to) have simple names for complex faults, such as these are.

course, in every use) the identification or the statement.[1] You are guilty of misreferring in using, in making your assertion, the *word* '1227', or of misnaming in using the *word* 'rhombus': but you are guilty of making a misidentification or of making a misstatement in using the *sentence* '1227 is a rhombus'. The issuing of the *whole* utterance cannot be an act of misnaming or of misreferring, nor, similarly, of naming (in my usage) or of referring.

Let us henceforward take it, not merely that the stage of linguistic legislation is over, but also that we are not, in issuing our utterances, guilty of sins against, or of sins through faults in, our accepted linguistic legislation.

There now arise four distinct uses to which we may put our sentence '1227 is a rhombus', four distinct speech-acts which, in uttering it as an assertion, we may be said to be performing —four species, if you like, of the generic speech-act of asserting. These will be called:

c-identifying, cap-fitting or placing;
b-identifying, bill-filling or casting;
stating;
instancing.

How does this complexity arise? For let it be repeated that in none of these performances are we to be taken as in any way legislating, but only as performing in accordance with the terms and purposes of an accepted legislation. And furthermore we are still excluding a complication of great importance,

[1] Sometimes we use 'the identification', like 'the description' and unlike 'the statement', for, we may say, a *part* of the utterance: but I am using it only for the *whole* utterance, so as to assimilate identifying, as it should be assimilated, to stating and not to naming (in my use). Even if 'the identification' can be used, as is 'the name', for a part of the *utterance*, still 'identifying' is not a name for a part *of my performance in issuing* the utterance (as 'naming', in my use, always is), but for the whole of it. That part of our utterance is a name or a reference says nothing to prejudge the type of assertive speech-act to which our whole performance in issuing the utterance belongs: but that part of it is an identification or a description tells us precisely that (in, of course, our simplified speech-situations).

which will be introduced only later, namely, that our vocabulary may be 'inadequate' to the variety presented by the world we are to talk about: we are still taking our legislation as adequate in the sense that every item in the world is of one type only, which matches precisely the sense of one name only. Complexity arises, nevertheless, owing to the complexity, which may escape notice, of the notions of 'fitting' and 'matching'.

We have already noticed in passing, in the case of name-giving and sense-giving, the distinction in point of *direction* between allotting an X to a Y and allotting a Y to an X. In a similar way, when we operate in accordance with such legislation, there is a difference in *direction of fit* between fitting a name to an item (or an item *with* the name) and fitting an item to a name (or a name *with* the item). These differ as fitting a nut with a bolt differs from fitting a bolt with a nut. We may be 'given' a name, and purport to produce an item of a type which matches (or is matched by) the sense of that name: this production we declare by uttering an assertion of form S with the given name as T-word and the reference of the produced item as I-word. To utter an assertion in this way is to fit an item to a name. Conversely, we may be 'given' an item, and purport to produce a name with a sense which matches (or is matched by) the type of that item: this production we declare by uttering an assertion of form S with the reference of the given item as I-word and the produced name as T-word. To utter an assertion in this way is to fit a name to an item.

But there is also another distinction to be drawn. We fit the name to the item or the item to the name on the ground that the *type* of the item and the *sense* of the name *match*. But in matching X and Y, there is a distinction between matching X *to* Y and matching Y *to* X, which may be called a distinction in point of *onus of match*. We are apt to overlook this with the verb 'match'[1] (especially where it is being taken to mean

---

[1] If X matches Y, Y matches X: just as, if X fits Y, Y fits X. But if I match X to Y, I do not match Y to X, any more than, if I fit X to Y, I fit Y to X.

'match *exactly*'): but if we consider the analogous word 'assimilate', the distinction between assimilating X to Y, where the onus of assimilability is on X, and assimilating Y to X, where the onus of assimilability is on Y, is clear enough. We go wrong in assimilating because we are mistaken about or misrepresent the nature of the member, X in the first case and Y in the second, on which the onus of assimilability rests. When we ask whether we should assimilate X to Y, the question is *whether* X has the qualities Y *has*: a simile, 'A is like B', is a bad simile not because B has not the features which A has or has features which A has not, but because A has not the features which B has or has features which B has not.

These two distinctions generate our four different performances in uttering '1227 is a rhombus', which are, in the form of a diagram:

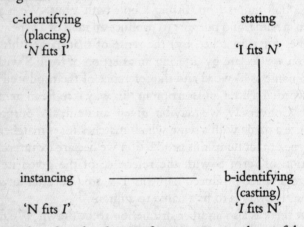

c-identifying (placing) 'N fits I'	stating 'I fits N'
instancing 'N fits *I*'	b-identifying (casting) '*I* fits N'

To explain first the choice of terms. We use the useful word 'identify', understandably enough, in two opposite ways: we may speak of 'identifying it (as a daphnia)' when you hand it to me and ask me if I can identify it, and I say that it is a daphnia: but we also speak of 'identifying a daphnia' (or 'identifying the daphnia') when you hand me a slide and ask me if I can identify a daphnia (or the daphnia) in it. In the first case we are finding a cap to fit a given object: hence the name 'cap-fitting' or 'c-identifying'. We are trying to 'place' it. But in the second case we are trying to find an object to fill a given bill: hence the name 'b-identifying' or 'bill-filling'. We 'cast' this thing as the daphnia.[1] The terms 'stating' and 'instancing' should need no explanation: to instance is to cite I as an instance of T.

In the diagram the connecting lines, horizontal and vertical, indicate the way in which the members of each pair connected are similar to each other, as follows:

> The *horizontal line* indicates that the *direction of fit* is the same. In both placing and stating we are fitting names to given items, in both instancing and casting we are fitting items to given names. In the verbalizations given in the diagram, that which is being fitted *to* is shown by italics, in contrast to that which is being fitted *with*, which is not in italics.

> The *vertical line* indicates that the *onus of match* is the same. In both placing and instancing the type of the item is taken for granted and the question might be whether the sense of the T-word is such as really to match it: in both stating and casting the sense of the T-word is taken for granted, and the question might be whether the type of the item is really such as to match it. In the verbalizations given in the diagram, that, name or item, on the sense or type of which lies the onus of match is put as the subject.

Or again:

> To *place* we have to find a pattern to match to this sample.
> To *state* we have to find a pattern to match this sample to.
> To *instance* we have to find a sample to match this pattern to.
> To *cast* we have to find a sample to match to this pattern.

Or again, the differences and likenesses between the four

---

[1] Contrast the questions: (a) *What* (part of speech) is the word underlined in the following sentence: He was going <u>downhill</u>? (b) *Which* is the adverb in the following sentence: He was going downhill? Answers: (a) An adverb (cap-fitting); (b) 'Downhill' (bill-filling). We might even christen c-identifying 'what-identifying' and b-identifying 'which-identifying'.

performances may be brought out by considering wherein, if any one of them is faultily executed, the fault lies:

To *misidentify* (= misplace) shows that we have gone wrong in our matching through failure to appreciate, to keep clearly before ourselves for the purpose of this matching, the sense of the name (T-word). 'I see now, I was wrong to identify it as magenta: magenta, of course, on reflection, is not what this is'. The mistake is due, we might say, using a word more obviously appropriate in more complicated situations than S_0, to 'misconception' of the sense.

Misidentifying must be carefully distinguished from what we have called 'misnaming'. There, the name is 'wrong' even though, and whether or not, the sense, wrongly allotted to it, does match the type of the item: whereas here the name is 'wrong' *because* the sense, rightly allotted to it, does *not* match the type of the item. If I have misnamed, I should not have said it was a 'rhombus': if I have misidentified, I should not have said it was a rhombus. (Ambiguity of 'said'.)

It may be asked, Does not misidentifying remain, nevertheless, itself a (merely) 'linguistic' mistake? This is reminiscent of the argument that misstatement is impossible, which so long entangled the Greeks, and is perhaps hard to answer because 'linguistic' is vague. The basic point, never to be surrendered, is that mistakes in matching are possible, do occur, and that they may be due to faulty grasp of *either* of the two elements being matched. Just as we can (do) advert to the same item and yet match its type to differing patterns (misperception), so we can advert to the same sense and match it to differing types of items. If it is indeed hard to imagine our making such a mistake in such a simple situation as S_0, perhaps after all it is equally hard to imagine, here, misperception and consequent misstatement. (Yet in one way our model of patterns and samples may be helpful; for it suggests that agreement as to the 'sense' of some name, a term we have admitted to be not ultimate in speech theory, is in the last resort established by agreement upon the *items* the types of which are to be standards, leaving those types themselves still to be appraised by perception and so liable to the, admittedly possible, errors of perception.)

To *misinstance* likewise reveals misconception of the sense of the name. It is to be distinguished from misreferring: there, the reference is 'wrong' even *though* the sense *does* match the type, whereas here the reference is 'wrong' *because* the sense does *not* match the type. I should not have said '1227' was one: or, I should not have said 1227 was one.

To *misstate* shows that we do not correctly appraise the type of the item: it is due, we may say in our simple situation, to *misperceiving* the sample.

To *misidentify* (= miscast) likewise reveals misperception of the type of the item.

This brings out the similarity between placing and instancing and again between stating and casting. In another way, we might bring out the similarity between placing and stating on the one hand and between instancing and casting on the other: to a misplacing or a misstatement we respond with 'But 1227 *isn't* a *rhombus*', but to a misinstance or a miscasting we respond with 'But 1227 *isn't* a rhombus'. (Needless to say, we cannot so respond in S_0, where we are not equipped with negation: to introduce negation alters the situation—though of course I have no wish to suggest that negation is 'posterior' to affirmation, or that assimilating even 'makes sense' without contrasting.)

Finally, one further and perhaps less clear way of bringing out the contrast between placing and stating, and likewise between instancing and casting. In both placing and stating we fit the name to the item, but in placing the interest is in linking *the name to the type* via the sense, whereas in stating the interest is in linking *the sense to the item* via the type: it is primarily, we may say, the *type* that we identify[1] but primarily the *item* about which we state. Similarly, in both instancing and casting we

[1] It should be unnecessary to point out that I am never using 'identify' here in the sense of identifying an item as the same item again, which is a feat demanding a speech-situation far more complex than S_0. Moreover, in a situation where, say, a single item may have more than one feature, the sense of 'identify' will suffer a sea-change.

fit the item to the name, but it is primarily the *type* that we instance and primarily the *item* that we cast.

It is now time to inject a first dose of complexity into our model of the speech-situation. We shall now suppose that there occur in the world to be talked about items of types which do not exactly match any of the patterns in our stock (the sense of any of our names), though they may be more or less similar to one or to more than one of those patterns. This new model situation will be called by the name 'Speech-situation S_1'.

It is to be noted that each item in the world is still being assumed to be of *one type only*—or to possess, we may say, one feature only, or to be assessable in one dimension only. For example, if our original patterns are colours, they may be a (certain shade of) red, a (certain shade of) blue and a (certain shade of) yellow. Then in S_0, every item which occurs will be either a red (of the pattern shade) or a blue (of the pattern shade) or a yellow (of the pattern shade): but in S_1, items may occur of any colour—they may be (what we should ordinarily call) white, and so resemble none of the patterns, or none more than another, or (what we should ordinarily call) pink, and so resemble one of our patterns appreciably and none of the others at all, or (what we should ordinarily call) purple, and so resemble two of our patterns equally but the rest not at all, or (what we should ordinarily call) crimson and so resemble one of our patterns most closely but another appreciably and the rest not at all, and so on. But in S_1 none of the items must be conceived as having, for example, shape or size to be talked about as well as colour, though they might have, for example, shape but no colour. It is only in some further model of the speech-situation, to be called say 'S_2' but not here discussed, that we might introduce the complication that the *same* item may possess more than one feature or be of more than one type or be assessable in more than one dimension.

It is obvious that the 'complication' here introduced in S_1 is inevitable in most actual speech-situations. The actual world is, to all human intents and purposes, indefinitely various; but we cannot handle an indefinitely large vocabulary; nor, generally speaking, do we wish to insist on the minutest detectable differences, but rather on relative similarities; nor, with our limited experience both as individuals and as a race, can we anticipate in our vocabulary vagaries of nature which have yet to be revealed.

Faced, then, with some such item in S_1, the type of which does not exactly match the sense of any one of the names in our stock, what courses are open to us? We can of course (as with the resources in speech-acts available in S_0 we must, to be correct) say nothing—in default of some fresh legislation: and this we shall still do if the type of the recalcitrant item resembles none of our patterns at all, or none more than another. More generally, however, the type of the item resembling the sense of some one of our names *sufficiently* well, and more closely than it resembles the senses of others of our names, we may say, using that name, '1228 is a polygon'. When we speak in this way, a new set of terms becomes appropriate for the four different speech-acts which, in saying '1228 is a polygon', we may be performing. The four performances are distinguished, as in S_0, by means of direction of fit and onus of match, but we now term them:

Calling	Describing
Exemplifying	Classing

When we *call*[1] 1228 a polygon or *describe* it as a polygon, it is admitted, by the use of these terms for our speech-acts, that the name does not exactly fit the item—because in the one case the sense does not exactly match to the type and in the other case the type does not exactly match to the sense.

If we are accused of *wrongly* calling 1228 a polygon, or of *mis*calling it a polygon, then we are accused of *abusing language*, of doing violence to language. In calling 1228 a polygon, we admit a multiformity into our pattern, we modify or stretch

[1] Not: call 1228 a 'polygon'. Ambiguity of 'call'.

the sense of our name, and future uses of the name will be influenced by the precedent here set. If on the other hand we are accused of wrongly *describing*, or of *mis*describing, 1228 as a polygon, we are accused of doing violence *to the facts*. In describing 1228 as a polygon we impose admittedly a uniformity on our specimens, we are simplifying or neglecting the specificity of the type of the item 1228, and we are committing ourselves thereby to a certain view of it.

In the same way, briefly, when we give *examples* as opposed to instances we admit a multiformity in the pattern to which justice is not done by one specimen, and when we *class* some item as a polygon, as opposed to identifying (casting) it as a polygon, we admit to a neglect of the full specificity of the item.

Two warnings may be here repeated, concerning the 'ordinary' use of such terms as 'call' and 'describe'. Firstly, these same terms may be used of speech-acts performed in envisaged speech-situations *other* than S_1, for example in a speech situation in which the same item may possess more than one feature, to draw attention to features of such speech-acts other than (though no doubt connected with) the features just described above. Secondly, it is likely enough that our ordinary use of the terms is fairly loose, that we do not always distinguish carefully between them, although there is a distinction which can be marked by their means. Contrast, for example, the following:

(1) You call that crimson? But surely no crimson can have so much blue in it? That is not what crimson is at all.

You describe it as crimson? But look, it has a lot of blue in it. It is not really like crimson at all.

(2) He calls me a dictator, in spite of the fact that I have notoriously always acted only on the advice of Parliament!

He describes me as a dictator, whereas in fact, as he must have known, I have always acted only on the advice of Parliament.

If many such examples are studied, the watershed between calling and describing appears to take shape.

Though cases in which we shall have to call, describe, &c., instead of, in black-and-white terms, identifying, stating, &c., are sure to arise continually, we feel ourselves sometimes bound to cope with them as they arise by means of fresh linguistic legislation. In calling there is indeed already implicit an element of legislation by precedent—this is case law and will regularly be necessary: but we may also demand statute law. Naturally, if the type of an item is highly novel, and does not appreciably resemble any of our stock of patterns, or none rather than another, it will be preferable not to call it or describe it by any of the names in our existent vocabulary, but rather to allot this type to some altogether new name as its sense: this is legislation of the kind already familiar in S_0. But suppose the new type does match fairly well one, or more than one, of our existing stock of patterns, suppose 1228 is genuinely *like* a red, i.e. our hitherto familiar specific red. Our fresh legislation will then take the typical S_1 form of classification and differentiation. That is, we shall not merely allot a new name, a 'specific' name, say 'crimson', to the type, but we shall also adopt the convention that *crimson is a sort of red*, thus giving the explicitness of statute law to the modification in the sense of the name 'red' and recognizing 'red' as the name of a multiform pattern, i.e. as a generic name. This legislation will show itself, in our restricted language, by the phenomenon of entailment between sentences of form S, which now appears for the first time: henceforward, '1228 is a crimson' will entail '1228 is a red'. The phenomenon merely of incompatibility was already present even in S_0, for even there '1227 is a red' was incompatible, according to our legislation, with '1227 is a green'.

In the above account we have not, of course, dealt with by any means all of the kinds of case that arise in S_1. We have discussed the case where the novel type is like up to a point but not beyond it, the sense of one of our available names, but not appreciably like the sense of any other—the case, we may say, where there is only one name for more than one variety of type (calling) or more than one variety of type for a single name (describing). But there are also, say, cases where the type resembles up to a point more than one of our available patterns —where, we may say, there are two names to call one type by, or a single type which may be described by two names. Such different varieties of cases lead appropriately now to the introduction of specific words (differentiation) and now to the introduction of generic words (classification). It should be unnecessary further to point out that in a fully-fledged language we have, of course, numerous additional devices for coping with the kind of cases arising typically in S_1, devices such as the useful words 'like', 'real', &c.: but in S_1 our language is still restricted to sentences of the form S.

This sort of investigation of the nature of speech-acts might go on more or less indefinitely. I propose to stop at this point, where we have barely begun upon the complexities of 'calling', 'describing', &c. Obviously what is here written is imperfect and probably it is wrong in many ways: but what I should like to have succeeded in doing is in calling renewed attention to the following points:

1. Names for speech-acts are more numerous, more specialized, more ambiguous and more significant than is ordinarily allowed for: none of them can be safely used in philosophy in a general way (for example, 'statement' or 'description') without more investigation than they have, I think, yet received. Here of course we have been concerned with only a few speech-acts of a single family, but naturally there are other whole families besides.

2. To some extent we probably do, even in ordinary language, make use of models of the speech-situation in using the terms that we do for speech-acts. At any rate, the construction of such models can help towards clarifying the varieties of speech-act which are possible. Any such model, even the simplest, seems bound to be fairly complicated—too complicated for the standard subject-predicate or class-membership

model. Moreover, we seem bound to use a whole series of different models, because *the difference between one named speech-act and another often resides principally in a difference between the speech-situations envisaged for their respective performances.*

I have touched not merely upon very few speech-acts, but also upon only very few features of these, and in highly simplified situations only. A feature, for example, in which different speech-acts even of the same family may differ very much is that commonly discussed in an entirely general way under the name of 'truth': even, say, with speech-acts which are assertions, we often prefer for one a different term of approbation from that which we prefer for another, and usually for good and understandable reasons. This, however, I shall not pursue here, but instead conclude by giving a short example of how a small variation in our model of the speech-situation, this time on the *language* side rather than on the side of the world, will have repercussions on the speech-acts we perform.

Hitherto we have confined ourselves, in our sentence form S, to *affirmative* assertions. But if we now introduce a second sentence form 'SN', viz.

$$\text{'I is not a T',}$$

we find that this, unlike form S, is not equally usable for the performance of all four of our speech-acts in S_0. By introducing this sentence form, we bring out a resemblance not hitherto pointed out, between c-identifying and b-identifying in contrast with stating and instancing, which might be symbolized in our diagram by linking them with a *diagonal* line, thus:

c-identifying   stating

instancing   b-identifying

A sentence of form SN will be correct on any occasion of its utterance if the type of the item referred to by 'I' and the sense of the name 'T' do *not* match—where 'I is a T' assimilates sense and type, 'I is not a T' contrasts them. We may call this speech-situation, which is the same as S_0 except for the introduction of the negative sentence form SN, 'speech-situation S_{0N}'.

When in situation S_{0N} I utter the sentence '1229 is not a T', then I may be *stating* something about 1229, but I cannot be identifying it—to say that 1229 is not something is not to identify it. In both stating and identifying our utterance is intended to fit a name to, to pin a label to, the item: but there was a difference between the two performances in point of onus of match. And it now appears that where the interest is in matching a sense to the type, nothing is achieved to the purpose by the production of a sense which does *not* match the type. To tell us that 1229 is not a T is not to tell us what it is, nor to identify it. But where, on the other hand, the interest is in matching the type to a sense, something is achieved to the purpose even by the discovery that the type does not match some or any one particular sense. We identify 1229 as *red* as opposed to *blue*, &c., but we state that 1229 *is* red as opposed to is *not* red.

In a similar but opposite manner, when I utter the sentence '1229 is not a T', I may be giving a negative or counter instance, but I cannot be identifying (casting): there is no such thing as a negative or counter identification. In both instancing and casting I am fitting an item to the name: but where I am matching the sense to a type something significant is achieved even by a refusal to match, whereas where I am matching a type to the sense, nothing is achieved by a failure to match. We identify (cast) *1229* as a square, as opposed to *1228*, &c., but we instance 1229 as a square as opposed to not a square.

So far, it has been said that the sentence form SN is in order when we are matching *the* (given) sense/type to *a* (produced) type/sense, but not in order when we are matching *a* (produced) sense/type to *the* (given) type/sense. The same distinction can be put in another way and in our old terms as resulting from a combination of the two distinctions of direction of fit and onus of match, as shown by the following table on p. 200. In this table we may say that with both c- and b-identifying the direction of fit is *parallel* to the onus of match, whereas with both stating and instancing the direction and onus are *opposite*. In identifying we fit the name to the item because the sense of the former matches the type of the latter, or we fit the item to the name because the type of the former matches the sense of the latter: but in stating and instancing we fit the name/item to the item/name because the type/sense of the *latter* matches the sense/type of the *former*. In the verbalizations given in our original diagram, parallelism is shown by the subject of the sentence being in italics.

	Direction of Fit	Onus of Match
c-identifying . . .	N to I	S to T
stating . . .	N to I	T to S
instancing . . .	I to N	S to T
b-identifying . . .	I to N	T to S

We cannot, in either sense of 'identify', identify I as not a T: to identify as not is nonsense for not to identify. Whereas, therefore, the use of the affirmative sentence form S will not decide whether we are identifying or stating or instancing, the use of the negative sentence form SN makes it clear that we must be either stating or instancing. In similar ways other variations in the permitted forms of sentence will in general have effects on the varieties of speech-acts which, in uttering them, we may be performing. (Though in general of course also the use of any one sentence form does not tie us down to the performance of some *one* particular variety of speech-act.)

7

UNFAIR TO FACTS

THIS paper goes back to an old controversy between Strawson and me about truth. Of course comments on comments, criticisms of criticisms, are subject to the law of diminishing fleas, but I think there are here some misconceptions still to be cleared up, some of which seem to be still prevalent in generally sensible quarters.

In this old paper I gave (somewhat qualified) support to the common English expression that a true statement is one which 'corresponds with the facts'. I professed not to like this, in its own way doubtless unexceptionable, terminology, and preferred some jargon of my own, in which 'facts' and 'corresponds' do not occur at all, as a description of the conditions which must be satisfied if we are to say of a statement that it is true. Strawson in general, though with reservations, accepted, I believe, that description, but contended that, nevertheless, to say a certain statement is true is not to *assert that* those conditions are satisfied but to do something else such as *endorsing* the statement said to 'be true'. This was the principal issue, I think, between us, but we are not concerned with it here.

Now Strawson expended a good deal of ammunition on three words occurring in my paper—'statement', 'corresponds', and 'facts', giving at times, I think, the impression that I had given a pretty myth-eaten description even of the conditions which must obtain if we are to say of a statement that it is true. And this he claimed was due to my misunderstandings about the uses of these three words. I propose therefore to consider one of them, namely 'fact' (which I remember Ryle said at the time I should give more attention to). I choose 'fact' because, although the use of this word was not at all essential to my account of truth, (indeed I only mentioned it to point out that it caused confusion) I do find that I think Strawson's own account of the word incorrect, and that I do not for a minute believe, with him, that 'facts' are pseudo-entities and the notion of 'fitting the facts' a useless notion.

By way of preliminary softening up, I shall take Strawson's two boldest and negative lines, and try to argue that they are unplausible and based on insufficient consideration of ordinary usage. Then I shall take his two more sophisticated and positive contentions.

I. What I am referring to as his two boldest and negative lines are these:

(i) There is a (logically fundamental) type-difference between 'facts' and things-genuinely-in-the-world, such as things, persons and events.

(ii) 'Corresponds with the facts' is a mere idiom, as it were a 'fused' idiom, not to be taken at all at its apparent face-value.

(i) Taking the first of these: how is this alleged type-difference shown? Strawson points out, truly enough, that 'while we certainly say a statement corresponds to (fits, is borne out by, agrees with) the facts, as a variant on saying that it is true, we *never* say that it corresponds to the thing, person, &c., it is about'.[1] This is partly said, I think, to refute my analysis of 'corresponds with the facts' in terms of (among other things) the persons, &c., that the statement refers to: but it will not suffice for this, because, of course, that analysis was offered *as a whole* as an analysis of the *whole* expression 'corresponds with the facts': to substitute part of the analysis for part of the analysandum is a well-known short way with analyses. Still, here is a case, certainly, in which 'things', 'events', &c., are used differently from 'facts'. And certainly there are important

[1] *Proceedings of the Aristotelian Society*, Supplementary Volume xxiv.

differences between these words. But firstly, there are important similarities also.

For example, although we perhaps rarely, and perhaps only in strained senses, say that a 'thing' (e.g. the German Navy) is a fact, and perhaps never say that a person is a fact, still, things and persons are far from being all that the ordinary man, and even Strawson, would admit to be genuinely things-in-the-world whatever exactly that may mean. Phenomena, events, situations, states of affairs are commonly supposed to be genuinely-in-the-world, and even Strawson admits events are so. Yet surely of all of these we can say that they *are facts*. The collapse of the Germans is an event and is a fact—was an event and was a fact.

Strawson, however, seems to suppose that anything of which we say '. . . is a fact' is, automatically, *not* something in the world. Thus:

> What 'makes the statement' that the cat has mange 'true' is not the cat, but the *condition* of the cat, i.e. the fact that the cat has mange. The only plausible candidate for the position of what (in the world) makes the statement true is the fact it states; but the fact it states is not something in the world.[1]

I cannot swallow this because it seems to me quite plain:

(1) that the condition of the cat is a fact;
(2) that the condition of the cat is something-in-the-world—if I understand that expression at all.

How can Strawson have come to say that the condition of the cat is *not* something in the world?

It seems to me that the trouble may arise through not observing certain rather easily overlooked boundaries between what may and may not be done with the word 'fact'.

There are two things we might very well, in of course a paedagogic way, say:

(*a*) what makes the statement that the cat has mange true

[1] *Proceedings of the Aristotelian Society*, Supplementary Volume xxiv, p. 135.

is the condition of the cat (together, of course, with the meanings of the words);

(b) what makes the statement that the cat has mange true is the fact that the cat has mange.

(The second seems to me a *bit* unhelpful and off-colour, but let it pass.)

But now from these two we most certainly can*not* infer

The condition [or 'mangy condition'] of the cat is *the fact that* the cat has mange,

nor

The condition [or 'mangy condition'] of the cat is *the fact that* this statement [or 'the statement that the cat has mange'] states.

We cannot infer these things, because, for whatever reason, they don't make sense. We do not, I think (for whatever reason), *ever* say anything of the following form:

x is *the fact that* this statement [or 'the statement that S'] states

whatever be substituted for *x*.

Nor do we in general say anything of the form

x is *the fact that* S

whatever be substituted for *x* (to this there are some exceptions: e.g. It is the fact that S, Still more surprising is the fact that S, What I object to is the fact that S, The last straw is the fact that S).

It appears to me, perhaps wrongly, that Strawson is led, by his 'i.e.', into supposing that the condition of the cat *is* the fact that the cat has mange, which according to me is not sense.

To this he is helped by his doctrine, to be discussed shortly, that ' "Fact" is wedded to "that"–clauses'. For it would of course be good sense to say that

The condition of the cat *is a fact*:

and if we believe in adding 'that'–clauses we shall ask *what* fact, and reply 'The fact that the cat has mange'. But the question *what* fact, like its answer, does not make sense.

Having thus got so far as reducing 'the condition of the cat' to 'the fact that the statement states', Strawson is then ready to proclaim, on the strength of his other principal doctrine, that 'Facts are what statements state, not what they are about', that the condition of the cat is a pseudo-entity.

To sum this up. According to me

1. The condition of the cat is a fact, and is something in the world.
2. It is nonsense to say: the condition of the cat—or with only irrelevant exceptions anything else—*is the fact that* anything at all.
3. 'Fact' with 'that' and 'fact' without 'that' behave differently.
   a. *x is a fact* is all right   b. *x is the fact that* is wrong.

Here I should say (or admit?) that there is, I think, one important and perhaps obvious difference between 'fact' and say 'event' or 'phenomenon'—a difference which for all I know might qualify as a logically fundamental type-difference. But this is very far from making 'facts' to be *not* 'things-in-the-world'. It seems to me, on the contrary, that to say that something is a fact *is* at least in part precisely to say that it is something in the world: much more that than—though perhaps also to a minor extent also—to classify it as being some special kind of something-in-the-world. To a considerable extent 'being a fact' seems to resemble 'existing' in the sorts of way that have led it to be held that 'existence is not a predicate'. One might compare:

Cows are animals	with	Fevers are diseases
Cows are things		Fevers are conditions
Cows exist		Fevers are facts
There are such things as cows		There are such conditions as fevers

Or one might say: it is as true and yet as queer to say that 'Facts are things-in-the-world' as that 'Entities are things-in-the-world'. Or one might say that 'fact' resembles 'person':

'persons' are not, of course, facts and facts are not persons but to say so-and-so is a person or a fact is in part at least to say so-and-so is real. (We do not on the whole like, there is oxymoron in, imaginary 'facts' or 'imaginary persons'—we prefer imaginary characters. In this way 'fact' does differ from say 'event'.)

I believe—but this is speculative—that it could be shown that some of the odd phenomena notorious about the word 'fact' could be shown to be connected with this 'existential' side of it (some of which, however, have been much exaggerated!), e.g. that we do not say that 'a fact was at a certain time' but that 'at a certain time it was a fact'.

(ii) Secondly, how is Strawson really to handle the good English expression 'corresponds with the facts' (and incidentally a good many others that go along with it)? For he claims that 'the demand for something in the world to which the statement corresponds when it is true' is a *wholly* mistaken demand and that 'fact' is a name for a pseudo-entity invented to satisfy this bogus demand. But this is to treat a wholesome English expression as though it were a philosopher's invented expression; to treat 'facts' as though they were in the same position as 'propositions' taking these to be pseudo-entities invented to answer the bogus demand 'what is it that sentences when meaningful mean?' How come that English has invented so unhappy an expression? It seems to me that Strawson has two rather different lines here, neither of which will do.

One thing we might try is to say that 'corresponds with the facts' is a 'fused' idiom precisely equivalent to 'is true'. It is in no way to be understood as meaning that anything 'corresponds' with anything in the way that that word ordinarily means, or as implying that there are such things as 'facts', or that anything is related in any way to anything—(for that matter, I suppose, no assertion is made about the statement *at all* when we say it 'corresponds with the facts', any more than when we say it 'is true'). This seems to me quite unplausible—why *should not* we be meaning by it that there is some sort of relation between something and something (no doubt not so simple as it sounds)? Strawson actually allows that when I say a map corresponds with the topography of the countryside I *am* talking about a relation between something and something, yet still contends that I am *not* when I say a statement corresponds with the facts. But how is this plausible —for we may remind ourselves that it is quite possible to say of a map that it does not correspond with the facts (e.g. a situation-map) and of a statement that it does not correspond with the topography. (Or should we go back, then, on the admission that 'corresponds' does mean a relation in the case of maps—say that topography is what maps map, not what maps are about, &c.!)

A second, and surely rather different, line, is the following. For the good English 'corresponds with the facts' or 'fits the facts' we substitute the quite unEnglish 'corresponds with *the fact that so and so*' or 'fits *the fact that so-and-so*' and proceed to claim that this is somehow tautological. This is a method which seems to be becoming fashionable. Strawson writes, 'What could fit more perfectly the fact that it is raining than the statement that it is raining? Of course statements and facts fit. They were made for each other.' But in answer to this: surely it is not sense either to ask whether the statement that S fits the fact that S or to state that it either does or does not. And I may add that it seems to me, *pace* Mrs. Daitz, equally nonsense to ask whether the statement that S fits or corresponds to the fact that F, where 'F' is *different* from 'S' not identical with it (though of course it is *not* nonsense to ask something that sounds rather similar to this, viz. whether the statement that S *squares with* or '*does justice to*' the fact that F ('F' ≠ 'S')). But even, further, if we allowed the expression: the statement that S fits the fact that S, surely we cannot allow the suggestion of 'statements and facts were made *for each other*'. To begin with, obviously, some statements *do not* fit the facts; we need not elaborate on this. But even if we take it as: '*True* statements fit the facts', '*True* statements and facts are made for each other' we cannot agree that there is any more sense in saying they are 'made for each other', or if there is sense, any more malice in saying it, than there would be in saying, on the ground that 'well-aimed shots hit their marks', that marks and shots (well-aimed) are made for each other.

It may be said—before we proceed further—why bother? Why raise this cry 'Unfair to facts'? There are two reasons I think.

1. It seems in the past to have been, at least often, inexpedient to say 'Facts are not things-in-the-world'. This misled, for example, Bradley, who had some by no means ill-deserved cold water to pour upon facts, at the crucial point. Still, on the other hand, no doubt it may for some purposes also be expedient to give ourselves a jolt by suggesting that 'there are no facts'.

2. More important altogether, to my mind, than this is the following. The expression 'fitting the facts' is *not* by any means an isolated idiom in our language. It seems to have a very intimate connexion with a whole series of adverbs and adjectives used in appraising statements—I mean, 'precise', 'exact', 'rough', 'accurate', and the like, and their cognate adverbs. All these are connected with the notion of fitting and measuring in ordinary contexts, and it can scarcely be fortuitous that they, along with fitting and corresponding, have been taken over as a group to the sphere of statements and facts. Now to some extent the use of this galaxy of words in connexion with statements *may* be a transferred use; yet no one would surely deny that these constitute serious and important notions which can be, and should be, elucidated. I should certainly go much farther and claim—as I have done before—that these are the important terms to elucidate when we address ourselves to the problem of 'truth', just as, not 'freedom' but notions like duress and accident, are what require elucidation when we worry about 'freedom'. Yet all these terms are commonly dismissed along with the supposed useless 'fitting the facts'.

To give an illustration of this. Warnock, in his excellent book on Berkeley, says that Berkeley's complaint is that ordinary language does not *fit the facts* (or, as he says at other times, is inaccurate or inexact or loose or imprecise). Warnock says this is a confusion: for 'fits the facts (exactly?)' is simply equivalent to 'is true'—and he reduces the notion to helplessness by the same device as Strawson did: he asks, e.g.

What statement could possibly fit the fact that there is a table in my study more exactly than the statement 'There is a table in my study'?[1]

and says

It is really tautologous to say that any true statement exactly fits the facts; it exactly fits those facts, or that fact, which it states.

It would be most unreasonable to object to a statement because it fails to state facts which it does not state.[2]

Having thus disposed of 'fitting the facts', Warnock considers all the rest—inaccuracy,[3] looseness, &c. (but he does not distinguish between these!) as apparently disposed of, and offers us as the only reasonable complaint against statements which could very well, by confusion, be intended by, for example, Berkeley, this: that the statement is 'logically complex' and can be analysed into more verbose but logically simpler expressions. Such an analysis does not he says 'fit the facts' any better but is merely more explicit or more detailed—less concentrated. Well, maybe this does occur (if it is a single phenomenon?); maybe it was what Berkeley meant, though this would need proving; but all the same inaccuracy, looseness, and the rest do *also* occur, are important, are distinct, and they cannot be dismissed from consideration by this perverted little rigmarole about 'fitting the facts'.

II. Now I shall set out what I take to be Strawson's main positive contentions about the word 'fact'. I think that others too hold the same beliefs.

---

[1] G. J. Warnock, *Berkeley*, Pelican Books, 1953, p. 240.
[2] Ibid.
[3] The relation between a rough, loose, inaccurate, inexact, imprecise, &c. statement and the facts is a most important matter for elucidation.

i. 'Fact', says Strawson, 'is wedded to that-clauses'.[1] He does not explain this overmuch. But I think it is meant to be a statement about English usage: and one impression he conveys to his readers and I think himself is that, wherever we get the word 'fact' occurring in a sentence without a 'that-clause' we at least *could* insert a that-clause after it, even if we do not already actually 'supply' such a clause in some way mentally. We have seen already two instances of his acting on this principle.

ii. 'Facts', says Strawson, 'are what statements (when true) state; they are not what statements are about.' This seems to be a philosophical contention, based upon the linguistic contention I above. And it is this philosophical contention which leads him to say that facts are not anything genuinely-in-the-world, but pseudo-entities.

Now let us confront i: 'Fact is wedded to that-clauses' with the evidence of the Dictionary. If it is indeed so wedded, it leads, I fear, a double life. It was not born in wedlock, its marriage was a marriage of convenience and it continues to lead a flourishing bachelor existence.

The Dictionary (*Oxford English Dictionary*) does not take much account of 'fact that'. 'Fact that', along with 'fact of', is given as a comparatively recent linguistic device for avoiding gerundial constructions as the subjects of sentences or as the domains of prepositions: i.e. in order not to say 'I was unaware of the kitchen's being draughty' or 'the kitchen's being draughty annoyed him', we say 'I was unaware of the fact that the kitchen was draughty' or 'the fact that the kitchen was draughty annoyed him': it is compared with 'circumstance that'. No use of 'fact of' is given earlier than the eighteenth century: examples of 'fact that' are not given, but may even be later. I believe that if we consult even, say, the philosophers of the eighteenth century we can readily satisfy ourselves that 'fact that' is not in use; and the Dictionary's account is borne out by our experience of the general tendency nowadays to adopt similar novel 'that'-constructions with other words, like 'circumstance', 'event', 'situation'. (A later feature of such usages of course, is that the 'that' gets dropped out—'in case' for 'in the case that' and 'in the event' for 'in the event that'.)

To complete the history of the word according to the Dictionary. For the first 200 years of its use (sixteenth and seventeenth centuries) it meant (cf. 'feat') a deed or action, either the thing done or the doing of the thing, and more especially a criminal action; during the eighteenth century this use gradually died out in favour of a more extended meaning which began to appear already in the seventeenth century: a fact is now *something that has really occurred* (even classical Latin extended *factum* to mean 'event' or 'occurrence')[1] or something that is actually the case (a further extension to the meaning of '*factum*' found in scholastic Latin). *Hence* and thereafter it came to mean something *known* to have really occurred, and *hence* (according to the Dictionary) a particular *truth* known by observation or authentic testimony, by contrast with what is merely inferred or a conjecture or a fiction.

From this brief history, I take it as obvious that: (i) 'Fact' was in origin a name for 'something in the world', if we may take it that a past action or past actual event or occurrence is 'something in the world', and there is no reason whatever to doubt that it often still is so. (ii) Any connexion between 'fact' and 'knowledge', and still more between 'fact' and 'truth' (in particular the use of 'a fact' as equivalent to 'a truth'), is a derivative and comparatively late connexion. (iii) The expression 'fact that' is later still, and was introduced as a grammatical convenience, because of the already existing meaning of 'fact'. To explain the meaning of 'fact' in terms of the expression 'fact that' is to invert the real order of things—just as much as it would be to explain the meaning of 'circumstance' in terms of 'circumstance that' (or 'situation' in terms of 'situation that' and so on: indeed, one may suspect that we have here one pretty general method of misunderstanding or misrepresenting what language is up to).

[1] Actual event or occurrence, of course.

I should further take it as fairly plain that (iv) when 'facts' or 'a fact' occur in general in modern English, the usage is just what it was in the eighteenth century. When we say 'The mangy condition of the cat is a fact' we mean it is an actual state of affairs; when we say 'What are the facts?' we mean 'what is the actual state of affairs?', 'what has actually occurred?' or the like. This is the meaning, too, in such common expressions as 'an *accomplished* fact' or 'He has had no personal experience of the facts he reports'. And finally, I take it that (v) the expression 'The fact that S' *means* 'a certain fact [or actual occurrence, &c.], viz. that correctly described [or reported, &c.] by saying now "S" [or at other times "S" with a change of tense].' It was to this that I referred when I said that 'the fact that' is a way of speaking compendiously about words and world together. It is a usage grammatically *like* (not of course in all ways the same as) the *apposition* usage with proper names, as when we say 'The person Caesar' which we should interpret as 'a certain person [or actual man, &c.], viz. the one designated by the name "Caesar"'.

And two further clear points about 'the fact that':

(vi) 'The fact that S' is a totally different occurrence of 'the fact that' from that in say '*The fact that* he stated'. In other words, even if 'fact' were wedded to that-clauses, there are different that-clauses.

(vii) I feel—but cannot I confess sufficiently 'explain', probably for want of terminology—that somehow this explanation of the special form of expression 'the fact that S' should be what accounts (*a*) for our inability to say things of the form 'the mangy condition of the cat *is* the fact that the cat has mange' (or 'the cat's having mange *is* the fact that the cat has mange') and likewise possibly (*b*) for the queerness of the problem that Ramsey and Moore discussed as to whether 'the fact that S' is a name or a description or what on earth?

Compare persons and facts again: is there a parallel between
'Cicero' 'The cat has mange'

Cicero $\left\{\begin{array}{l}\text{The cat's having mange}\\\text{The mangy condition of the cat}\end{array}\right.$

The person Cicero   The fact that the cat has mange

Thus (a)

To say 'the mangy condition of the cat *is* the fact that the
cat has mange' is like saying 'Cicero is the person Cicero'.
These two forms of expression are not designed for combination in this manner. But why? Nor for that matter is 'Tully is
the person Cicero', only rather ' "Cicero" is the name of the
person Cicero'.

'Tully' is a name of the same person as 'Cicero': so 'Everest
is so high' is a statement of the same fact as 'Gaurisankar is so
high'. 'Everest is so high' is a statement of the fact that Everest
is so high.

Also (b) asking whether 'The fact that S' is a name or a
description is like asking whether 'the person Cicero' is a name.
But we seem to lack a name for this type of expression and a
description of its role and limitations.

Now let us ask, what was Strawson actually arguing in
saying 'Fact is wedded to that-clauses'. He was thinking of its
use in connexion with certain verbs.

'Facts', he says, 'are known, stated, learnt, forgotten, overlooked, commented on, communicated, or noticed. (Each of
these verbs may be followed by a "that"-clause or a "the fact
that"-clause.)'[1] This is not, I think, very clear.

1. It is not clear whether it is meant that *wherever* we have
a sentence in which one of these verbs occurs with 'fact' as its
object we could put a that-clause or the-fact-that-clause in place
of the object, or only that we *sometimes* can.

2. It is not clear whether it matters whether 'fact' occurring
in the original sentence as object of one or another of these
verbs is to be singular or plural, with the definite or indefinite
article or neither.

[1] *Proceedings of the Aristotelian Society*, Supplementary Volume xxiv,
p. 136.

3. It is not clear whether, if we do substitute a that-clause or a the-fact-that-clause for 'fact' the meaning of the original sentence is to be considered altered or unaltered.

But I *think* the impression Strawson conveys both to himself and to his readers is that, given any of these verbs, the following three forms of sentence are equally good English and somehow interchangeable.

(a) *Fact-form.*   He verbed a/the fact/facts
(b) *That-form.*   He verbed that S
(c) *The fact-that-form.* He verbed the fact that S.

But it will be found that the verbs in his list behave differently with respect to these three forms of sentence. (With some, such as 'comment on', it is not the case that all three forms make sense: we cannot 'comment on that'.)

The best example of what Strawson is after seems to be the verb 'forget':

> He forgot a fact or the facts
> He forgot that S
> He forgot the fact that S.

These seem all good English, and reasonably interchangeable— of course the second two specify what it was he forgot whereas the first does not, but this is fair enough and nothing to boggle at.

And, of course, with the verb 'state' also, all three forms of sentence make sense (though not all are equally usual):

> He stated a fact
> He stated that S
> He stated the fact that S.

But here there is a great difference between the second and the other two. With 'forget', the fact-form entails the that-form, and conversely; but with 'states' this is not so. 'He stated that S' does not entail 'he stated a fact'.

Similarly, with 'state' certain forms of sentence are good sense which are not good sense in the same way with 'forget' or 'know':

> What he stated was a fact
> In stating that S he stated a fact.

But not

> What he forgot or knew was a fact[1]
> In forgetting that S he forgot a fact.

All that this shows is, of course, that 'state' is not, like 'know' and 'forget', a success or achievement word in Ryle's sense. To know that or to notice that is to know or notice a fact; but to state that is not necessarily to state a fact. 'State' may be wedded to that-clauses; but 'fact' is wedded to neither.

This is of course notorious enough. But surely it is also enough to cast doubt on 'Statements and facts are made for each other'. Even 'Knowledge and facts are made for each other' or 'Forgetfulness and facts were made for each other' would contain more truth—though even then one would be inclined to protest that there may very well be facts that nobody knows or ever will know, and that to say the facts are made for the knowledge is curious.

Strawson also produces a list of other verbs, presumably *un*connected with 'that'-clauses, which he suggests *are* connected with things-in-the-world (things, persons, events) but not with facts, viz. 'witness', 'hear', 'see', 'break', 'overturn', 'interrupt', 'prolong', &c. But surely we can witness facts? And observe them and have personal acquaintance with them. I cannot see that there is a clear distinction here.

However, we have seen I think in general enough from the dictionary, and from the troubles that arise when we insert that-clauses indiscriminately, to abandon the doctrine that fact is wedded to that-clauses. Let us now turn to the second doctrine which was that:

> 'Facts are what statements (when true) state: they are not what statements are about.'

Take the second clause first, about which I shall not say much. The main thing I feel about it is that 'about' is too

---

[1] Point of the joke about the Bourbons 'forgetting nothing'.

vague a word to bear the weight Strawson wants to put on it. If we take other verbs, for example, facts are both what we forget and what we forget about, both what we know and what we know about (as well as 'of'); verbally we can say that 'the number of the planets' is both what a statement is about and what that same statement states. Moreover, Strawson would admit, I think, that a statement can be about a fact, or about the fact that . . . I do not, however, wish to insist that Strawson could not make out a case for this clause of his doctrine.

What I do wish to insist is that the first clause—'Facts are what statements, when true, state' is most misleading. Undoubtedly we should agree that 'True statements state facts'; but if we convert it in Strawson's manner we certainly give ourselves the impression that this is somehow or other a 'definition' of facts. It gives, and I think is meant to give, the impression of reducing 'facts' to an accusative so deeply and hopelessly internal that their status as 'entities' is hopelessly compromised.

Strawson represents us as asking: 'What do true statements state?' and giving ourselves the bogus and unhelpful answer 'Facts', much as philosophers are supposed to have asked themselves 'What do meaningful sentences mean?' and to have given themselves the bogus answer 'propositions'. Yet there is nothing in the form of such questions to make them necessarily, along with their answer, bogus. Strawson himself is prepared to ask, for example, 'What do statements refer to?' and to answer 'Things, persons or events'. Nor need we by any means take our answer (e.g. Things are what statements refer to) to be a definition of 'things' or in some manner unwholesomely analytic.

To shake off this hypnotism of the internal accusative, this vague menace of the analytic, consider a few parallel examples:

Births are what birth-certificates, when accurate, certify.

Persons are what surnames, when borne, are the surnames of.

Women are what men, when they marry, marry.

Wives are what men, when they marry, marry.
Animals are what portraits, when faithful, portray.
Sitters are what portraits, when faithful, portray.
Events are what narratives, when true, narrate.
History is what narratives, when true, narrate.

Which, if any of these, is Strawson's sentence to be taken to resemble? Does it in particular resemble the 'Events are what narratives, when true, narrate' case? And would it make sense to go on: 'they are not what narratives are about'? At any rate, one thing is plain, that, whatever the analyticity or internal accusatives or what not involved in any of these pronouncements, none of them have the slightest tendency to convince us that births, persons, or events, women (or even wives), animals (or even sitters) are *not* 'things or happenings on the surface of the globe'.

Why then worry about 'facts'?

There seems, on closer inspection, to be some trouble about the expression 'What statements state'. How is it to be taken?

Let us agree by all means that 'true statements state facts', and that somehow or in some sense this is, if you like, 'true by definition'—though keeping of course an open mind as to *which* definition—that, for example, of 'fact' or that of 'true statement'. But now if we put this in the shape

Facts are what true statements state

it has to be understood that this variety of 'what' ('what statements state' 'What he stated') is a highly 'ambiguous' one—or rather, that there are different uses for the expression 'what he stated'.

To take an illustration: compare:

(a) what he stated was true, [or 'was a truth'].
(b) what he stated was a fact.

In these two sentences 'what he stated' is not grammatically identical. For in (a) we can substitute for 'what he stated' the expression 'his statement'; whereas in (b) we cannot do this;

'his statement was a fact', if it had any meaning, would anyhow mean something quite different from 'what he stated was a fact'.[1]

Or again, contrast both (a) and (b) alike with yet another use of 'what he stated'. In reply to the question 'what did he state?' we might be told '(He stated) that S', i.e. we get

(c) what he stated was that S.

That this differs from the use of 'what he stated' in (a) and (b) is plain; but the difference may be brought out by considering how odd it would be, to give to the question 'What did he state?' the answer 'A fact' or 'A truth'. These could only be given, on the contrary, as answers to the quite different yes-or-no-type questions 'Was what he stated a fact?' or 'Was what he stated true (a truth)'.

We can in fact distinguish at least five different ways in which 'What' is used in connexion with 'state', which are immediately relevant here. 'State', in this respect, is typical of a large group of words used in talking about communication, and I shall illustrate the five different uses concerned by means of the analogous verb to 'signal'.

Let us take a simple model situation in which all we are concerned to do is to signal targets as they bob up in an aperture. The targets are of various different recognizable types and there is an appointed signal (say a flag of a special colour) for each different type of target. Very well then—the targets keep on bobbing up, and we keep on wagging flags—the convention of reference being the simple one (non-'verbal' or rather non 'flag-al') that each signal refers to the contemporary occupant of the aperture. Now, in what ways can we use the expression 'what we signal'?

(I) There are two uses in which we can use the expression

---

[1] This is of course in line with the fact that in 'It is true that S' we can insert 'to state' after 'is true'; whereas in 'It is a fact that S' we cannot insert 'to state'. Strawson says there is no nuance except of style between 'It is true that' and 'It is a fact that'; yet he himself admits that the former 'glances at' the making of a statement, whereas the latter does not.

'What we signal is always . . .'. Perhaps not very helpful or usual except for paedagogic purposes. viz.

(1) 'What we signal is always a target'. Cf. 'What we state is always a fact'.

(2) 'What we signal is always a signal'. Cf. 'What we state is always a statement'.

There is no conflict between these pronouncements; nor is it either necessary or legitimate, in order to 'reconcile' them, to conclude that 'targets are signals': they are *not*, nor are facts statements, by the same token! All that is needed is to realize that 'what we signal' has two uses—or that 'signal' can take two varieties of accusative, both, interestingly enough, completely 'internal'. (1) means that whenever we signal we signal something as a target, signals are as such signals of targets; so whenever we state we state something as a fact, statements are as such statements of fact.[1]

(2) of course is highly paedagogic, though harmless. It would be very paedagogic to say 'we signal signals' or 'we state statements'—though parallel to saying, for example, 'we plan plans'. Such remarks instruct us as follows: whenever we say 'we plan (signal, state) so-and-so' there will be something of which we can say that it was our plan (signal, statement). (1) and (2) alike are only of use in giving instructions about the meaning and use of the verb 'signal' and the substantive 'signal'.

But now further (II), when we do *not* use the 'always' and the 'we' of paedagogic generalization, we use 'what . . . signal (state)' in quite different ways, as follows:

(3) 'What we signal is sometimes, but not always, a target'. 'What we state is sometimes, but not always, a fact'.

(4) 'What we signal is sometimes, but not always, (a) correct (signal).

'What we state is sometimes, but not always, true' (a truth).

---

[1] Of course we are excluding from treatment throughout the expression 'statement of opinion', interesting enough in itself but not relevant here.

It is in use (3) that we speak when we say, for example, 'What he stated then was a fact but what she stated thereafter was not a fact'; and in use (4) that we speak when we say, for example, 'What he stated then was true but what she stated thereafter was not'.

The uses of 'what we signal' in (3) and (4) are of course *connected*, but they are *not* identical. If they were *identical* we should get the absurd conclusion that

A target is (a) correct (signal)

and the conclusion, equally absurd I think, that

A fact is a true statement (a truth).

The actual connexion between (3) and (4) is not so simple, though simple enough:

> If, and only if, and because what we signal (3) is a target, then what we signal (4) is correct; and, derivatively, if, and only if, but not because what we signal (4) is correct, then what we signal (3) is a target.

There is an obvious connexion between 'what we signal' in the sense (3) and 'what we signal' in the paedagogic sense (1); and likewise between sense (2) and sense (4). Perhaps, indeed, we might even say that the difference between (1) and (3) and again between (2) and (4), is not so much a difference between senses or uses of 'what we signal' as rather a difference between senses or uses of 'what we signal *is*'. But at any rate there is a radical distinction between 'what we signal' in (1) and (3) together and in (2) and (4) together—between what we signal as a *target* (actual or—paedagogically—putative) and on the other hand as a *signal* (correct or incorrect). And just as, in the signalling case, there is not the slightest temptation to say

'Targets are not things in the world'
'Targets are (correct) signals'

so there should be no temptation to say

'Facts are not things-in-the-world'
'Facts are true statements'.

But finally (III) there is yet another use of 'what we signal', or of 'what we signal is' where 'what we signal' is neither *always* x, as in (1) and (2), nor always either x or not x, as in (3) and (4).

In this use (5).

—what we signal is now red, now green, now purple
—what we state is now that S, now that T, now that U.

To sum up, then,

Facts are what true statements state

is like

Targets are what correct signals signal

and has no more tendency to prove that facts are pseudo-entities than that targets are. And if we choose to say that either is being defined in terms of the other, we should say the other way round.

Or again: from the two unexceptionable
(1) He stated a fact
(2) He stated that S

we can indeed get:

'what he stated was a fact'
'what he stated was that S'.

But we cannot possibly make an inference from these such as

a fact is that S or that T, &c.

(which makes it look like a 'bogus entity') because 'what he stated' does not mean the same in the two premisses.

8

A PLEA FOR EXCUSES[1]

THE subject of this paper, *Excuses*, is one not to be treated, but only to be introduced, within such limits. It is, or might be, the name of a whole branch, even a ramiculated branch, of philosophy, or at least of one fashion of philosophy. I shall try, therefore, first to state *what* the subject is, *why* it is worth studying, and *how* it may be studied, all this at a regrettably lofty level: and then I shall illustrate, in more congenial but desultory detail, some of the methods to be used, together with their limitations, and some of the unexpected results to be expected and lessons to be learned. Much, of course, of the amusement, and of the instruction, comes in drawing the coverts of the microglot, in hounding down the minutiae, and to this I can do no more here than incite you. But I owe it to the subject to say, that it has long afforded me what philosophy is so often thought, and made, barren of—the fun of discovery, the pleasures of co-operation, and the satisfaction of reaching agreement.

What, then, is the subject? I am here using the word 'excuses' *for a title*, but it would be unwise to freeze too fast to this one noun and its partner verb: indeed for some time I used to use 'extenuation' instead. Still, on the whole 'excuses' is probably the most central and embracing term in the field, although this includes others of importance—'plea', 'defence', 'justification', and so on. When, then, do we 'excuse' conduct, our own or somebody else's? When are 'excuses' proffered?

In general, the situation is one where someone is *accused* of

[1] Reprinted from *Proceedings of the Aristotelian Society*, 1956-7, by courtesy of the editor.

having done something, or (if that will keep it any cleaner) where someone is *said* to have done something which is bad, wrong, inept, unwelcome, or in some other of the numerous possible ways untoward. Thereupon he, or someone on his behalf, will try to defend his conduct or to get him out of it.

One way of going about this is to admit flatly that he, X, did do that very thing, A, but to argue that it was a good thing, or the right or sensible thing, or a permissible thing to do, either in general or at least in the special circumstances of the occasion. To take this line is to *justify* the action, to give reasons for doing it: not to say, to brazen it out, to glory in it, or the like.

A different way of going about it is to admit that it wasn't a good thing to have done, but to argue that it is not quite fair or correct to say *baldly* 'X did A'. We may say it isn't fair just to say X did it; perhaps he was under somebody's influence, or was nudged. Or, it isn't fair to say baldly he *did* A; it may have been partly accidental, or an unintentional slip. Or, it isn't fair to say he did simply A—he was really doing something quite different and A was only incidental, or he was looking at the whole thing quite differently. Naturally these arguments can be combined or overlap or run into each other.

In the one defence, briefly, we accept responsibility but deny that it was bad: in the other, we admit that it was bad but don't accept full, or even any, responsibility.

By and large, justifications can be kept distinct from excuses, and I shall not be so anxious to talk about them because they have enjoyed more than their fair share of philosophical attention. But the two certainly can be confused, and can *seem* to go very near to each other, even if they do not perhaps actually do so. You dropped the tea-tray: Certainly, but an emotional storm was about to break out: or, Yes, but there was a wasp. In each case the defence, very soundly, insists on a fuller description of the event in its context; but the first is a justification, the second an excuse. Again, if the objection is to the use of such a dyslogistic verb as 'murdered', this may be on the ground that the killing was done in battle (justification) or on the ground that it was only accidental if reckless (excuse). It is arguable that we do not use the terms justification and excuse as carefully as we might; a miscellany of even less clear terms, such as 'extenuation', 'palliation', 'mitigation', hovers uneasily between partial justification and partial excuse; and when we plead, say, provocation, there is genuine uncertainty or ambiguity as to what we mean—is *he* partly responsible, because he roused a violent impulse or passion in me, so that it wasn't truly or merely me acting 'of my own accord' (excuse)? Or is it rather that, he having done me such injury, I was entitled to retaliate (justification)? Such doubts merely make it the more urgent to clear up the usage of these various terms. But that the defences I have for convenience labelled 'justification' and 'excuse' are in principle distinct can scarcely be doubted.

This then is the sort of situation we have to consider under 'excuses'. I will only further point out how very wide a field it covers. We have, of course, to bring in the opposite numbers of excuses—the expressions that *aggravate*, such as 'deliberately', 'on purpose', and so on, if only for the reason that an excuse often takes the form of a rebuttal of one of these. But we have also to bring in a large number of expressions which at first blush look not so much like excuses as like accusations— 'clumsiness', 'tactlessness', 'thoughtlessness', and the like. Because it has always to be remembered that few excuses get us out of it *completely*: the average excuse, in a poor situation, gets us only out of the fire into the frying pan—but still, of course, any frying pan in a fire. If I have broken your dish or your romance, maybe the best defence I can find will be clumsiness.

Why, if this is what 'excuses' are, should we trouble to investigate them? It might be thought reason enough that their production has always bulked so large among human activities. But to moral philosophy in particular a study of them will contribute in special ways, both positively towards the development of a cautious, latter-day version of conduct, and negatively towards the correction of older and hastier theories.

In ethics we study, I suppose, the good and the bad, the right and the wrong, and this must be for the most part in some connexion with conduct or the doing of actions. Yet before we consider what actions are good or bad, right or wrong, it is proper to consider first what is meant by, and what not, and what is included under, and what not, the expression 'doing an action' or 'doing something'. These are expressions still too little examined on their own account and merits, just as the general notion of 'saying something' is still too lightly passed over in logic. There is indeed a vague and comforting idea in the background that, after all, in the last analysis, doing an action must come down to the making of physical movements with parts of the body; but this is about as true as that saying something must, in the last analysis, come down to making movements of the tongue.

The beginning of sense, not to say wisdom, is to realize that 'doing an action', as used in philosophy,[1] is a highly abstract expression—it is a stand-in used in the place of any (or almost any?) verb with a personal subject, in the same sort of way that 'thing' is a stand-in for any (or when we remember, almost any) noun substantive, and 'quality' a stand-in for the adjective. Nobody, to be sure, relies on such dummies quite implicitly quite indefinitely. Yet notoriously it is possible to arrive at, or to derive the idea for, an over-simplified metaphysics from the obsession with 'things' and their 'qualities'. In a similar way, less commonly recognized even in these semi-sophisticated times, we fall for the myth of the verb. We treat the expression 'doing an action' no longer as a stand-in for a verb with a personal subject, as which it has no doubt some uses, and might have more if the range of verbs were not left unspecified, but as a self-explanatory, ground-level description, one which brings adequately into the open the essential features of every-

[1] This use has little to do with the more down-to-earth occurrences of 'action' in ordinary speech.

thing that comes, by simple inspection, under it. We scarcely notice even the most patent exceptions or difficulties (is to think something, or to say something, or to try to do something, to do an action?), any more than we fret, in the *ivresse des grandes profondeurs*, as to whether flames are things or events. So we come easily to think of our behaviour over any time, and of a life as a whole, as consisting in doing now action A, next action B, then action C, and so on, just as elsewhere we come to think of the world as consisting of this, that and the other substance or material thing, each with its properties. All 'actions' are, as actions (meaning what?), equal, composing a quarrel with striking a match, winning a war with sneezing: worse still, we assimilate them one and all to the supposedly most obvious and easy cases, such as posting letters or moving fingers, just as we assimilate all 'things' to horses or beds.

If we are to continue to use this expression in sober philosophy, we need to ask such questions as: Is to sneeze to do an action? Or is to breathe, or to see, or to checkmate, or each one of countless others? In short, for what range of verbs, as used on what occasions, is 'doing an action' a stand-in? What have they in common, and what do those excluded severally lack? Again we need to ask how we decide what is the correct name for 'the' action that somebody did—and what, indeed, are the rules for the use of 'the' action, 'an' action, 'one' action, a 'part' or 'phase' of an action and the like. Further, we need to realize that even the 'simplest' named actions are not so simple— certainly are not the mere makings of physical movements, and to ask what more, then, comes in (intentions? conventions?) and what does not (motives?), and what is the detail of the complicated internal machinery we use in 'acting'—the receipt of intelligence, the appreciation of the situation, the invocation of principles, the planning, the control of execution and the rest.

In two main ways the study of excuses can throw light on these fundamental matters. First, to examine excuses is to examine cases where there has been some abnormality or failure: and as so often, the abnormal will throw light on the normal, will help us to penetrate the blinding veil of ease and obviousness that hides the mechanisms of the natural successful act. It rapidly becomes plain that the breakdowns signalized by the various excuses are of radically different kinds, affecting different parts or stages of the machinery, which the excuses consequently pick out and sort out for us. Further, it emerges that not *every* slip-up occurs in connexion with *every*thing that could be called an 'action', that not every excuse is apt with every verb—far indeed from it: and this provides us with one means of introducing some classification into the vast miscellany of 'actions'. If we classify them according to the particular selection of breakdowns to which each is liable, this should assign them their places in some family group or groups of actions, or in some model of the machinery of acting.

In this sort of way, the philosophical study of conduct can get off to a positive fresh start. But by the way, and more negatively, a number of traditional cruces or mistakes in this field can be resolved or removed. First among these comes the problem of Freedom. While it has been the tradition to present this as the 'positive' term requiring elucidation, there is little doubt that to say we acted 'freely' (in the philosopher's use, which is only faintly related to the everyday use) is to say only that we acted *not* un-freely, in one or another of the many heterogeneous ways of so acting (under duress, or what not). Like 'real', 'free' is only used to rule out the suggestion of some or all of its recognized antitheses. As 'truth' is not a name for a characteristic of assertions, so 'freedom' is not a name for a characteristic of actions, but the name of a dimension in which actions are assessed. In examining all the ways in which each action may not be 'free', i.e. the cases in which it will not do to say simply 'X did A', we may hope to dispose of the problem of Freedom. Aristotle has often been chidden for talking about excuses or pleas and overlooking 'the real problem': in my own case, it was when I began to see the injustice of this charge that I first became interested in excuses.

There is much to be said for the view that, philosophical tradition apart, Responsibility would be a better candidate for the role here assigned to Freedom. If ordinary language is to be our guide, it is to evade responsibility, or full responsibility, that we most often make excuses, and I have used the word myself in this way above. But in fact 'responsibility' too seems not really apt in all cases: I do not exactly evade responsibility when I plead clumsiness or tactlessness, nor, often, when I plead that I only did it unwillingly or reluctantly, and still less if I plead that I had in the circumstances no choice: here I was constrained and have an excuse (or justification), yet may accept responsibility. It may be, then, that at least two key terms, Freedom and Responsibility, are needed: the relation between them is not clear, and it may be hoped that the investigation of excuses will contribute towards its clarification.[1]

So much, then, for ways in which the study of excuses may throw light on ethics. But there are also reasons why it is an attractive subject methodologically, at least if we are to proceed from 'ordinary language', that is, by examining *what we should say when*, and so why and what we should mean by it. Perhaps this method, at least as *one* philosophical method, scarcely requires justification at present—too evidently, there is gold in them thar hills: more opportune would be a warning about the care and thoroughness needed if it is not to fall into disrepute. I will, however, justify it very briefly.

First, words are our tools, and, as a minimum, we should use clean tools: we should know what we mean and what we do not, and we must forearm ourselves against the traps that

---

[1] Another well-flogged horse in these same stakes is Blame. At least two things seem confused together under this term. Sometimes when I blame X for doing A, say for breaking the vase, it is a question simply or mainly of my disapproval of A, breaking the vase, which unquestionably X did: but sometimes it is, rather, a question simply or mainly of how far I think X responsible for A, which unquestionably was bad. Hence if somebody says he blames me for something, I may answer by giving a *justification*, so that he will cease to disapprove of what I did, or else by giving an *excuse*, so that he will cease to hold me, at least entirely and in every way, responsible for doing it.

language sets us. Secondly, words are not (except in their own little corner) facts or things: we need therefore to prise them off the world, to hold them apart from and against it, so that we can realize their inadequacies and arbitrariness, and can re-look at the world without blinkers. Thirdly, and more hopefully, our common stock of words embodies all the distinctions men have found worth drawing, and the connexions they have found worth marking, in the lifetimes of many generations: these surely are likely to be more numerous, more sound, since they have stood up to the long test of the survival of the fittest, and more subtle, at least in all ordinary and reasonably practical matters, than any that you or I are likely to think up in our arm-chairs of an afternoon—the most favoured alternative method.

In view of the prevalence of the slogan 'ordinary language', and of such names as 'linguistic' or 'analytic' philosophy or 'the analysis of language', one thing needs specially emphasizing to counter misunderstandings. When we examine what we should say when, what words we should use in what situations, we are looking again not *merely* at words (or 'meanings', whatever they may be) but also at the realities we use the words to talk about: we are using a sharpened awareness of words to sharpen our perception of, though not as the final arbiter of, the phenomena. For this reason I think it might be better to use, for this way of doing philosophy, some less misleading name than those given above—for instance, 'linguistic phenomenology', only that is rather a mouthful.

Using, then, such a method, it is plainly preferable to investigate a field where ordinary language is rich and subtle, as it is in the pressingly practical matter of Excuses, but certainly is not in the matter, say, of Time. At the same time we should prefer a field which is not too much trodden into bogs or tracks by traditional philosophy, for in that case even 'ordinary' language will often have become infected with the jargon of extinct theories, and our own prejudices too, as the upholders or imbibers of theoretical views, will be too readily, and often insensibly, engaged. Here too, Excuses form an admirable topic; we can discuss at least clumsiness, or absence of mind, or inconsiderateness, even spontaneousness, without remembering what Kant thought, and so progress by degrees even to discussing deliberation without for once remembering Aristotle or self-control without Plato. Granted that our subject is, as already claimed for it, neighbouring, analogous or germane in some way to some notorious centre of philosophical trouble, then, with these two further requirements satisfied, we should be certain of what we are after: a good site for *field work* in philosophy. Here at last we should be able to unfreeze, to loosen up and get going on agreeing about discoveries, however small, and on agreeing about how to reach agreement.[1] How much it is to be wished that similar field work will soon be undertaken in, say, aesthetics; if only we could forget for a while about the beautiful and get down instead to the dainty and the dumpy.

There are, I know, or are supposed to be, snags in 'linguistic' philosophy, which those not very familiar with it find, sometimes not without glee or relief, daunting. But with snags, as with nettles, the thing to do is to grasp them—and to climb above them. I will mention two in particular, over which the study of excuses may help to encourage us. The first is the snag of Loose (or Divergent or Alternative) Usage; and the second the crux of the Last Word. Do we all say the same, and only the same, things in the same situations? Don't usages differ? And, Why should what we all ordinarily say be the only or the best or final way of putting it? Why should it even be true?

Well, people's usages do vary, and we do talk loosely, and we do say different things apparently indifferently. But first, not nearly as much as one would think. When we come down to cases, it transpires in the very great majority that what we had thought was our wanting to say different things of and in *the same* situation was really not so—we had simply imagined the

[1] All of which was seen and claimed by Socrates, when he first betook himself to the way of Words.

situation *slightly* differently: which is all too easy to do, because of course no situation (and we are dealing with *imagined* situations) is ever 'completely' described. The more we imagine the situation in detail, with a background of story—and it is worth employing the most idiosyncratic or, sometimes, boring means to stimulate and to discipline our wretched imaginations—the less we find we disagree about what we should say. Nevertheless, *sometimes* we do ultimately disagree: sometimes we must allow a usage to be, though appalling, yet actual; sometimes we should genuinely use either or both of two different descriptions. But why should this daunt us? All that is happening is entirely explicable. If our usages disagree, then you use 'X' where I use 'Y', or more probably (and more intriguingly) your conceptual system is different from mine, though very likely it is at least equally consistent and serviceable: in short, we can find *why* we disagree—you choose to classify in one way, I in another. If the usage is loose, we can understand the temptation that leads to it, and the distinctions that it blurs: if there are 'alternative' descriptions, then the situation can be described or can be 'structured' in two ways, or perhaps it is one where, for current purposes, the two alternatives come down to the same. A disagreement as to what we should say is not to be shied off, but to be pounced upon: for the explanation of it can hardly fail to be illuminating. If we light on an electron that rotates the wrong way, that is a discovery, a portent to be followed up, not a reason for chucking physics: and by the same token, a genuinely loose or eccentric talker is a rare specimen to be prized.

As practice in learning to handle this bogey, in learning the essential *rubrics*, we could scarcely hope for a more promising exercise than the study of excuses. Here, surely, is just the sort of situation where people will say 'almost anything', because they are so flurried, or so anxious to get off. 'It was a mistake', 'It was an accident'—how readily these can *appear* indifferent, and even be used together. Yet, a story or two, and everybody will not merely agree that they are completely different, but even discover for himself what the difference is and what each means.[1]

Then, for the Last Word. Certainly ordinary language has no claim to be the last word, if there is such a thing. It embodies, indeed, something better than the metaphysics of the Stone Age, namely, as was said, the inherited experience and acumen of many generations of men. But then, that acumen has been concentrated primarily upon the practical business of life. If a distinction works well for practical purposes in ordinary life (no mean feat, for even ordinary life is full of hard cases), then there is sure to be something in it, it will not mark nothing: yet this is likely enough to be not the best way of arranging things if our interests are more extensive or intellectual than the ordinary. And again, that experience has been derived only from the sources available to ordinary men throughout most of civilized history: it has not been fed from the resources of the microscope and its successors. And it must be added too, that superstition and error and fantasy of all kinds do become incorporated in ordinary language and even sometimes stand up to the survival test (only, when they do, why should we not detect it?). Certainly, then, ordinary language is *not* the last word: in principle it can everywhere be supplemented and improved upon and superseded. Only remember, it *is* the *first* word.[2]

For this problem too the field of Excuses is a fruitful one. Here is matter both contentious and practically important for everybody, so that ordinary language is on its toes: yet also, on its back it has long had a bigger flea to bite it, in the shape

[1] You have a donkey, so have I, and they graze in the same field. The day comes when I conceive a dislike for mine. I go to shoot it, draw a bead on it, fire: the brute falls in its tracks. I inspect the victim, and find to my horror that it is *your* donkey. I appear on your doorstep with the remains and say—what? 'I say, old sport, I'm awfully sorry, &c., I've shot your donkey *by accident*'? Or '*by mistake*'? Then again, I go to shoot my donkey as before, draw a bead on it, fire—but as I do so, the beasts move, and to my horror yours falls. Again the scene on the doorstep—what do I say? 'By mistake'? Or 'by accident'?

[2] And forget, for once and for a while, that other curious question 'Is it true?' May we?

of the Law, and both again have lately attracted the attentions of yet another, and at least a healthily growing, flea, in the shape of psychology. In the law a constant stream of actual cases, more novel and more tortuous than the mere imagination could contrive, are brought up *for decision*—that is, formulae for docketing them must somehow be found. Hence it is necessary first to be careful with, but also to be brutal with, to torture, to fake and to override, ordinary language: we cannot here evade or forget the whole affair. (In ordinary life we dismiss the puzzles that crop up about time, but we cannot do that indefinitely in physics.) Psychology likewise produces novel cases, but it also produces new methods for bringing phenomena under observation and study: moreover, unlike the law, it has an unbiased interest in the totality of them and is unpressed for decision. Hence its own special and constant need to supplement, to revise and to supersede the classifications of both ordinary life and the law. We have, then, ample material for practice in learning to handle the bogey of the Last Word, however it should be handled.

Suppose, then, that we set out to investigate excuses, what are the methods and resources initially available? Our object is to imagine the varieties of situation in which we make excuses, and to examine the expressions used in making them. If we have a lively imagination, together perhaps with an ample experience of dereliction, we shall go far, only we need system: I do not know how many of you keep a list of the kinds of fool you make of yourselves. It is advisable to use systematic aids, of which there would appear to be three at least. I list them here in order of availability to the layman.

First we may use the dictionary—quite a concise one will do, but the use must be *thorough*. Two methods suggest themselves, both a little tedious, but repaying. One is to read the book through, listing all the words that seem relevant; this does not take as long as many suppose. The other is to start with a widish selection of obviously relevant terms, and to consult the dictionary under each: it will be found that, in the explanations of the various meanings of each, a surprising number of other terms occur, which are germane though of course not often synonymous. We then look up each of *these*, bringing in more for our bag from the 'definitions' given in each case; and when we have continued for a little, it will generally be found that the family circle begins to close, until ultimately it is complete and we come only upon repetitions. This method has the advantage of grouping the terms into convenient clusters—but of course a good deal will depend upon the comprehensiveness of our initial selection.

Working the dictionary, it is interesting to find that a high percentage of the terms connected with excuses prove to be *adverbs*, a type of word which has not enjoyed so large a share of the philosophical limelight as the noun, substantive or adjective, and the verb: this is natural because, as was said, the tenor of so many excuses is that I did it but only *in a way*, not just flatly like that—i.e. the verb needs modifying. Besides adverbs, however, there are other words of all kinds, including numerous abstract nouns, 'misconception,' 'accident', 'purpose', and the like, and a few verbs too, which often hold key positions for the grouping of excuses into classes at a high level ('couldn't help', 'didn't mean to', 'didn't realize', or again 'intend', and 'attempt'). In connexion with the nouns another neglected class of words is prominent, namely, prepositions. Not merely does it matter considerably which preposition, often of several, is being used with a given substantive, but further the prepositions deserve study on their own account. For the question suggests itself, Why are the nouns in one group governed by 'under', in another by 'on', in yet another by 'by' or 'through' or 'from' or 'for' or 'with', and so on? It will be disappointing if there prove to be no good reasons for such groupings.

Our second source-book will naturally be the law. This will provide us with an immense miscellany of untoward cases, and also with a useful list of recognized pleas, together with a good deal of acute analysis of both. No one who tries this resource will long be in doubt, I think, that the common law, and in particular the law of tort, is the richest storehouse; crime and contract contribute some special additions of their own, but tort is altogether more comprehensive and more flexible. But even here, and still more with so old and hardened a branch of the law as crime, much caution is needed with the arguments of counsel and the dicta or decisions of judges: acute though these are, it has always to be remembered that, in legal cases—

(1) there is the overriding requirement that a decision be reached, and a relatively black or white decision—guilty or not guilty—for the plaintiff or for the defendant;

(2) there is the general requirement that the charge or action and the pleadings be brought under one or another of the heads and procedures that have come in the course of history to be accepted by the Courts. These, though fairly numerous, are still few and stereotyped in comparison with the accusations and defences of daily life. Moreover contentions of many kinds are beneath the law, as too trivial, or outside it, as too purely moral—for example, inconsiderateness;

(3) there is the general requirement that we argue from and abide by precedents. The value of this in the law is unquestionable, but it can certainly lead to distortions of ordinary beliefs and expressions.

For such reasons as these, obviously closely connected and stemming from the nature and function of the law, practising lawyers and jurists are by no means so careful as they might be to give to our ordinary expressions their ordinary meanings and applications. There is special pleading and evasion, stretching and strait-jacketing, besides the invention of technical terms, or technical senses for common terms. Nevertheless, it is a perpetual and salutary surprise to discover how much is to be learned from the law; and it is to be added that if a distinction drawn is a sound one, even though not yet recognized in law, a lawyer can be relied upon to take note of it, for it may be dangerous not to—if he does not, his opponent may.

Finally, the third source-book is psychology, with which I include such studies as anthropology and animal behaviour. Here I speak with even more trepidation than about the Law. But this at least is clear, that some varieties of behaviour, some ways of acting or explanations of the doing of actions, are here noticed and classified which have not been observed or named by ordinary men and hallowed by ordinary language, though perhaps they often might have been so if they had been of more practical importance. There is real danger in contempt for the 'jargon' of psychology, at least when it sets out to supplement, and at least sometimes when it sets out to supplant, the language of ordinary life.

With these sources, and with the aid of the imagination, it will go hard if we cannot arrive at the meanings of large numbers of expressions and at the understanding and classification of large numbers of 'actions'. Then we shall comprehend clearly much that, before, we only made use of *ad hoc*. Definition, I would add, explanatory definition, should stand high among our aims: it is not enough to show how clever we are by showing how obscure everything is. Clarity, too, I know, has been said to be not enough: but perhaps it will be time to go into that when we are within measurable distance of achieving clarity on some matter.

So much for the cackle. It remains to make a few remarks, not, I am afraid, in any very coherent order, about the types of significant result to be obtained and the more general lessons to be learned from the study of Excuses.

1. *No modification without aberration.* When it is stated that X did A, there is a temptation to suppose that given some, indeed perhaps *any*, expression modifying the verb we shall be entitled to insert either it or its opposite or negation in our statement: that is, we shall be entitled to ask, typically, 'Did X do A Mly or not Mly?' (e.g. 'Did X murder Y voluntarily or involuntarily?'), and to answer one or the other. Or as a minimum it is supposed that if X did A there must be at least *one*

modifying expression that we could, justifiably and informatively, insert with the verb. In the great majority of cases of the use of the great majority of verbs ('murder' perhaps is not one of the majority) such suppositions are quite unjustified. The natural economy of language dictates that for the *standard* case covered by any normal verb—not, perhaps, a verb of omen such as 'murder', but a verb like 'eat' or 'kick' or 'croquet'— no modifying expression is required or even permissible. Only if we do the action named in some *special* way or circumstances, different from those in which such an act is naturally done (and of course both the normal and the abnormal differ according to what verb in particular is in question) is a modifying expression called for, or even in order. I sit in my chair, in the usual way—I am not in a daze or influenced by threats or the like: here, it will not do to say either that I sat in it intentionally or that I did not sit in it intentionally,[1] nor yet that I sat in it automatically or from habit or what you will. It is bedtime, I am alone, I yawn: but I do not yawn involuntarily (or voluntarily!), nor yet deliberately. To yawn in any such peculiar way is just not to just yawn.

2. *Limitation of application.* Expressions modifying verbs, typically adverbs, have limited ranges of application. That is, given any adverb of excuse, such as 'unwittingly' or 'spontaneously' or 'impulsively', it will not be found that it makes good sense to attach it to any and every verb of 'action' in any and every context: indeed, it will often apply only to a comparatively narrow range of such verbs. Something in the lad's upturned face appealed to him, he threw a brick at it—'spontaneously'? The interest then is to discover why some actions can be excused in a particular way but not others, particularly perhaps the latter.[2] This will largely elucidate the meaning of the excuse, and at the same time will illuminate the

[1] Caveat or hedge: of course we can say 'I did *not* sit in it "intentionally"' as a way simply of repudiating the suggestion that I sat in it intentionally.

[2] For we are sometimes not so good at observing what we *can't* say as what we can, yet the first is pretty regularly the more revealing.

characteristics typical of the group of 'actions' it picks out: very often too it will throw light on some detail of the machinery of 'action' in general (see 4), or on our standards of acceptable conduct (see 5). It is specially important in the case of some of the terms most favoured by philosophers or jurists to realize that at least in ordinary speech (disregarding back-seepage of jargon) they are not used so universally or so dichotomistically. For example, take 'voluntarily' and 'involuntarily': we may join the army or make a gift voluntarily, we may hiccough or make a small gesture involuntarily, and the more we consider further actions which we might naturally be said to do in either of these ways, the more circumscribed and unlike each other do the two classes become, until we even doubt whether there is *any* verb with which both adverbs are equally in place. Perhaps there are some such; but at least sometimes when we may think we have found one it is an illusion, an apparent exception that really does prove the rule. I can perhaps 'break a cup' voluntarily, *if* that is done, say, as an act of self-impoverishment: and I can perhaps break another involuntarily, *if*, say, I make an involuntary movement which breaks it. Here, plainly, the two acts described each as 'breaking a cup' are really very different, and the one is similar to acts typical of the 'voluntary' class, the other to acts typical of the 'involuntary' class.

3. *The importance of Negations and Opposites*. 'Voluntarily' and 'involuntarily', then, are not opposed in the obvious sort of way that they are made to be in philosophy or jurisprudence. The 'opposite', or rather 'opposites', of 'voluntarily' might be 'under constraint' of some sort, duress or obligation or influence:[1] the opposite of 'involuntarily' might be 'deliberately' or 'on purpose' or the like. Such divergences in opposites indicate that 'voluntarily' and 'involuntarily', in spite of their apparent connexion, are fish from very different kettles. In general, it will pay us to take nothing for granted or as obvious

---

[1] But remember, when I sign a cheque in the normal way, I do *not* do so *either* 'voluntarily' *or* 'under constraint'.

about negations and opposites. It does not pay to assume that a word must have an opposite, or one opposite, whether it is a 'positive' word like 'wilfully' or a 'negative' word like 'inadvertently'. Rather, we should be asking ourselves such questions as why there is no use for the adverb 'advertently'. For above all it will not do to assume that the 'positive' word must be around to wear the trousers; commonly enough the 'negative' (looking) word marks the (positive) abnormality, while the 'positive' word, *if* it exists, merely serves to rule out the suggestion of that abnormality. It is natural enough, in view of what was said in (1) above, for the 'positive' word not to be found at all in some cases. I do an act A_1 (say, crush a snail) *inadvertently* if, in the course of executing by means of movements of my bodily parts some other act A_2 (say, in walking down the public path) I fail to exercise such meticulous supervision over the courses of those movements as would have been needed to ensure that they did not bring about the untoward event (here, the impact on the snail).[1] By claiming that A_1 was inadvertent we place it, where we imply it belongs, on this special level, in a class of incidental happenings which must occur in the doing of any physical act. To lift the act out of this class, we need and possess the expression 'not . . . inadvertently': 'advertently', if used for this purpose, would suggest that, if the act was not done inadvertently, then it must have been done noticing what I was doing, which is far from necessarily the case (e.g. if I did it absent-mindedly), or at least that there is *something* in common to the ways of doing all acts not done inadvertently, which is not the case. Again, there is no use for

---

[1] Or analogously: I do an act A_1 (say, divulge my age, or imply you are a liar), *inadvertently* if, in the course of executing by the use of some medium of communication some other act A_2 (say, reminiscing about my war service) I fail to exercise such meticulous supervision over the choice and arrangement of the signs as would have been needed to ensure that. . . . It is interesting to note how such adverbs lead parallel lives, one in connexion with physical actions ('doing') and the other in connexion with acts of communication ('saying'), or sometimes also in connexion with acts of 'thinking' ('inadvertently assumed').

'advertently' at the *same* level as 'inadvertently': in passing the butter I do not knock over the cream-jug, though I do (inadvertently) knock over the teacup—yet I do not by-pass the cream-jug *advertently*: for at this level, below supervision in detail, *anything* that we do is, if you like, inadvertent, though we only call it so, and indeed only call it something we have done, if there is something untoward about it.

A further point of interest in studying so-called 'negative' terms is the manner of their formation. Why are the words in one group formed with *un-* or *in-*, those in another with *-less* ('aimless', 'reckless', 'heedless', &c.), and those in another with *mis-* ('mistake', 'misconception', 'misjudgement', &c.)? Why care*less*ly but *in*attentively? Perhaps care and attention, so often linked, are rather different. Here are remunerative exercises.

4. *The machinery of action.* Not merely do adverbial expressions pick out classes of actions, they also pick out the internal detail of the machinery of doing actions, or the departments into which the business of doing actions is organized. There is for example the stage at which we have actually to *carry out* some action upon which we embark—perhaps we have to make certain bodily movements or to make a speech. In the course of actually *doing* these things (getting weaving) we have to pay (some) attention to what we are doing and to take (some) care to guard against (likely) dangers: we may need to use judgement or tact: we must exercise sufficient control over our bodily parts: and so on. Inattention, carelessness, errors of judgement, tactlessness, clumsiness, all these and others are ills (with attendant excuses) which affect one specific stage in the machinery of action, the *executive* stage, the stage where we *muff* it. But there are many other departments in the business too, each of which is to be traced and mapped through its cluster of appropriate verbs and adverbs. Obviously there are departments of intelligence and planning, of decision and resolve, and so on: but I shall mention one in particular, too often overlooked, where troubles and excuses abound. It

happens to us, in military life, to be in receipt of excellent intelligence, to be also in self-conscious possession of excellent principles (the five golden rules for winning victories), and yet to hit upon a plan of action which leads to disaster. One way in which this can happen is through failure at the stage of *appreciation* of the situation, that is at the stage where we are required to cast our excellent intelligence into such a form, under such heads and with such weights attached, that our equally excellent principles can be brought to bear on it properly, in a way to yield the right answer.[1] So too in real, or rather civilian, life, in moral or practical affairs, we can know the facts and yet look at them mistakenly or perversely, or not fully realize or appreciate something, or even be under a total misconception. Many expressions of excuse indicate failure at this particularly tricky stage: even thoughtlessness, inconsiderateness, lack of imagination, are perhaps less matters of failure in intelligence or planning than might be supposed, and more matters of failure to appreciate the situation. A course of E. M. Forster and we see things differently: yet perhaps we know no more and are no cleverer.

5. *Standards of the unacceptable.* It is characteristic of excuses to be 'unacceptable': given, I suppose, almost any excuse, there will be cases of such a kind or of such gravity that 'we will not accept' it. It is interesting to detect the standards and codes we thus invoke. The extent of the supervision we exercise over the execution of any act can never be quite unlimited, and usually is expected to fall within fairly definite limits ('due care and attention') in the case of acts of some general kind, though of course we set very different limits in different cases. We may plead that we trod on the snail inadvertently: but not on a baby—you ought to look where you are putting your great feet. Of course it *was* (*really*), if you like, inadvertence: but that word constitutes a plea, which is not going to be

---

[1] We know all about how to do quadratics: we know all the needful facts about pipes, cisterns, hours and plumbers: yet we reach the answer '$3\frac{3}{4}$ men'. We have failed to cast our facts correctly into mathematical form.

allowed, because of standards. And if you try it on, you will be subscribing to such dreadful standards that your last state will be worse than your first. Or again, we set different standards, and will accept different excuses, in the case of acts which are rule-governed, like spelling, and which we are expected absolutely to get right, from those we set and accept for less stereotyped actions: a wrong spelling may be a slip, but hardly an accident, a winged beater may be an accident, but hardly a slip.

6. *Combination, dissociation and complication*. A belief in opposites and dichotomies encourages, among other things, a blindness to the combinations and dissociations of adverbs that are possible, even to such obvious facts as that we can act at once on impulse and intentionally, or that we can do an action intentionally yet for all that not deliberately, still less on purpose. We walk along the cliff, and I feel a sudden impulse to push you over, which I promptly do: I acted on impulse, yet I certainly intended to push you over, and may even have devised a little ruse to achieve it: yet even then I did not act deliberately, for I did not (stop to) ask myself whether to do it or not.

It is worth bearing in mind, too, the general rule that we must not expect to find simple labels for complicated cases. If a mistake results in an accident, it will not do to ask whether 'it' was an accident or a mistake, or to demand some briefer description of 'it'. Here the natural economy of language operates: if the words already available for simple cases suffice in combination to describe a complicated case, there will be need for special reasons before a special new word is invented for the complication. Besides, however well-equipped our language, it can never be forearmed against all possible cases that may arise and call for description: fact is richer than diction.

7. *Regina* v. *Finney*. Often the complexity and difficulty of a case is considerable. I will quote the case of *Regina* v. *Finney*:[1]

[1] A somewhat distressing favourite in the class that Hart used to conduct with me in the years soon after the war. The italics are mine.

Shrewsbury Assizes.   1874.   12 Cox 625.

Prisoner was indicted for the manslaughter of Thomas Watkins.

The Prisoner was an attendant at a lunatic asylum. Being in charge of a lunatic, who was bathing, he turned on hot water into the bath, and thereby scalded him to death. The facts appeared to be truly set forth in the statement of the prisoner made before the committing magistrate, as follows: 'I had bathed Watkins, and had loosed the bath out. *I intended putting in a clean bath*, and asked Watkins if he would get out. At this time *my attention was drawn* to the next bath by the new attendant, who was asking me a question; and *my attention was taken from the bath* where Watkins was. I put my hand down to turn water on in the bath where Thomas Watkins was. *I did not intend to turn the hot water*, and *I made a mistake in the tap. I did not know what I had done until* I heard Thomas Watkins shout out; and *I did not find my mistake out till* I saw the steam from the water. You cannot get water in this bath when they are drawing water at the other bath; but at other times it shoots out like a water gun when the other baths are not in use. . . .'

(It was proved that the lunatic had such possession of his faculties as would enable him to understand what was said to him, and to get out of the bath.)

A. Young (for Prisoner). The death *resulted from accident*. There was no such *culpable negligence* on the part of the prisoner as will support this indictment. A *culpable mistake*, or some degree of *culpable negligence*, causing death, will not support a charge of manslaughter; unless the *negligence* be so gross as to be *reckless*. (R. v. Noakes.)

Lush, J. To render a person liable for *neglect of duty* there must be such a degree of culpability as to amount to *gross negligence* on his part. If you accept the prisoner's own statement, you find no such amount of *negligence* as would come within this definition. It is not every little *trip or mistake* that will make a man so liable. It was the duty of the attendant not to let hot water into the bath while the patient was therein. According to the prisoner's own account, *he did not believe that* he was letting the hot water in while the deceased remained there. The lunatic was, we have heard, a man capable of getting out by himself and of understanding what was said to him. He was told to get out. A new attendant who had come on this day, was at an adjoining bath and he *took off the prisoner's attention*. Now, if the prisoner, knowing that the man was in the bath, had turned on the tap, and turned on the hot instead of the cold water, I should have said there was gross negligence; for he ought to have looked to see. But from his own account he had told the deceased to get out, and *thought he had got out*. If you think that indicates gross *carelessness*, then you should find the prisoner guilty of manslaughter. But if you think it *inadvertence* not amounting to culpability—i.e., what is properly termed an *accident*—then the prisoner is not liable.

Verdict, Not guilty.

In this case there are two morals that I will point:

(i) Both counsel and judge make very free use of a large number of terms of excuse, using several as though they were, and even stating them to be, indifferent or equivalent when they are not, and presenting as alternatives those that are not.

(ii) It is constantly difficult to be sure *what* act it is that counsel or judge is suggesting might be qualified by what expression of excuse.

The learned judge's concluding direction is a paradigm of these faults.[1] Finney, by contrast, stands out as an evident master of the Queen's English. He is explicit as to each of his acts and states, mental and physical: he uses different, and the correct, adverbs in connexion with each: and he makes no attempt to boil down.

8. *Small distinctions, and big too.* It should go without saying that terms of excuse are not equivalent, and that it matters which we use: we need to distinguish inadvertence not merely from (save the mark) such things as mistake and accident, but from such nearer neighbours as, say, aberration and absence

---

[1] Not but what he probably manages to convey his meaning somehow or other. Judges seem to acquire a knack of conveying meaning, and even carrying conviction, through the use of a pithy Anglo-Saxon which sometimes has literally no meaning at all. Wishing to distinguish the case of shooting at a post in the belief that it was an enemy, as *not* an 'attempt', from the case of picking an empty pocket in the belief that money was in it, which *is* an 'attempt', the judge explains that in shooting at the post 'the man is never on the thing at all'.

of mind. By imagining cases with vividness and fullness we should be able to decide in which precise terms to describe, say, Miss Plimsoll's action in writing, so carefully, 'DAIRY' on her fine new book: we should be able to distinguish between sheer, mere, pure, and simple mistake or inadvertence. Yet unfortunately, at least when in the grip of thought, we fail not merely at these stiffer hurdles. We equate even—I have seen it done—'inadvertently' with 'automatically': as though to say I trod on your toe inadvertently means to say I trod on it automatically. Or we collapse succumbing to temptation into losing control of ourselves—a bad patch, this, for telescoping.[1]

All this is not so much a *lesson* from the study of excuses as the very object of it.

9. *The exact phrase and its place in the sentence*. It is not enough, either, to attend simply to the 'key' word: notice must also be taken of the full and exact form of the expression used. In considering mistakes, we have to consider seriatim 'by mistake', 'owing to a mistake', 'mistakenly', 'it was a mistake to', 'to make a mistake in or over or about', 'to be mistaken about', and so on: in considering purpose, we have to consider 'on', 'with the', 'for the', &c., besides 'purposeful', 'purposeless', and the like. These varying expressions may function quite differently—and usually do, or why should we burden ourselves with more than one of them?

Care must be taken too to observe the precise position of an adverbial expression in the sentence. This should of course indicate what verb it is being used to modify: but more than that, the position can also affect the *sense* of the expression,

---

[1] Plato, I suppose, and after him Aristotle, fastened this confusion upon us, as bad in its day and way as the later, grotesque, confusion of moral weakness with weakness of will. I am very partial to ice cream, and a bombe is served divided into segments corresponding one to one with the persons at High Table: I am tempted to help myself to two segments and do so, thus succumbing to temptation and even conceivably (but why necessarily?) going against my principles. But do I lose control of myself? Do I raven, do I snatch the morsels from the dish and wolf them down, impervious to the consternation of my colleagues? Not a bit of it. We often succumb to temptation with calm and even with finesse.

i.e. the way in which it modifies that verb. Compare, for example:

> a_1 He clumsily trod on the snail.
> a_2 Clumsily he trod on the snail.
> b_1 He trod clumsily on the snail.
> b_2 He trod on the snail clumsily.

Here, in a_1 and a_2 we describe his treading on the creature at all as a piece of clumsiness, incidental, we imply, to his performance of some other action: but with b_1 and b_2 to tread on it is, very likely, his aim or policy, what we criticize is his execution of the feat.[1] Many adverbs, though far from all (not, for example, 'purposely') are used in these two typically different ways.

10. *The style of performance*. With some adverbs the distinction between the two senses referred to in the last paragraph is carried a stage further. 'He ate his soup deliberately' may mean, like 'He deliberately ate his soup', that his eating his soup was a deliberate act, one perhaps that he thought would annoy somebody, as it would more commonly if he deliberately ate *my* soup, and which he decided to do: but it will often mean that he went through the performance of eating his soup in a noteworthy manner or *style*—pause after each mouthful, careful choice of point of entry for the spoon, sucking of moustaches, and so on. That is, it will mean that he ate *with* deliberation rather than *after* deliberation. The style of the performance, slow and unhurried, is understandably called 'deliberate' because each movement *has the typical look* of a deliberate act: but it is scarcely being said that the making of each motion *is* a deliberate act or that he is 'literally' deliberating. This case, then, is more extreme than that of 'clumsily', which does in both uses describe literally a manner of performing.

---

[1] As a matter of fact, most of these examples *can* be understood the other way, especially if we allow ourselves inflexions of the voice, or commas, or contexts. a_2 might be a poetic inversion for b_2: b_1, perhaps with commas round the 'clumsily', might be used for a_1: and so on. Still, the two senses are clearly enough distinguishable.

It is worth watching out for this secondary use when scrutinizing any particular adverbial expression: when it definitely does not exist, the reason is worth inquiring into. Sometimes it is very hard to be sure whether it does exist or does not: it does, one would think, with 'carelessly', it does not with 'inadvertently', but does it or does it not with 'absent-mindedly' or 'aimlessly'? In some cases a word akin to but distinct from the primary adverb is used for this special role of describing a style of performance: we use 'purposefully' in this way, but never 'purposely'.

11. *What modifies what?* The Judge in *Regina* v. *Finney* does not make clear what event is being excused in what way. 'If you think that indicates gross carelessness, then. . . . But if you think it inadvertence not amounting to culpability—i.e. what is properly called an accident—then. . . .' Apparently he means that Finney may have *turned on the hot tap* inadvertently:[1] does he mean also that the tap may have been turned accidentally, or rather that *Watkins may have been scalded* and killed accidentally? And was the carelessness in turning the tap or in thinking Watkins had got out? Many disputes as to what excuse we should properly use arise because we will not trouble to state explicitly *what* is being excused.

To do so is all the more vital because it is in principle always open to us, along various lines, to describe or refer to 'what I did' in so many different ways. This is altogether too large a theme to elaborate here. Apart from the more general and obvious problems of the use of 'tendentious' descriptive terms, there are many special problems in the particular case of

[1] What Finney says is different: he says he 'made a mistake in the tap'. This is the basic use of 'mistake', where we simply, and not necessarily accountably, take the wrong one. Finney here attempts to account for his mistake, by saying that his attention was distracted. But suppose the order is 'Right turn' and I turn left: no doubt the sergeant will insinuate that my attention was distracted, or that I cannot distinguish my right from my left—but it was not and I can, this was a simple, pure mistake. As often happens. Neither I nor the sergeant will suggest that there was any accident, or any inadvertence either. If Finney had turned the hot tap inadvertently, then it would have been knocked, say, in reaching for the cold tap: a different story.

'actions'. Should we say, are we saying, that he took her money, or that he robbed her? That he knocked a ball into a hole, or that he sank a putt? That he said 'Done', or that he accepted an offer? How far, that is, are motives, intentions and conventions to be part of the description of actions? And more especially here, what is *an* or *one* or *the* action? For we can generally split up what might be named as one action in several distinct ways, into different *stretches* or *phases* or *stages*. Stages have already been mentioned: we can dismantle the machinery of the act, and describe (and excuse) separately the intelligence, the appreciation, the planning, the decision, the execution and so forth. Phases are rather different: we can say that he painted a picture or fought a campaign, or else we can say that first he laid on this stroke of paint and then that, first he fought this action and then that. Stretches are different again: a single term descriptive of what he did may be made to cover either a smaller or a larger stretch of events, those excluded by the narrower description being then called 'consequences' or 'results' or 'effects' or the like of his act. So here we can describe Finney's act *either* as turning on the hot tap, which he did by mistake, with the result that Watkins was scalded, *or* as scalding Watkins, which he did *not* do by mistake.

It is very evident that the problems of excuses and those of the different descriptions of actions are throughout bound up with each other.

12. *Trailing clouds of etymology*. It is these considerations that bring us up so forcibly against some of the most difficult words in the whole story of Excuses, such words as 'result', 'effect', and 'consequence', or again as 'intention', 'purpose', and 'motive'. I will mention two points of method which are, experience has convinced me, indispensable aids at these levels.

One is that a word never—well, hardly ever—shakes off its etymology and its formation. In spite of all changes in and extensions of and additions to its meanings, and indeed rather pervading and governing these, there will still persist the old idea. In an *accident* something befalls: by *mistake* you take the wrong one: in *error* you stray: when you act *deliberately* you act after weighing it up (*not* after thinking out ways and means). It is worth asking ourselves whether we know the etymology of 'result' or of 'spontaneously', and worth remembering that 'unwillingly' and 'involuntarily' come from very different sources.

And the second point is connected with this. Going back into the history of a word, very often into Latin, we come back pretty commonly to pictures or *models* of how things happen or are done. These models may be fairly sophisticated and recent, as is perhaps the case with 'motive' or 'impulse', but one of the commonest and most primitive types of model is one which is apt to baffle us through its very naturalness and simplicity. We take *some very simple action*, like shoving a stone, usually as done by and viewed by oneself, and use *this*, with the features distinguishable in it, as our model in terms of which to talk about other actions and events: and we continue to do so, scarcely realizing it, even when these other actions are pretty remote and perhaps much more interesting to us in their own right than the acts originally used in constructing the model ever were, and even when the model is really distorting the facts rather than helping us to observe them. In primitive cases we may get to see clearly the differences between, say, 'results', 'effects', and 'consequences', and yet discover that these differences are no longer clear, and the terms themselves no longer of real service to us, in the more complicated cases where we had been bandying them about most freely. A model must be recognized for what it is. 'Causing', I suppose, was a notion taken from a man's own experience of doing simple actions, and by primitive man every event was construed in terms of this model: every event has a cause, that is, every event is an action done by somebody—if not by a man, then by a quasi-man, a spirit. When, later, events which are *not* actions are realized to be such, we still say that they must be 'caused', and the word snares us: we are struggling to ascribe to it a new, unanthropomorphic meaning, yet constantly, in searching for its analysis, we unearth and incorporate the lineaments of the ancient model. As happened even to Hume, and consequently to Kant. Examining such a word historically, we may well find that it has been extended to cases that have by now too tenuous a relation to the model case, that it is a source of confusion and superstition.

There is too another danger in words that invoke models, half-forgotten or not. It must be remembered that there is no necessity whatsoever that the various models used in creating our vocabulary, primitive or recent, should all fit together neatly as parts into one single, total model or scheme of, for instance, the doing of actions. It is possible, and indeed highly likely, that our assortment of models will include some, or many, that are overlapping, conflicting, or more generally simply *disparate*.[1]

13. In spite of the wide and acute observation of the phenomena of action embodied in ordinary speech, modern scientists have been able, it seems to me, to reveal its inadequacy at numerous points, if only because they have had access to more comprehensive data and have studied them with more catholic and dispassionate interest than the ordinary man, or even the lawyer, has had occasion to do. I will conclude with two examples.

Observation of animal behaviour shows that regularly, when an animal is embarked on some recognizable pattern of behaviour but meets in the course of it with an insuperable

---

[1] This is by way of a general warning in philosophy. It seems to be too readily assumed that if we can only discover the true meanings of each of a cluster of key terms, usually historic terms, that we use in some particular field (as, for example, 'right', 'good' and the rest in morals), then it must without question transpire that each will fit into place in some single, interlocking, consistent, conceptual scheme. Not only is there no reason to assume this, but all historical probability is against it, especially in the case of a language derived from such various civilizations as ours is. We may cheerfully use, and with weight, terms which are not so much head-on incompatible as simply disparate, which just do not fit in or even on. Just as we cheerfully subscribe to, or have the grace to be torn between, simply disparate ideals—why *must* there be a conceivable amalgam, the Good Life for Man?

obstacle, it will betake itself to energetic, but quite unrelated, activity of some wild kind, such as standing on its head. This phenomenon is called 'displacement behaviour' and is well identifiable. If now, in the light of this, we look back at ordinary human life, we see that displacement behaviour bulks quite large in it: yet we have apparently no word, or at least no clear and simple word, for it. If, when thwarted, we stand on our heads or wiggle our toes, then we are not exactly *just* standing on our heads, don't you know, in the ordinary way, yet is there any convenient adverbial expression we can insert to do the trick? 'In desperation'?

Take, again, 'compulsive' behaviour, however exactly psychologists define it, compulsive washing for example. There are of course hints in ordinary speech that we do things in this way—'just feel I have to', 'shouldn't feel comfortable unless I did', and the like: but there is no adverbial expression satisfactorily pre-empted for it, as 'compulsively' is. This is understandable enough, since compulsive behaviour, like displacement behaviour, is not in general going to be of great practical importance.

Here I leave and commend the subject to you.

9

IFS AND CANS[1]

ARE *cans* constitutionally iffy? Whenever, that is, we say that we can do something, or could do something, or could have done something, is there an *if* in the offing—suppressed, it may be, but due nevertheless to appear when we set out our sentence in full or when we give an explanation of its meaning?

Again, if and when there *is* an *if*-clause appended to a main clause which contains a *can* or *could* or *could have*, what sort ot an *if* is it? What is the meaning of the *if*, or what is the effect or the point of combining this *if*-clause with the main clause?

These are large questions, to which philosophers, among them some whom I most respect, have given small answers: and it is two such answers, given recently by English philosophers, that I propose to consider. Both, I believe, are mistaken, yet something is to be learned from examining them. In philosophy, there are many mistakes that it is no disgrace to have made: to make a first-water, ground-floor mistake, so far from being easy, takes one (*one*) form of philosophical genius.[2]

Many of you will have read a short but justly admired book written by Professor G. E. Moore of Cambridge, which is called simply *Ethics*. In it, there is a point where Moore, who is engaged in discussing Right and Wrong, says that if we are to discuss whether any act that has been done was right or wrong then we are bound to discuss what the person concerned *could have* done instead of what he did in fact do. And this, he thinks,

[1] Reprinted from the *Proceedings of the British Academy*, 1956, by courtesy of the editor.
[2] Plato, Descartes, and Leibniz all had this form of genius, besides of course others.

may lead to an entanglement in the problem, so-called, of Free Will: because, though few would deny, at least expressly, that a man could have done something other than what he did actually do *if he had chosen*, many people would deny that he *could* (absolutely) have done any such other thing. Hence Moore is led to ask whether it is ever true, and if so in what sense, that a man could have done something other than what he did actually do. And it is with his answer to this question, not with its bearings upon the meanings of *right* and *wrong* or upon the problem of Free Will, that we are concerned.

With his usual shrewdness Moore begins by insisting that there is at least *one* proper sense in which we can say that a man can do something he does not do or could have done something he did not do—even though there may perhaps be *other* senses of *can* and *could have* in which we cannot say such things. This sense he illustrates by the sentence 'I could have walked a mile in 20 minutes this morning, but I certainly could not have run two miles in 5 minutes': we are to take it that in fact the speaker did not do either of the two things mentioned, but this in no way hinders us from drawing the very common and necessary distinction between undone acts that we could have done and undone acts that we could not have done. So it is certain that, at least in *some* sense, we often could have done things that we did not actually do.

Why then, Moore goes on to ask, should anyone try to deny this? And he replies that people do so (we may call them 'determinists') because they hold that everything that happens has a *cause* which precedes it, which is to say that once the cause has occurred the thing itself is *bound* to occur and *nothing* else *could* ever have happened instead.

However, on examining further the 20-minute-mile example, Moore argues that there is much reason to think that 'could have' in such cases simply means 'could have *if* I had chosen', or, as perhaps we had better say in order to avoid a possible complication (these are Moore's words), simply means '*should* have if I had chosen'. And if this *is* all it means, then there is after all no conflict between our conviction that we often could have, in this sense, done things that we did not actually do and the determinist's theory: for he certainly holds himself that I often, and perhaps even always, should have done something different from what I did do *if I had chosen* to do that different thing, since my choosing differently would constitute a change in the causal antecedents of my subsequent act, which would therefore, on his theory, naturally itself be different. If, therefore, the determinist nevertheless asserts that in *some* sense of 'could have' I could *not* ever have done anything different from what I did actually do, this must simply be a second sense[1] of 'could have' different from that which it has in the 20-minute-mile example.

In the remainder of his chapter, Moore argues that quite possibly his first sense of 'could have', in which it simply means 'could or should have if I had chosen', is all we need to satisfy our hankerings after Free Will, or at least is so if conjoined in some way with yet a third sense of 'could have' in which sense 'I could have done something different' means 'I might, for all anyone could know for certain beforehand, have done something different'. This third kind of 'could have' might, I think, be held to be a vulgarism, 'could' being used incorrectly for 'might': but in any case we shall not be concerned with it here.

In the upshot, then, Moore leaves us with only one important sense in which it can be said that I could have done something that I did not do: he is not convinced that any other sense is necessary, nor has he any clear idea what such another sense would be: and he is convinced that, on his interpretation of 'could have', even the determinist can, and indeed must, say that I could very often have done things I did not do. To summarize his suggestions (he does not put them forward with complete conviction) once again:

1. 'Could have' simply means 'could have if I had chosen'.
2. For 'could have if I had chosen' we may substitute 'should have if I had chosen'.

[1] About which Moore has no more to tell us.

3. The *if*-clauses in these expressions state the causal conditions upon which it would have followed that I could or should have done the thing different from what I did actually do.

Moore does not state this third point expressly himself: but it seems clear, in view of the connexions he alleges between his interpretation of 'could have' and the determinist theory, that he did believe it, presumably taking it as obvious.

There are then three questions to be asked:

1. Does 'could have if I had chosen' mean the same, in general or ever, as 'should have if I had chosen?'
2. In either of these expressions, is the *if* the *if* of causal condition?
3. In sentences having *can* or *could have* as main verb, are we required or entitled always to supply an *if*-clause, and in particular the clause 'if I had chosen'?

It appears to me that the answer in each case is No.

1. Anyone, surely, would admit that in general *could* is very different indeed from *should* or *would*.[1] What a man *could* do is not at all the same as what he *would* do: perhaps he could shoot you if you were within range, but that is not in the least to say that he would. And it seems clear to me, in our present example, that 'I could have run a mile if I had chosen' and 'I should have run a mile if I had chosen' mean quite different things, though unfortunately it is not so clear exactly what either of them, especially the latter, does mean. 'I should have run a mile in 20 minutes this morning if I had chosen' seems to me an unusual, not to say queer, specimen of English: but if I had to interpret it, I should take it to mean the same as 'If I had chosen to run a mile in 20 minutes this morning, I should (jolly well) have done so', that is, it would be an assertion of my strength

---

[1] Since Moore has couched his example in the first person, he uses 'should' in the apodosis: but of course in the third person, everyone would use 'would'. For brevity, I shall in what follows generally use 'should' to do duty for both persons.

of character, in that I put my decisions into execution (an assertion which is, however, more naturally made, as I have now made it, with the *if*-clause preceding the main clause). I should certainly not myself understand it to mean that if I had made a certain choice my making that choice would have caused me to do something. But in whichever of these ways we understand it, it is quite different from 'I *could* have walked a mile in 20 minutes this morning if I had chosen', which surely says something rather about my opportunities or powers. Moore, unfortunately, does not explain why he thinks we are entitled to make this all-important transition from 'could' to 'should', beyond saying that by doing so we 'avoid a possible complication'. Later I shall make some suggestions which may in part explain why he was tempted to make the transition: but nothing can justify it.

2. Moore, as I pointed out above, did not discuss what sort of *if* it is that we have in 'I can if I choose' or in 'I could have if I had chosen' or in 'I should have if I had chosen'. Generally, philosophers, as also grammarians, have a favourite, if somewhat blurred and diffuse, idea of an *if*-clause as a 'conditional' clause: putting our example schematically as 'If *p*, then *q*', then it will be said that *q* follows from *p*, typically either in the sense that *p* entails *q* or in the sense that *p* is a *cause* of *q*, though other important variations are possible. And it seems to be on these lines that Moore is thinking of the *if* in 'I can if I choose'. But now, it is characteristic of this general sort of *if*, that from 'If *p* then *q*' we *can* draw the inference 'If not *q*, then not *p*', whereas we can *not* infer either 'Whether or not *p*, then *q*' or '*q*' simpliciter. For example, from 'If I run, I pant' we *can* infer 'If I do not pant, I do not run' (or, as we should rather say, 'If I am not panting, I am not running'), whereas we can *not* infer either 'I pant, whether I run or not' or 'I pant' (at least in the sense of 'I am panting'). If, to avoid these troubles with the English tenses, which are unfortunately prevalent but are not allowed to matter, we put the example in the past tense, then from 'If I ran, I panted' it *does* follow that 'If I did not pant,

I did not run', but it does *not* follow either that 'I panted whether or not I ran' or that 'I panted' period. These possibilities and impossibilities of inference are typical of the *if* of causal condition: but they are precisely reversed in the case of 'I can if I choose' or 'I could have if I had chosen'. For from these we should not draw the curious inferences that 'If I cannot, I do not choose to' or that 'If I could not have, I had not chosen to' (or 'did not choose to'), whatever these sentences may be supposed to mean. But on the contrary, from 'I can if I choose' we certainly should infer that 'I can, whether I choose to or not' and indeed that 'I can' period: and from 'I could have if I had chosen' we should similarly infer that 'I could have, whether I chose to or not' and that anyway 'I could have' period. So that, whatever this *if* means, it is evidently not the *if* of causal condition.

This becomes even clearer when we observe that it is quite common *elsewhere* to find an ordinary causal conditional *if* in connexion with a *can*, and that then there is no doubt about it, as for example in the sentence 'I can squeeze through if I am thin enough', which *does* imply that 'If I cannot squeeze through I am not thin enough', and of course does *not* imply that 'I can squeeze through'. 'I can if I choose' is precisely different from this.

Nor does *can* have to be a very special and peculiar verb for *if*s which are not causal conditional to be found in connexion with it: all kinds of *if*s are found with all kinds of verbs. Consider for example the *if* in 'There are biscuits on the sideboard if you want them', where the verb is the highly ordinary *are*, but the *if* is more like that in 'I can if I choose' than that in 'I panted if I ran': for we can certainly infer from it that 'There are biscuits on the sideboard whether you want them or not' and that anyway 'There are biscuits on the sideboard', whereas it would be folly to infer that 'If there are no biscuits on the sideboard you do not want them', or to understand the meaning to be that you have only to want biscuits to cause them to be on the sideboard.

The *if*, then, in 'I can if I choose' is not the causal conditional *if*. What of the *if* in 'I shall if I choose'? At first glance, we see that this is quite different (one more reason for refusing to substitute *shall* for *can* or *should have* for *could have*). For from 'I shall if I choose' we clearly cannot infer that 'I shall whether I choose to or not' or simply that 'I shall'. But on the other hand, can we infer, either, that 'If I shan't I don't choose to'? (Or should it be rather 'If I don't I don't choose to'?) I think not, as we shall see: but even if some such inference can be drawn, it would still be patently wrong to conclude that the meaning of 'I shall if I choose' is that my choosing to do the thing is sufficient to cause me inevitably to do it or has as a consequence that I shall do it, which, unless I am mistaken, is what Moore was supposing it to mean. This may be seen if we compare 'I shall ruin him if I choose' with 'I shall ruin him if I am extravagant'. The latter sentence does indeed obviously state what would be the consequence of the fulfilment of a condition specified in the *if*-clause—but then, the first sentence has clearly different characteristics from the second. In the first, it makes good sense in general to stress the 'shall', but in the second it does not.[1] This is a symptom of the fact that in the first sentence 'I shall' is the present of that mysterious old verb *shall*, whereas in the second 'shall' is simply being used as an auxiliary, without any meaning of its own, to form the future indicative of 'ruin'.

I expect you will be more than ready at this point to hear something a little more positive about the meanings of these curious expressions 'I can if I choose' and 'I shall if I choose'. Let us take the former first, and concentrate upon the *if*. The dictionary tells us that the words from which our *if* is descended expressed, or even meant, 'doubt' or 'hesitation' or 'condition' or 'stipulation'. Of these, 'condition' has been given a prodigious innings by grammarians, lexicographers, and philosophers alike: it is time for 'doubt' and 'hesitation' to

---

[1] In general, though of course in some contexts it does: e.g. 'I may very easily ruin him, and I *shall* if I am extravagant', where 'shall' is stressed to point the contrast with 'may'.

be remembered, and these do indeed seem to be the notions present in 'I can if I choose'. We could give, on different occasions and in different contexts, many different interpretations of this sentence, which is of a somewhat primitive and *loose-jointed* type. Here are some:

> I can, quaere do I choose to?
> I can, but do I choose to?
> I can, but perhaps I don't choose to
> I can, but then I should have to choose to, and what about *that*?
> I can, but would it really be reasonable to choose to?
> I can, but whether I choose to is another question
> I can, I have only to choose to
> I can, in case I (should) choose to,
> and so on.

These interpretations are not, of course, all the same: which it is that we mean will usually be clear from the context (otherwise we should prefer another expression), but sometimes it can be brought out by stress, on the 'if' or the 'choose' for example. What is common to them all is simply that the *assertion*, positive and complete, that 'I can', is linked to the *raising of the question* whether I choose to, which may be relevant in a variety of ways.[1]

Ifs of the kind I have been trying to describe are common enough, for example the *if* in our example 'There are biscuits on the sideboard if you want them'. I do not know whether you want biscuits or not, but in case you do, I point out that there are some on the sideboard. It is tempting, I know, to 'expand' our sentence here to this: 'There are biscuits on the sideboard *which you can (or may) take* if you want them': but this, legitimate or not, will not make much difference, for we are still left with 'can (or may) if you want', which is (here) just like 'can

---

[1] If there were space, we should consider other germane expressions: e.g. 'I can do it or not as I choose', 'I can do whichever I choose' (*quidlibet*). In particular, 'I can whether I choose to or not' means 'I can, but whether I choose to or not is an open question': it does *not* mean 'I can on condition that I choose and likewise on condition that I don't', which is absurd.

if you choose' or 'can if you like', so that the *if* is still the *if* of doubt or hesitation, not the *if* of condition.[1]

I will mention two further points, very briefly, about 'I can if I choose', important but not so relevant to our discussion here. Sometimes the *can* will be the *can*, and the choice the choice, of legal or other *right*, at other times these words will refer to practicability or feasibility: consequently, we should sometimes interpret our sentence in some such way as 'I am entitled to do it (if I choose)', and at other times in some such way as 'I am capable of doing it (if I choose)'. We, of course, are concerned with interpretations of this second kind. It would be nice if we always said 'I *may* if I choose' when we wished to refer to our rights, as perhaps our nannies once told us to: but the interlocking histories of *can* and *may* are far too chequered for there to be any such rule in practice.[2] The second point is that *choose* is an important word in its own right, and needs careful interpretation: 'I can if I like' is not the same, although the 'can' and the 'if' may be the same in both, as 'I can if I choose'. Choice is always between alternatives, that is between several courses to be weighed in the same scale against each other, the one to be *preferred*. 'You can vote whichever way you choose' is different from 'You can vote whichever way you like'.

And now for something about 'I *shall* if I choose'—what sort of *if* have we here? The point to notice is, that 'I shall' is not an assertion of *fact* but an expression of *intention*, verging towards the giving of some variety of undertaking: and the *if*, conse-

[1] An account on these lines should probably be given also of an excellent example given to me by Mr. P. T. Geach: 'I paid you back yesterday, if you remember.' This is much the same as 'I paid you back yesterday, don't you remember?' It does not mean that your now remembering that I did so is a condition, causal or other, of my having paid you back yesterday.

[2] Formerly I believed that the meaning of 'I can if I choose' was something like 'I can, I have the choice', and that the point of the *if*-clause was to make clear that the 'can' in the main clause was the 'can' of right. This account, however, does not do justice to the role of the 'if', and also unduly restricts in general the meaning of 'choice'.

quently, is the *if* not of condition but of *stipulation*. In sentences like:

> I shall | marry him if I choose
> I intend | to marry him if I choose
> I promise | to marry him if he will have me

the *if*-clause is a part of the object phrase governed by the initial verb ('shall', 'intend', 'promise'), if this is an allowable way of putting it: or again, the *if* qualifies the *content* of the undertaking given, or of the intention announced, it does *not* qualify the giving of the undertaking. Why, we may ask, is it perverse to draw from 'I intend to marry him if I choose' the inference 'If I do not intend to marry him I do not choose to'? Because 'I intend to marry him if I choose' is not like 'I panted if I ran' in this important respect: 'I panted if I ran' does not assert anything 'categorically' about me—it does not assert that I did pant, and hence it is far from surprising to infer something. beginning 'If I did not pant': but 'I intend to marry him if I choose' (and the same goes for 'I shall marry him if I choose') *is* a 'categorical' expression of intention, and hence it is paradoxical to make an inference leading off with 'If I do *not* intend'.

3. Our third question was as to when we are entitled or required to supply *if*-clauses with *can* or *could have* as main verb.

Here there is one thing to be clear about at the start. There are *two* quite distinct and incompatible views that may be put forward concerning *if*s and *can*s, which are fatally easy to confuse with each other. One view is that wherever we have *can* or *could have* as our main verb, an *if*-clause must always be understood or supplied, if it is not actually present, in order to complete the sense of the sentence. The other view is that the meaning of 'can' or 'could have' can be more clearly reproduced by *some other verb* (notably 'shall' or 'should have') with an *if*-clause appended to *it*. The first view is that an *if* is required to *complete* a *can*-sentence: the second view is that an *if* is required in the *analysis* of a *can*-sentence. The suggestion of Moore that 'could have' means 'could have if I had chosen' is a suggestion of the first kind: but the suggestion also made by Moore that it means 'should have if I had chosen' is a suggestion of the second kind. It may be because it is so easy (apparently) to confuse these two kinds of theory that Moore was tempted to talk as though 'should have' could mean the same as 'could have'.

Now we are concerned at this moment solely with the *first* sort of view, namely that *can*-sentences are not complete without an *if*-clause. And if we think, as Moore was for the most part thinking, about 'could have' (rather than 'can'), it is easy to see why it may be tempting to allege that it always requires an *if*-clause with it. For it is natural to construe 'could have' as a past subjunctive or 'conditional', which is practically as much as to say that it needs a *conditional* clause with it. And of course it is quite true that 'could have' *may* be, and very often is, a past conditional: but it is *also* true that 'could have' may be and often is the *past (definite) indicative* of the verb *can*. Sometimes 'I could have' is equivalent to the Latin 'Potui' and means 'I *was* in a position to': sometimes it is equivalent to the Latin 'Potuissem' and means 'I *should have been* in a position to'. Exactly similar is the double role of 'could', which is sometimes a conditional meaning 'should be able to', but also sometimes a past indicative (indefinite) meaning 'was able to': no one can doubt this if he considers such contrasted examples as 'I could do it 20 years ago' and 'I could do it if I had a thingummy.' It is not so much that 'could' or 'could have' is ambiguous, as rather that two parts of the verb *can* take the same shape.

Once it is realized that 'could have' can be a past indicative, the general temptation to supply *if*-clauses with it vanishes: at least there is no more temptation to supply them with 'could have' than with 'can'. If we ask how a Roman would have said 'I could have ruined you this morning (although I didn't)', it is clear that he would have used 'potui', and that his sentence is complete without any conditional clause. But more than this, if he had wished to add 'if I had chosen', and however he had expressed that in Latin, he would still not have changed his 'potui' to 'potuissem': but this is precisely what he *would* have done if he had been tacking on some other, more 'normal' kind of *if*-clause, such as 'if I had had one more vote'.[1]

That is to say, the 'could have' in 'could have if I had chosen' is a past indicative, *not* a past conditional, despite the fact that there is what would, I suppose, be called a 'conditional' clause, that is an *if*-clause, with it. And this is, of course, why we can make the inferences that, as we saw, we can make from 'I could have if I had chosen', notably the inference to 'I could have' absolutely. Hence we see how mistaken Moore was in contrasting 'I could have if I had chosen' with the 'absolute' sense of 'I could have': we might almost go so far as to say that the addition of the 'conditional' clause 'if I had chosen' makes it certain that (in Moore's language) the sense of 'could have' is the absolute sense, or as I should prefer to put it, that the mood of 'could have' is indicative.

It might at this point be worth considering in general whether it makes sense to suppose that a language could contain any verb such as *can* has been argued or implied to be, namely one that can never occur without an *if*-clause appended to it. At least if the *if* is the normal 'conditional' *if* this would seem very difficult. For let the verb in question be *to X*: then we shall never say simply 'I X', but always 'I X if I Y': but then also, according to the accepted rules, if it is true that 'I X if I Y', and *also* true (which it must surely sometimes be) that 'I do, in fact, Y', it must surely follow that 'I X', simpliciter, without any *if* about it any longer. Perhaps this was the 'possible complication' that led Moore to switch from the suggestion that 'I could have' (in one sense) has always to be *expanded* to 'I could have if' to the suggestion that it has always to be *analysed* as 'I should have if':

[1] If the *if*-clause is 'if I had chosen', then I *was* able, *was* actually in a position, to ruin you: hence 'potui'. But if the *if*-clause expresses a genuine *unfulfilled condition*, then plainly I was *not* actually in a position to ruin you, hence not 'potui' but 'potuissem'. My colleague Mr. R. M. Nisbet has pointed out to me the interesting discussion of this point in S. A. Handford, *The Latin Subjunctive*, pp. 130 ff. It is interesting that although this author well appreciates the Latin usage, he still takes it for granted that in English the 'could have' is universally subjunctive or conditional.

for of course the argument I have just given does not suffice to show that there could not be some verb which has always to be *analysed* as something containing a conditional *if*-clause: suggestions that this is in fact the case with some verbs are common in philosophy, and I do not propose to argue this point, though I think that doubt might well be felt about it. The only sort of 'verb' I can think of that might always demand a conditional clause with it is an 'auxiliary' verb, if there is one, which is used solely to form subjunctive or conditional moods (whatever exactly they may be) of other verbs: but however this may be, it is quite clear that *can*, and I should be prepared also to add *shall* and *will* and *may*, are not in this position.

To summarize, then, what has been here said in reply to Moore's suggestions in his book:

(a) 'I could have if I had chosen' does not mean the same as 'I should have if I had chosen'.

(b) In neither of these expressions is the *if*-clause a 'normal conditional' clause, connecting antecedent to consequent as cause to effect.

(c) To argue that *can* always requires an *if*-clause with it to complete the sense is totally different from arguing that *can*-sentences are always to be analysed into sentences containing *if*-clauses.

(d) Neither *can* nor any other verb always requires a conditional *if*-clause after it: even 'could have', when a past indicative, does not require such a clause: and in 'I could have if I had chosen' the verb is in fact a past indicative, not a past subjunctive or conditional.

Even, however, if all these contentions are true so far, we must recognize that it may nevertheless still be the case that *can*, *could*, and *could have*, even when used as indicatives, are to be analysed as meaning *shall*, *should*, and *should have*, used as auxiliaries of tense or mood with another verb (i.e. so as to make that other verb into a future or subjunctive), followed by a conditional *if*-clause. There is some plausibility,[1] for example, in the suggestion that 'I can do X' means 'I shall succeed in doing X, if I try' and 'I could have done X' means 'I should have succeeded in doing X, if I had tried'.

It is indeed odd that Moore should have plumped so simply, in giving his account whether of the necessary supplementation or of the analysis of 'could have', for the one particular *if*-clause 'if I had chosen', which happens to be particularly exposed to the above objections, without even mentioning the possibility of invoking other *if*-clauses, at least in some cases. Perhaps the reason was that *choose* (a word itself much in need of discussion) presented itself as well fitted to bridge the gulf between determinists and free-willers, which *try* might not so readily do. But as a matter of fact Moore does himself at one point give an analysis of 'I could have done X' which is different in an interesting way from his usual version, although confusible with it. At a crucial point in his argument, he chooses for his example 'The ship could have gone faster', and the suggestion is made that this is equivalent to 'The ship *would* have gone faster *if her officers had chosen*'. This may well seem plausible, but so far from being in line, as Moore apparently thinks, with his general analysis, it differs from it in two important respects:

---

[1] Plausibility, but no more. Consider the case where I miss a very short putt and kick myself because I could have holed it. It is not that I should have holed it if I had tried: I did try, and missed. It is not that I should have holed it if conditions had been different: that might of course be so, but I am talking about conditions as they precisely were, and asserting that I could have holed it. There is the rub. Nor does 'I can hole it this time' mean that I shall hole it this time if I try or if anything else: for I may try and miss, and yet not be convinced that I could not have done it; indeed, further experiments may confirm my belief that I could have done it that time although I did not.

But if I tried my hardest, say, and missed, surely there *must* have been *something* that caused me to fail, that made me unable to succeed? So that I *could not* have holed it. Well, a modern belief in science, in there being an explanation of everything, may make us assent to this argument. But such a belief is not in line with the traditional beliefs enshrined in the word *can*: according to *them*, a human ability or power or capacity is inherently liable not to produce success, on occasion, and that for no reason (or are bad luck and bad form sometimes reasons?).

(a) the subject of the *if*-clause ('her officers') is different from the subject of the main clause ('the ship'), the subject of the original sentence:

(b) the verb in the *if*-clause following 'chosen' is different from the verb in the main clause, the verb in the original sentence. We do not readily observe this because of the ellipsis after 'chosen': but plainly the verb must be, not 'to go faster', but 'to make her go faster' or, for example, 'to open the throttle'.

These two features are dictated by the fact that a ship is inanimate. We do not wish seriously to ascribe free will to inanimate objects, and the 'could' of the original sentence is perhaps only justifiable (as opposed to 'might') because it is readily realized that some person's free will is in question.

If we follow up the lines of this new type of analysis, we should have to examine the relations between 'I could have won' and 'I could, or should, have won if I had chosen to lob' and 'I could, or should, have won if he had chosen to lob'. I will do no more here than point out that the difference between 'could' and 'should' remains as before, and that the sense of 'I could have won', if it really is one, in which it means something of the sort 'I should have won if he had chosen to lob' or 'to let me win' (the parallel to the ship example), is of little importance—the 'if' here is of course the conditional *if*.

It is time now to turn to a second discussion of *ifs* and *cans*. Quite recently my colleague Mr. Nowell-Smith, in another little book called *Ethics*, also reaches a point in his argument at which he has to examine the sentence 'He could have acted otherwise', that is, could have done something that he did not in fact do. His reason for doing so is that, unless we can truly say this of people, we might find ourselves unable to blame people for things, and this would be generally regretted. This reason is not unrelated to Moore's reason for embarking on his earlier discussion, and Nowell-Smith's views show some resemblances to Moore's: perhaps this is because Nowell-Smith, like Moore at the time he wrote his book is willing, if not anxious, to come to terms with determinism.

Nowell-Smith begins his discussion by saying (p. 274) that ' "could have" is a modal phrase, and modal phrases are not normally used to make categorical statements'. I am not myself at all sure what exactly a 'modal phrase' is, so I cannot discuss this assertion: but I do not think this matters, because he proceeds to give us two other examples of modal phrases, viz. 'might have' and 'would have',[1] and to tell us first what they are not (which I omit) and then what they are:

'Would have' and 'might have' are clearly suppressed hypotheticals, incomplete without an 'if . . .' or an 'if . . . not . . .'. Nobody would say 'Jones would have won the championship' unless (a) he believed that Jones did not win and (b) he was prepared to add 'if he had entered' or 'if he had not sprained his ankle' or some such clause.

Here (a) is actually incorrect—we can say 'Jones would (still) have won the championship, (even) if Hagen had entered'—but this does not concern us. (b), however, seems to be fairly correct, at least as far as concerns 'would have' (in the case of 'might have' it might well be doubted[2]). So we have it that, when Nowell-Smith says that 'would have' is a 'suppressed hypo-

---

[1] Also perhaps 'may have', for he discusses 'It *might* have rained last Thursday' in terms that seem really to apply to 'It *may* have rained last Thursday'.

[2] I refrain here from questioning it in the case of 'would have'. Yet 'would' is agreed to be often a past indicative of the old verb *will*, requiring no *if*-clause: and I think myself that in, say, 'X would have hanged him, but Y was against it' 'would have' is likewise a past indicative—indeed it is from this sort of example that we can see how the past tenses of *will* have come to be used as auxiliaries of mood for forming the conditionals of other verbs.

To state what seem to be some grammatical facts (omitting all reference to the use of the words concerned in expressing wishes):

Could have is sometimes a past indicative, sometimes a past subjunctive of the verb *can*. When it is the main verb and is a subjunctive, it does require a conditional clause with it. *Can* and its parts are *not* used as auxiliaries of tense or mood to form tenses or moods of other verbs.

Would have, whether or not it is used as a past indicative or subjunctive of the verb *will*, is now commonly used (*should have* in the first person) as an auxiliary for forming the past subjunctive of other verbs: hence if it is the main verb it does in general require a conditional clause with it.

thetical' he means that it requires the addition of an *if*-clause to complete the sense. And he goes on to say that 'could have' sentences also (though not so obviously) 'express hypotheticals', if not always at least in important cases, such as notably those where we say someone could have done something he did not actually do: in these cases 'could have' . . . is equivalent to 'would have . . . if . . .'.

It will be clear at once that Nowell-Smith, like Moore, is not distinguishing between the contention that 'could have' *requires supplementation by* an *if*-clause and the quite different contention that *its analysis contains* an *if*-clause.[1] On the whole it seems plain that it is the second (analysis) view that he wishes to argue for: but the argument he produces is that 'could have' is (in important cases) like 'would have', the point about which is that it needs an *if*-clause to complete it—as though this, which is an argument in favour of the *first* view, told in favour of the second view. But it cannot possibly do so: and in any event *could have* is liable, as we have already seen, to be in important cases a past indicative, so that the contention that it is like *would have* in requiring a conditional *if*-clause is unfounded.

Nevertheless, it must be allowed that Nowell-Smith may still be right in urging that 'could have' *means* 'would have if' and that, as he eventually adds, 'can' means 'will if'. What has he to say in support of this?

He propounds two examples for discussion, which I think do not differ greatly, so I shall quote only the first. Here it is:

He could have read *Emma* in bed last night, though he actually read *Persuasion*; but he could not have read *Werther*, because he does not know German.

---

[1] It is true that he uses two different expressions: 'would have' *is* a (suppressed) hypothetical, while 'could have' sentences *express* hypotheticals. But it does not look as if any distinction is intended, and if it is, the protracted initial analogy between 'could have' and 'would have' seems irrelevant and misleading. Moreover, discussing the (unimportant) case of 'It could have been a Morris', he writes that 'it would be absurd to ask under what conditions it *could or would* have been a Morris' (my italics): this seems to show an indifference to the distinction that I am insisting on.

This is evidently of the same kind as Moore's 20-minute-mile example. The first thing that Nowell-Smith urges is that such a 'could have' statement is not a categorical, or a 'straight-forward' categorical, statement. And his argument in favour of this view is derived from the way in which we should establish its truth or falsity. No inspection of what the man actually did will, he says, verify directly that he could have done something else (here, read *Emma*) which he did not do: rather, we should, to establish this, have to show

(a) that he has performed tasks of similar difficulty sufficiently often to preclude the possibility of a fluke, and (b) that nothing prevented him on this occasion. For example, we should have to establish that there was a copy of *Emma* in the house.

To refute it, on the other hand, we should have to show either 'that some necessary condition was absent' (there was no copy of *Emma*)' or 'that the capacity was absent'. That is, let us say, we have to show on the one hand that he had both the ability and the opportunity to read *Emma*, or on the other hand that he lacked either the ability or the opportunity.

Nowell-Smith seems, at least at first, to be less interested in the matter of opportunity: for he says that we can establish 'directly', i.e. by considering what the facts at the time actually were, at least that he did *not* have the opportunity, that is, that something did prevent him, and he does not seem daunted by the obviously greater difficulty of establishing, in order to establish that he *could* have done it, the general negative that *there was nothing* to prevent him. At any rate, it is at first upon our manner of establishing that he had (or had not) the *ability* to do this thing that he did not do that Nowell-Smith fastens in order to support his assertion that the 'could have' statement is not categorical. That the man had the *ability* to read *Emma* can *not*, he says, be established 'directly', i.e. by observing what happened on that past occasion, but only by considering what prowess he has displayed in the face of similar tasks in the past on other occasions, or displays now when put to the test: the argument that we have perforce to use is an 'inductive' one (and, he adds, none the worse for that).

Now let us pass all this, at least for the sake of argument.[1] What interests us is to discover why Nowell-Smith thinks that these considerations show that 'He had the ability to read *Emma*' is not a categorical statement. I confess I fail to follow the argument:

The very fact that evidence for or against 'could have' statements must be drawn from occasions other than that to which they refer is enough to show that 'He could have acted otherwise' is not a straightforward categorical statement.

But do we really know what is meant by a 'straightforward categorical statement'? Certainly it is not the case that statements made on the strength of inductive evidence are in general not categorical—for example, the statement that the next mule born will prove sterile: this seems categorical enough. Perhaps this example should be ruled out as not in point, on the ground that here there *will some day* be 'direct' evidence relevant to the assertion, even if it is not available at the moment. Could the same, I wonder, be said of the inductive conclusion 'All mules are sterile'? Or is that not categorical? I know that this has been interpreted by some philosophers to mean 'If anything is a mule then it is sterile', but I see no reason to support that curious interpretation.

The situation becomes still more puzzling when we remember that Nowell-Smith is about to generalize his theory, and to assert, not merely that 'could have' means 'would have . . . if', but also that 'can' means 'shall or will . . . if'. Suppose then that I assert 'I can here and now lift my finger,' and translate this as 'I shall lift my finger if . . .': then surely this will be 'directly' verified if the conditions are satisfied and I do proceed to lift the

[1] Yet I think it is not hard to see that we cannot establish 'directly', at least in many cases, that something 'prevented' him: he was drugged or dazzled, which prevented him from reading, which establishes that he could not have read—but how do we know that being drugged or dazzled 'prevents' people from reading? Surely on 'inductive' evidence? And, in short, to be prevented is to be rendered unable.

finger? If this is correct, and if the theory is indeed a general one, then there seems to be no point in insisting on the non-availability of 'direct' evidence, which is only a feature of certain cases. Incidentally, it is not in fact the case that to say 'He could have done it' is always used in a way to imply that he did not in fact do it: we make a list of the suspects in a murder case, all of whom we think could have done it and one of whom we think did do it. True, this is not Nowell-Smith's case: but unless we are prepared to assert that the 'could have' in his case differs in meaning from that in the murder case, and so to rule out the latter as irrelevant, we are in danger of having to admit that even 'could have' sentences can be 'directly' verified in favourable cases. For study of the facts of that past occasion can prove to us that he did it, and hence that our original 'He could have' was correct.[1]

However, to proceed. Whether or not we should describe our conclusion here as 'categorical' it seems that it should still be a conclusion of the form 'he *could* have done so and so', and not in the least a conclusion concerning what he *would* have done. We are interested, remember, in his abilities: we want to know whether he could have read *Emma* yesterday: we ascertain that he did read it the day before yesterday, and that he does read it today: we conclude that he could have read it yesterday. But it does not appear that this says anything about what he *would* have done yesterday or in what circumstances: certainly, we are now convinced, he *could* have read it yesterday, but *would* he have, considering that he had read it only the day before? Moreover, supposing the view is that our conclusion is not of the 'could have' but of the 'would have if' form, nothing has yet been said to establish this, nor to tell us what follows the 'if'. To establish that he would have read it yesterday

---

[1] There are, I should myself think, good reasons for not speaking of 'I can lift my finger' as being directly verified when I proceed to lift it, and likewise for not speaking of 'He could have done it' as being directly verified by the discovery that he did do it. But on Nowell-Smith's account I think that these would count as direct verifications.

if . . ., we shall need evidence not merely as to his abilities and opportunities, but also as to his character, motives, and so on.

It may indeed be thought, and it seems that Nowell-Smith does at least partly think this, that what follows the 'if' should be suppliable from the consideration that to say he could have, in the full sense, is to say not merely that he had the ability, which is what we have hitherto concentrated on, but also that he had the *opportunity*. For to establish *this*, do we not have to establish that certain *conditions* were satisfied, as for instance that there was a copy of *Emma* available? Very well. But here there is surely a confusion: we allow that, in saying that he could have, I do assert or imply that certain *conditions*, those of opportunity, *were satisfied*: but this is totally different from allowing that, in saying that he could have, I *assert something conditional*. It is, certainly, entirely possible to assert something conditional such as 'he could have read *Emma* yesterday if there had been a copy available', *could* being then of course a subjunctive: but to say this sort of thing is precisely not to say the sort of thing that we say when we say 'He could have acted otherwise', where 'could have' is an indicative—implying, as we now do, that there was no copy available, we imply that *pro tanto* he could *not* have acted otherwise. And the same will be true if we try saying 'He would have read *Emma* yesterday if there had been a copy available': this too certainly implies that he could not in fact have read it, and so cannot by any means be what we mean by saying that he could have read it.

In the concluding paragraph of his discussion, Nowell-Smith does finally undertake to give us his analysis not merely of 'could have', but also of 'can' (which he says means 'will if'). And this last feature is very much to be welcomed, because if an analysis is being consciously given of 'can' at least we shall at length be clear of confusions connected with the idea that 'could have' is necessarily a subjunctive.[1]

---

[1] It must, however, be pointed out once again that if we are to discuss the assertion that somebody *can* (now) do something, the previous arguments that our assertions are not categorical because they are based on induction and

The argument of the last paragraph runs as follows. It is 'logically odd' to say something of this kind (I am slightly emending Nowell-Smith's formula, but only in ways that are favourable to it and demanded by his own argument):

Smith has the ability to run a mile, has the opportunity to run a mile, has a preponderant motive for running a mile, but does not in fact do so.

From this it follows directly, says Nowell-Smith, that 'can' means 'will if', that is, I suppose, that 'Smith can run a mile' *means* 'If Smith has the opportunity to run a mile and a preponderant motive for running it, he will run it'.

It seems, however, plain that nothing of the kind follows. This may be seen first by setting the argument out formally. Nowell-Smith's premiss is of the form

Not (p and q and r and not -s)

that is

Logically odd (ability+opportunity+motive+non-action).

Now from this we can indeed infer

$p \supset ((q \text{ and } r) \supset s),$

that is that

If he has the ability, then, if he has the opportunity and the motive, he will do it.

But we can*not infer* the converse

$((q \text{ and } r) \supset s) \supset p,$

or in other words that

If, when he has the opportunity and the motive, he does it, he has the ability to do it.

(I do not say this last is not something to which we should,

cannot be verified directly, whether they were good or not, must now be abandoned: because of course it *is* possible to verify this 'directly' by the method Nowell-Smith has specified in another connexion earlier, viz. by getting the man to try and seeing him succeed.

when so put into English, assent, only that it does not follow from Nowell-Smith's premiss: of course it follows merely from the premiss that he does it, that he has the ability to do it, according to ordinary English.) But unless this second, converse implication *does* follow, we cannot, according to the usual formal principles, infer that *p* is *equivalent* to, nor therefore that it means the same as, (*q* and *r*) ⊃ *s*, or in words that ability *means* that opportunity plus motive leads to action.

To put the same point non-formally. From the fact that, if three things are true together a fourth must also be true, we cannot argue that one of the three things *simply means* that if the other two are true the fourth will be true. If we could argue indeed in this way, then we should establish, from Nowell-Smith's premiss, not merely that

'He has the ability to do X' simply means that 'If he has the opportunity and the motive to do X, he will do X'

but also equally that

'He has the opportunity to do X' *simply means* that 'If he has the ability and the motive to do X, he will do X'

and likewise that

'He has a preponderant motive to do X' *simply means* that 'If he has the ability and the opportunity to do X, he will do X'.

For clearly we can perform the same operations on *q* and *r* as on *p*, since the three all occupy parallel positions in the premiss. But these are fantastic suggestions. Put shortly, Nowell-Smith is pointing out in his premiss that if a man both can and wants to (more than he wants to do anything else), he will: but from this it does not follow that 'he can' *simply means* that 'if he wants to he will'. Nowell-Smith is struggling to effect a transition from *can* to *will* which presents difficulties as great as those of the transition from *could* to *would*: he puts up his show of effecting it by importing the additional, and here irrelevant, concept of motive, which needless to say is in general very intimately connected with the question of what 'he will' do.

When, in conclusion, Nowell-Smith finally sets out his analysis of 'Smith could have read *Emma* last night', it is this:

He would have read it, if there had been a copy, if he had not been struck blind, &c., &c., and if he had wanted to read it more than he had wanted to read ⟨this should be 'do'⟩ anything else.

But so far from this being what we mean by saying he could have read it, it actually implies that he could *not* have read it, for more than adequate reasons: it implies that he was blind at the time, and so on. Here we see that Nowell-Smith actually does make the confusion I referred to above between a statement which implies or asserts that certain conditions *were* fulfilled and a conditional statement, i.e. a statement about what would have happened if those conditions had been fulfilled. This is unfortunately a confusion of a general kind that is not uncommon: I need only mention the classic instance of Keynes, who confused asserting on evidence h that p is probable with asserting that on evidence h p is probable, both of which can be ambiguously expressed by 'asserting that p is probable on evidence h', but only the former of which asserts that p is (really) probable. Here similarly there is a confusion between asserting on the supposition (or premiss) that he had a copy that he could/would have read it, and asserting that on the supposition that he had a copy he could/would have read it, both of which can be ambiguously expressed by 'asserting that he could/would have read it on the supposition that he had a copy', but only the former of which asserts that he (actually) could have read it.

To some extent, then, we learn from studying Nowell-Smith's arguments lessons similar to those that we learned in the case of Moore. But some are new, as for instance that many assertions about what a man *would have* done or *will do* depend, in critical cases, upon premisses about his *motives* as well as, or rather than, about his abilities or opportunities: hence these assertions cannot be what assertions about his abilities *mean*.[1]

[1] Yet here it must be pointed out once more that it has not been shown that *all* assertions about what he would have done are so dependent, so that this

On one point I may perhaps elaborate a little further. It has been maintained that *sometimes* when we say 'He could have done X' this is a conditional: it requires completion by an *if*-clause, typically 'if he had had the opportunity', and so does *not* require us, if we are to establish its truth, to establish that he did in fact have the opportunity. Sometimes on the other hand it is a past indicative, implying that he did have the opportunity: in which case we do, to establish its truth, have to establish that certain conditions were satisfied, but the assertion is *not* to be described as a conditional assertion.

Now while I have no wish to retract this account in general or in all cases, I doubt whether it is the whole story. Consider the case where what we wish to assert is that somebody had the opportunity to do something but lacked the ability—'He could have smashed that lob, if he had been any good at the smash': here the *if*-clause, which may of course be suppressed and understood, relates not to opportunity but to ability. Now although we might describe the whole sentence as 'conditional', it nevertheless manages to assert, by means of its main clause, something 'categorical' enough, viz. that he did have a certain opportunity. And in the same way Nowell-Smith's 'He could have read *Emma*, if he had had a copy', does seem to assert 'categorically' that he had a certain ability, although he lacked the opportunity to exercise it. Looking at it in this way, there is a temptation to say that 'could have' has, besides its 'all-in' *sense* several more *restricted senses*: this would be brought out if we said 'He could have smashed it, *only* he is no good at the smash' or 'He could have read *Emma* but he had no copy', where, we should say, 'could have' is being used in the restricted senses of opportunity or of ability[1] only, and is a past indicative, not a past conditional.

particular argument against the analysis of 'could have' as 'would have if' is not conclusive: in particular, it does not dispose of the possible suggestion that 'could have' means 'would have if he had *tried*', for here considerations of motive may be irrelevant.

[1] I talk here and throughout of 'ability' and 'opportunity' only: but I realize that other abstract nouns like 'capacity', 'skill', and even 'right' are

This view might be reinforced by considering examples with the simple 'can' itself. We are tempted to say that 'He can' sometimes means just that he has the ability, with *nothing said* about opportunity, sometimes *just* that he has the chance, with nothing said about ability, sometimes, however, that he really actually *fully can* here and now, having both ability and opportunity. Now nobody, I think, would be tempted to say that 'can,' where it means one of the two lesser things, for example, 'has the opportunity', i.e. 'can in the full sense if he has the ability', is grammatically a subjunctive or conditional. Perhaps, then, it was not correct to describe 'He could have', either, as always a conditional where it asserts ability or opportunity only, with nothing said about the other, or even where the other is denied to have existed.

The verb *can* is a peculiar one. Let us compare it for a moment with another peculiar verb, *know*, with which it shares some grammatical peculiarities, such as lack of a continuous present tense. When I say that somebody *knows* what the thing in my hand is, I may mean merely that he has the ability to identify it given the opportunity, or that he has the opportunity to identify it if he has the ability, or that he has both. What do we say about *know* here? Certainly we are not prone to invoke the idea of a conditional, but rather that of different senses, or perhaps the still obscure idea of the dispositional. I must be content here merely to say that I do not think that the old armoury of terms, such as 'mood' and 'sense', is altogether adequate for handling such awkward cases. The only point of which I feel certain is that such verbs as *can* and *know* have each an all-in, paradigm use, around which cluster and from which divagate, little by little and along different paths, a whole series of other uses, for many of which, though perhaps not for all, a synonymous expression ('opportunity', 'realize', and so on) can be found.

It is not unusual for an audience at a lecture to include some

equally involved. All these terms need listing and elucidating before we really get to grips with 'can'.

who prefer things to be important, and to them now, in case
there are any such present, there is owed a peroration. Why, in
short, does all this matter? First, then, it needs no emphasizing
that both *if* and *can* are highly prevalent and protean words,
perplexing both grammatically and philosophically: it is not
merely worth while, but essential, in these studies to discover
the facts about *if*s and *can*s, and to remove the confusions they
engender. In philosophy it is *can* in particular that we seem so
often to uncover, just when we had thought some problem
settled, grinning residually up at us like the frog at the bottom
of the beer mug. Furthermore and secondly, we have not here
been dissecting these two words in general or completely, but
in a special connexion which perhaps no one will hold trivial.
It has been alleged by very serious philosophers (not only the
two I have mentioned) that the things we ordinarily say about
what we can do and could have done may actually be consistent with determinism. It is hard to evade all attempt to
decide whether this allegation is true—hard even for those who,
like myself, are inclined to think that determinism itself is still
a name for nothing clear, that has been argued for only in-
coherently. At least I should like to claim that the arguments
considered tonight fail to show that it *is* true, and indeed in
failing go some way to show that it is *not*. Determinism, whatever it may be, may yet be the case, but at least it appears not
consistent with what we ordinarily say and presumably think.
And finally there is a third point. Reflecting on the arguments
in this lecture, we may well ask ourselves whether they might
not be as well assigned to grammar as to philosophy: and this,
I think, is a salutary question to end on. There are constant
references in contemporary philosophy, which notoriously is
much concerned with language, to a 'logical grammar' and a
'logical syntax' as though these were things distinct from ordinary grammarian's grammar and syntax: and certainly they do
seem, whatever exactly they may be, different from traditional
grammar. But grammar today is itself in a state of flux; for fifty
years or more it has been questioned on all hands and counts

whether what Dionysius Thrax once thought was the truth about Greek is the truth and the whole truth about all language and all languages. Do we know, then, that there will prove to be any ultimate boundary between 'logical grammar' and a revised and enlarged *Grammar*? In the history of human inquiry, philosophy has the place of the initial central sun, seminal and tumultuous: from time to time it throws off some portion of itself to take station as a science, a planet, cool and well regulated, progressing steadily towards a distant final state. This happened long ago at the birth of mathematics, and again at the birth of physics: only in the last century we have witnessed the same process once again, slow and at the time almost imperceptible, in the birth of the science of mathematical logic, through the joint labours of philosophers and mathematicians. Is it not possible that the next century may see the birth, through the joint labours of philosophers, grammarians, and numerous other students of language, of a true and comprehensive *science of language*? Then we shall have rid ourselves of one more part of philosophy (there will still be plenty left) in the only way we ever can get rid of philosophy, by kicking it upstairs.

PERFORMATIVE UTTERANCES

I

You are more than entitled not to know what the word 'performative' means. It is a new word and an ugly word, and perhaps it does not mean anything very much. But at any rate there is one thing in its favour, it is not a profound word. I remember once when I had been talking on this subject that somebody afterwards said: 'You know, I haven't the least idea what he means, unless it could be that he simply means what he says'. Well, that is what I should like to mean.

Let us consider first how this affair arises. We have not got to go very far back in the history of philosophy to find philosophers assuming more or less as a matter of course that the sole business, the sole interesting business, of any utterance—that is, of anything we say—is to be true or at least false. Of course they had always known that there are other kinds of things which we say—things like imperatives, the expressions of wishes, and exclamations—some of which had even been classified by grammarians, though it wasn't perhaps too easy to tell always which was which. But still philosophers have assumed that the only things that they are interested in are utterances which report facts or which describe situations truly or falsely. In recent times this kind of approach has been questioned—in two stages, I think. First of all people began to say: 'Well, if these things are true or false it ought to be possible to decide which they are, and if we can't decide which they are they aren't any good but are, in short, nonsense'. And this new approach did a great deal of good; a great many things which probably are nonsense were found to be such. It is not the case, I think, that all kinds of nonsense have been adequately classified yet, and perhaps some things have been dismissed as nonsense which really are not; but still this movement, the verification movement, was, in its way, excellent.

However, we then come to the second stage. After all, we set some limits to the amount of nonsense that we talk, or at least the amount of nonsense that we are prepared to admit we talk; and so people began to ask whether after all some of those things which, treated as statements, were in danger of being dismissed as nonsense did after all really set out to be statements at all. Mightn't they perhaps be intended not to report facts but to influence people in this way or that, or to let off steam in this way or that? Or perhaps at any rate some elements in these utterances performed such functions, or, for example, drew attention in some way (without actually reporting it) to some important feature of the circumstances in which the utterance was being made. On these lines people have now adopted a new slogan, the slogan of the 'different uses of language'. The old approach, the old statemental approach, is sometimes called even a fallacy, the descriptive fallacy.

Certainly there are a great many uses of language. It's rather a pity that people are apt to invoke a new use of language whenever they feel so inclined, to help them out of this, that, or the other well-known philosophical tangle; we need more of a framework in which to discuss these uses of language; and also I think we should not despair too easily and talk, as people are apt to do, about the *infinite* uses of language. Philosophers will do this when they have listed as many, let us say, as seventeen; but even if there were something like ten thousand uses of language, surely we could list them all in time. This, after all, is no larger than the number of species of beetle that entomologists have taken the pains to list. But whatever the defects of either of these movements—the 'verification' movement or the 'use of language' movement—at any rate they have effected, nobody could deny, a great revolution in philosophy and, many would say, the most salutary in its history. (Not, if you come to think of it, a very immodest claim.)

Now it is one such sort of use of language that I want to examine here. I want to discuss a kind of utterance which looks like a statement and grammatically, I suppose, would be classed as a statement, which is not nonsensical, and yet is not true or false. These are not going to be utterances which contain curious verbs like 'could' or 'might', or curious words like 'good', which many philosophers regard nowadays simply as danger signals. They will be perfectly straightforward utterances, with ordinary verbs in the first person singular present indicative active, and yet we shall see at once that they couldn't possibly be true or false. Furthermore, if a person makes an utterance of this sort we should say that he is *doing* something rather than merely *saying* something. This may sound a little odd, but the examples I shall give will in fact not be odd at all, and may even seem decidedly dull. Here are three or four. Suppose, for example, that in the course of a marriage ceremony I say, as people will, 'I do'—(sc. take this woman to be my lawful wedded wife). Or again, suppose that I tread on your toe and say 'I apologize'. Or again, suppose that I have the bottle of champagne in my hand and say 'I name this ship the *Queen Elizabeth*'. Or suppose I say 'I bet you sixpence it will rain tomorrow'. In all these cases it would be absurd to regard the thing that I say as a report of the performance of the action which is undoubtedly done—the action of betting, or christening, or apologizing. We should say rather that, in saying what I do, I actually perform that action. When I say 'I name this ship the *Queen Elizabeth*' I do not describe the christening ceremony, I actually perform the christening; and when I say 'I do' (sc. take this woman to be my lawful wedded wife), I am not reporting on a marriage, I am indulging in it.

Now these kinds of utterance are the ones that we call *performative* utterances. This is rather an ugly word, and a new word, but there seems to be no word already in existence to do the job. The nearest approach that I can think of is the word 'operative', as used by lawyers. Lawyers when talking about legal instruments will distinguish between the preamble, which recites the circumstances in which a transaction is effected, and on the other hand the operative part—the part of it which actually performs the legal act which it is the purpose of the instrument to perform. So the word 'operative' is very near to what we want. 'I give and bequeath my watch to my brother' would be an operative clause and is a performative utterance. However, the word 'operative' has other uses, and it seems preferable to have a word specially designed for the use we want.

Now at this point one might protest, perhaps even with some alarm, that I seem to be suggesting that marrying is simply saying a few words, that just saying a few words *is* marrying. Well, that certainly is not the case. The words have to be said in the appropriate circumstances, and this is a matter that will come up again later. But the one thing we must not suppose is that what is needed in addition to the saying of the words in such cases is the performance of some internal spiritual act, of which the words then are to be the report. It's very easy to slip into this view at least in difficult, portentous cases, though perhaps not so easy in simple cases like apologizing. In the case of promising—for example, 'I promise to be there tomorrow'—it's very easy to think that the utterance is simply the outward and visible (that is, verbal) sign of the performance of some inward spiritual act of promising, and this view has certainly been expressed in many classic places. There is the case of Euripides' Hippolytus, who said 'My tongue swore to, but my heart did not'—perhaps it should be 'mind' or 'spirit' rather than 'heart', but at any rate some kind of backstage artiste. Now it is clear from this sort of example that, if we slip into thinking that such utterances are reports, true or false, of the performance of inward and spiritual acts, we open a loophole to perjurers and welshers and bigamists and so on, so that there are disadvantages in being excessively solemn in this way. It is better, perhaps, to stick to the old saying that our word is our bond.

However, although these utterances do not themselves report facts and are not themselves true or false, saying these things does very often *imply* that certain things are true and not false, in some sense at least of that rather woolly word 'imply'. For example, when I say 'I do take this woman to be my lawful wedded wife', or some other formula in the marriage ceremony, I do imply that I'm not already married, with wife living, sane, undivorced, and the rest of it. But still it is very important to realize that to imply that something or other is true, is not at all the same as saying something which is true itself.

These performative utterances are not true or false, then. But they do suffer from certain disabilities of their own. They can fail to come off in special ways, and that is what I want to consider next. The various ways in which a performative utterance may be unsatisfactory we call, for the sake of a name, the infelicities; and an infelicity arises—that is to say, the utterance is unhappy—if certain rules, transparently simple rules, are broken. I will mention some of these rules and then give examples of some infringements.

First of all, it is obvious that the conventional procedure which by our utterance we are purporting to use must actually exist. In the examples given here this procedure will be a verbal one, a verbal procedure for marrying or giving or whatever it may be; but it should be borne in mind that there are many non-verbal procedures by which we can perform exactly the same acts as we perform by these verbal means. It's worth remembering too that a great many of the things we do are at least in part of this conventional kind. Philosophers at least are too apt to assume that an action is always in the last resort the making of a physical movement, whereas it's usually, at least in part, a matter of convention.

The first rule is, then, that the convention invoked must exist and be accepted. And the second rule, also a very obvious one, is that the circumstances in which we purport to invoke this procedure must be appropriate for its invocation. If this is not observed, then the act that we purport to perform would not come off—it will be, one might say, a misfire. This will also be the case if, for example, we do not carry through the procedure—whatever it may be—correctly and completely, without a flaw and without a hitch. If any of these rules are not observed, we say that the act which we purported to perform is void, without effect. If, for example, the purported act was an act of marrying, then we should say that we 'went through a form' of marriage, but we did not actually succeed in marrying.

Here are some examples of this kind of misfire. Suppose that, living in a country like our own, we wish to divorce our wife. We may try standing her in front of us squarely in the room and saying, in a voice loud enough for all to hear, 'I divorce you'. Now this procedure is not accepted. We shall not thereby have succeeded in divorcing our wife, at least in this country and others like it. This is a case where the convention,.we should say, does not exist or is not accepted. Again, suppose that, picking sides at a children's party, I say 'I pick George'. But George turns red in the face and says 'Not playing'. In that case I plainly, for some reason or another, have not picked George—whether because there is no convention that you can pick people who aren't playing, or because George in the circumstances is an inappropriate object for the procedure of picking. Or consider the case in which I say 'I appoint you Consul', and it turns out that you have been appointed already—or perhaps it may even transpire that you are a horse; here again we have the infelicity of inappropriate circumstances, inappropriate objects, or what not. Examples of flaws and hitches are perhaps scarcely necessary—one party in the marriage ceremony says 'I will', the other says 'I won't'; I say 'I bet sixpence', but nobody says 'Done', nobody takes up the offer. In all these and other such cases, the act which we purport to perform, or set out to perform, is not achieved.

But there is another and a rather different way in which this kind of utterance may go wrong. A good many of these verbal procedures are designed for use by people who hold certain beliefs or have certain feelings or intentions. And if you use one of these formulae when you do not have the requisite thoughts or feelings or intentions then there is an abuse of the procedure, there is insincerity. Take, for example, the expression, 'I congratulate you'. This is designed for use by people who are glad that the person addressed has achieved a certain feat, believe that he was personally responsible for the success, and so on. If I say 'I congratulate you' when I'm not pleased or when I don't believe that the credit was yours, then there is insincerity. Likewise if I say I promise to do something, without having the least intention of doing it or without believing it feasible. In these cases there is something wrong certainly, but it is not like a misfire. We should not say that I didn't in fact promise, but rather that I did promise but promised insincerely; I did congratulate you but the congratulations were hollow. And there may be an infelicity of a somewhat similar kind when the performative utterance commits the speaker to future conduct of a certain description and then in the future he does not in fact behave in the expected way. This is very obvious, of course, if I promise to do something and then break my promise, but there are many kinds of commitment of a rather less tangible form than that in the case of promising. For instance, I may say 'I welcome you', bidding you welcome to my home or wherever it may be, but then I proceed to treat you as though you were exceedingly unwelcome. In this case the procedure of saying 'I welcome you' has been abused in a way rather different from that of simple insincerity.

Now we might ask whether this list of infelicities is complete, whether the kinds of infelicity are mutually exclusive, and so forth. Well, it is not complete, and they are not mutually exclusive; they never are. Suppose that you are just about to name the ship, you have been appointed to name it, and you are just about to bang the bottle against the stem; but at that very moment some low type comes up, snatches the bottle out of your hand, breaks it on the stem, shouts out 'I name this ship the *Generalissimo Stalin*', and then for good measure kicks away the chocks. Well, we agree of course on several things. We agree that the ship certainly isn't now named the *Generalissimo Stalin*, and we agree that it's an infernal shame and so on and so forth. But we may not agree as to how we should classify the particular infelicity in this case. We might say that here is a case of a perfectly legitimate and agreed procedure which, however, has been invoked in the wrong circumstances, namely by the wrong person, this low type instead of the person appointed to do it. But on the other hand we might look at it differently and say that this is a case where the procedure has not as a whole been gone through correctly, because part of the procedure for naming a ship is that you should first of all get yourself appointed as the person to do the naming and that's what this fellow did not do. Thus the way we should classify infelicities in different cases will be perhaps rather a difficult matter, and may even in the last resort be a bit arbitrary. But of course lawyers, who have to deal very much with this kind of thing, have invented all kinds of technical terms and have made numerous rules about different kinds of cases, which enable them to classify fairly rapidly what in particular is wrong in any given case.

As for whether this list is complete, it certainly is not. One further way in which things may go wrong is, for example, through what in general may be called misunderstanding. You may not hear what I say, or you may understand me to refer to something different from what I intended to refer to, and so on. And apart from further additions which we might make to the list, there is the general over-riding consideration that, as we are performing an act when we issue these performative utterances, we may of course be doing so under duress or in some other circumstances which make us not entirely responsible for doing what we are doing. That would certainly be an unhappiness of a kind—any kind of non-responsibility might be called an unhappiness; but of course it is a quite different kind of thing from what we have been talking about. And I might mention that, quite differently again, we could be issuing any of these utterances, as we can issue an utterance of any kind whatsoever, in the course, for example, of acting a play or making a joke or writing a poem—in which case of course it would not be seriously meant and we shall not be able to say that we seriously performed the act concerned. If the poet says 'Go and catch a falling star' or whatever it may be, he doesn't seriously issue an order Considerations of this kind apply to any utterance at all, not merely to performatives.

That, then, is perhaps enough to be going on with. We have discussed the performative utterance and its infelicities. That equips us, we may suppose, with two shining new tools to crack the crib of reality maybe. It also equips us—it always does—with two shining new skids under our metaphysical feet. The question is how we use them.

II

So far we have been going firmly ahead, feeling the firm ground of prejudice glide away beneath our feet which is always rather exhilarating, but what next? You will be waiting for the bit when we bog down, the bit where we take it all back, and sure enough that's going to come but it will take time. First of all let us ask a rather simple question. How can we be sure, how can we tell, whether any utterance is to be classed as a performative or not? Surely, we feel, we ought to be able to do that. And we should obviously very much like to be able to say that there is a grammatical criterion for this, some grammatical means of deciding whether an utterance is performative. All the examples I have given hitherto do in fact have the same grammatical form; they all of them begin with the verb in the first person singular present indicative active—not just any kind of verb of course, but still they all are in fact of that form. Furthermore, with these verbs that I have used there is a typical asymmetry between the use of this person and tense of the verb and the use of the same verb in other persons and other tenses, and this asymmetry is rather an important clue.

For example, when we say 'I promise that . . .', the case is very different from when we say 'He promises that . . .', or in the past tense 'I promised that . . .'. For when we say 'I promise that . . .' we do perform an act of promising—we give a promise. What we do *not* do is to report on somebody's performing an act of promising—in particular, we do not report on somebody's use of the expression 'I promise'. We actually do use it and do the promising. But if I say 'He promises', or in the past tense 'I promised', I precisely do report on an act of promising, that is to say an act of using this formula 'I promise' —I report on a present act of promising by him, or on a past act of my own. There is thus a clear difference between our first person singular present indicative active, and other persons and tenses. This is brought out by the typical incident of little Willie whose uncle says he'll give him half-a-crown if he promises never to smoke till he's 55. Little Willie's anxious parent will say 'Of course he promises, don't you, Willie?' giving him a nudge, and little Willie just doesn't vouchsafe. The point here is that he must do the promising himself by saying 'I promise', and his parent is going too fast in saying he promises.

That, then, is a bit of a test for whether an utterance is performative or not, but it would not do to suppose that every performative utterance has to take this standard form. There is at least one other standard form, every bit as common as this one, where the verb is in the passive voice and in the second or third person, not in the first. The sort of case I mean is that of a notice inscribed 'Passengers are warned to cross the line by the bridge only', or of a document reading 'You are hereby authorized' to do so-and-so. These are undoubtedly performative, and in fact a signature is often required in order to show who it is that is doing the act of warning, or authorizing, or whatever it may be. Very typical of this kind of performative—especially liable to occur in written documents of course

—is that the little word 'hereby' either actually occurs or might naturally be inserted.

Unfortunately, however, we still can't possibly suggest that every utterance which is to be classed as a performative has to take one or another of these two, as we might call them, standard forms. After all it would be a very typical performative utterance to say 'I order you to shut the door'. This satisfies all the criteria. It is performing the act of ordering you to shut the door, and it is not true or false. But in the appropriate circumstances surely we could perform exactly the same act by simply saying 'Shut the door', in the imperative. Or again, suppose that somebody sticks up a notice 'This bull is dangerous', or simply 'Dangerous bull', or simply 'Bull'. Does this necessarily differ from sticking up a notice, appropriately signed, saying 'You are hereby warned that this bull is dangerous'? It seems that the simple notice 'Bull' can do just the same job as the more elaborate formula. Of course the difference is that if we just stick up 'Bull' it would not be quite clear that it is a warning; it might be there just for interest or information, like 'Wallaby' on the cage at the zoo, or 'Ancient Monument'. No doubt we should know from the nature of the case that it was a warning, but it would not be explicit.

Well, in view of this break-down of grammatical criteria, what we should like to suppose—and there is a good deal in this—is that any utterance which is performative could be reduced or expanded or analysed into one of these two standard forms beginning 'I . . .' so and so or beginning 'You (or he) hereby . . .' so and so. If there was any justification for this hope, as to some extent there is, then we might hope to make a list of all the verbs which can appear in these standard forms, and then we might classify the kinds of acts that can be performed by performative utterances. We might do this with the aid of a dictionary, using such a test as that already mentioned—whether there is the characteristic asymmetry between the first person singular present indicative active and the other persons and tenses—in order to decide whether a verb is to go into our

list or not. Now if we make such a list of verbs we do in fact
find that they fall into certain fairly well-marked classes. There
is the class of cases where we deliver verdicts and make esti-
mates and appraisals of various kinds. There is the class where
we give undertakings, commit ourselves in various ways by
saying something. There is the class where by saying something
we exercise various rights and powers, such as appointing and
voting and so on. And there are one or two other fairly well-
marked classes.

Suppose this task accomplished. Then we could call these
verbs in our list explicit performative verbs, and any utterance
that was reduced to one or the other of our standard forms we
could call an explicit performative utterance. 'I order you to
shut the door' would be an explicit performative utterance,
whereas 'Shut the door' would not—that is simply a 'primary'
performative utterance or whatever we like to call it. In using
the imperative we may be ordering you to shut the door, but
it just isn't made clear whether we are ordering you or
entreating you or imploring you or beseeching you or inciting
you or tempting you, or one or another of many other subtly
different acts which, in an unsophisticated primitive language,
are very likely not yet discriminated. But we need not over-
estimate the unsophistication of primitive languages. There
are a great many devices that can be used for making clear,
even at the primitive level, what act it is we are performing
when we say something—the tone of voice, cadence, gesture—
and above all we can rely upon the nature of the circumstances,
the context in which the utterance is issued. This very often
makes it quite unmistakable whether it is an order that is being
given or whether, say, I am simply urging you or entreating
you. We may, for instance, say something like this: 'Coming
from him I was bound to take it as an order'. Still, in spite of
all these devices, there is an unfortunate amount of ambiguity
and lack of discrimination in default of our explicit performative verbs. If I say something like 'I shall be there', it may not
be certain whether it is a promise, or an expression of intention,

or perhaps even a forecast of my future behaviour, of what is going to happen to me; and it may matter a good deal, at least in developed societies, precisely which of these things it is. And that is why the explicit performative verb is evolved—to make clear exactly which it is, how far it commits me and in what way, and so forth.

This is just one way in which language develops in tune with the society of which it is the language. The social habits of the society may considerably affect the question of which performative verbs are evolved and which, sometimes for rather irrelevant reasons, are not. For example, if I say 'You are a poltroon', it might be that I am censuring you or it might be that I am insulting you. Now since apparently society approves of censuring or reprimanding, we have here evolved a formula 'I reprimand you', or 'I censure you', which enables us expeditiously to get this desirable business over. But on the other hand, since apparently we don't approve of insulting, we have not evolved a simple formula 'I insult you', which might have done just as well.

By means of these explicit performative verbs and some other devices, then, we make explicit what precise act it is that we are performing when we issue our utterance. But here I would like to put in a word of warning. We must distinguish between the function of making explicit what act it is we are performing, and the quite different matter of *stating* what act it is we are performing. In issuing an explicit performative utterance we are not stating what act it is, we are showing or making explicit what act it is. We can draw a helpful parallel here with another case in which the act, the conventional act that we perform, is not a speech-act but a physical performance. Suppose I appear before you one day and bow deeply from the waist. Well, this is ambiguous. I may be simply observing the local flora, tying my shoe-lace, something of that kind; on the other hand, conceivably I might be doing obeisance to you. Well, to clear up this ambiguity we have some device such as raising the hat, saying 'Salaam', or something of that kind, to make it quite plain that the act being performed is the conventional one of doing obeisance rather than some other act. Now nobody would want to say that lifting your hat was stating that you were performing an act of obeisance; it certainly is not, but it does make it quite plain that you are. And so in the same way to say 'I warn you that . . .' or 'I order you to . . .' or 'I promise that . . .' is not to state that you are doing something, but makes it plain that you are—it does constitute your verbal performance, a performance of a particular kind.

So far we have been going along as though there was a quite clear difference between our performative utterances and what we have contrasted them with, statements or reports or descriptions. But now we begin to find that this distinction is not as clear as it might be. It's now that we begin to sink in a little. In the first place, of course, we may feel doubts as to how widely our performatives extend. If we think up some odd kinds of expression we use in odd cases, we might very well wonder whether or not they satisfy our rather vague criteria for being performative utterances. Suppose, for example, somebody says 'Hurrah'. Well, not true or false; he is performing the act of cheering. Does that make it a performative utterance in our sense or not? Or suppose he says 'Damn'; he is performing the act of swearing, and it is not true or false. Does that make it performative? We feel that in a way it does and yet it's rather different. Again, consider cases of 'suiting the action to the words'; these too may make us wonder whether perhaps the utterance should be classed as performative. Or sometimes, if somebody says 'I am sorry', we wonder whether this is just the same as 'I apologize'—in which case of course we have said it's a performative utterance—or whether perhaps it's to be taken as a description, true or false, of the state of his feelings. If he had said 'I feel perfectly awful about it', then we should think it must be meant to be a description of the state of his feelings. If he had said 'I apologize', we should feel this was clearly a performative utterance, going through the ritual of apologizing. But if he says 'I am sorry' there is an unfortunate hovering between the two. This phenomenon is quite common. We often find cases in which there is an obvious pure performative utterance and obvious other utterances connected with it which are not performative but descriptive, but on the other hand a good many in between where we're not quite sure which they are. On some occasions of course they are obviously used the one way, on some occasions the other way, but on some occasions they seem positively to revel in ambiguity.

Again, consider the case of the umpire when he says 'Out' or 'Over', or the jury's utterance when they say that they find the prisoner guilty. Of course, we say, these are cases of giving verdicts, performing the act of appraising and so forth, but still in a way they have some connexion with the facts. They seem to have something like the duty to be true or false, and seem not to be so very remote from statements. If the umpire says 'Over', this surely has at least something to do with six balls in fact having been delivered rather than seven, and so on. In fact in general we may remind ourselves that 'I state that . . .' does not look so very different from 'I warn you that . . .' or 'I promise to . . .'. It makes clear surely that the act that we are performing is an act of stating, and so functions just like 'I warn' or 'I order'. So isn't 'I state that . . .' a performative utterance? But then one may feel that utterances beginning 'I state that . . .' do have to be true or false, that they *are* statements.

Considerations of this sort, then, may well make us feel pretty unhappy. If we look back for a moment at our contrast between statements and performative utterances, we realize that we were taking statements very much on trust from, as we said, the traditional treatment. Statements, we had it, were to be true or false; performative utterances on the other hand were to be felicitous or infelicitous. They were the doing of something, whereas for all we said making statements was not doing something. Now this contrast surely, if we look back at it, is unsatisfactory. Of course statements are liable to be assessed in this matter of their correspondence or failure to correspond with the facts, that is, being true or false. But they are also liable to infelicity every bit as much as are performative utterances. In fact some troubles that have arisen in the study of statements recently can be shown to be simply troubles of infelicity. For example, it has been pointed out that there is something very odd about saying something like this: 'The cat is on the mat but I don't believe it is'. Now this is an outrageous thing to say, but it is not self-contradictory. There is no reason why the cat shouldn't be on the mat without my believing that it is. So how are we to classify what's wrong with this peculiar statement? If we remember now the doctrine of infelicity we shall see that the person who makes this remark about the cat is in much the same position as somebody who says something like this: 'I promise that I shall be there, but I haven't the least intention of being there'. Once again you can of course perfectly well promise to be there without having the least intention of being there, but there is something outrageous about saying it, about actually avowing the insincerity of the promise you give. In the same way there is insincerity in the case of the person who says 'The cat is on the mat but I don't believe it is', and he is actually avowing that insincerity —which makes a peculiar kind of nonsense.

A second case that has come to light is the one about John's children—the case where somebody is supposed to say 'All John's children are bald but John hasn't got any children'. Or perhaps somebody says 'All John's children are bald', when as a matter of fact—he doesn't say so—John has no children. Now those who study statements have worried about this; ought they to say that the statement 'All John's children are bald' is meaningless in this case? Well, if it is, it is not a bit like a great many other more standard kinds of meaninglessness; and we see, if we look back at our list of infelicities, that what is going wrong here is much the same as what goes wrong in, say, the case of a contract for the sale of a piece of land when the piece of land referred to does not exist. Now what we say in the case of this sale of land, which of course would be effected by a performative utterance, is that the sale is void—void for lack of reference or ambiguity of reference; and so we can see that the statement about all John's children is likewise void for lack of reference. And if the man actually says that John has no children in the same breath as saying they're all bald, he is making the same kind of outrageous utterance as the man who says 'The cat is on the mat and I don't believe it is', or the man who says 'I promise to but I don't intend to'.

In this way, then, ills that have been found to afflict statements can be precisely paralleled with ills that are characteristic of performative utterances. And after all when we state something or describe something or report something, we do perform an act which is every bit as much an act as an act of ordering or warning. There seems no good reason why stating should be given a specially unique position. Of course philosophers have been wont to talk as though you or I or anybody could just go round stating anything about anything and that would be perfectly in order, only there's just a little question: is it true or false? But besides the little question, is it true or false, there is surely the question: *is* it in order? Can you go round just making statements about anything? Suppose for example you say to me 'I'm feeling pretty mouldy this morning'. Well, I say to you 'You're not'; and you say 'What the devil do you mean, I'm not?' I say 'Oh nothing—I'm just stating you're not, is it true or false?' And you say 'Wait a bit about whether it's true or false, the question is what did you mean by making statements about somebody else's feelings? I told you I'm feeling pretty mouldy. You're just not in a position to say, to state that I'm not'. This brings out that you can't just make statements about other people's feelings (though you can make guesses if you like); and there are very many things which, having no knowledge of, not being in a position to pronounce about, you just can't state. What we need to do for the case of stating, and by the same token describing and reporting, is to take them a bit off their pedestal, to realize that they are speech-acts no less than all these other speech-acts that we have been mentioning and talking about as performative.

Then let us look for a moment at our original contrast between the performative and the statement from the other side. In handling performatives we have been putting it all the time as though the only thing that a performative utterance had to do was to be felicitous, to come off, not to be a misfire, not to be an abuse. Yes, but that's not the end of the matter. At least in the case of many utterances which, on what we have said, we should have to class as performative—cases where we say 'I warn you to . . .', 'I advise you to . . .' and so on—there will be other questions besides simply: was it in order, was it all right, as a piece of advice or a warning, did it come off? After that surely there will·be the question: was it good or sound advice? Was it a justified warning? Or in the case, let us say, of a verdict or an estimate: was it a good estimate, or a sound verdict? And these are questions that can only be decided by considering how the content of the verdict or estimate is related in some way to fact, or to evidence available about the facts. This is to say that we do require to assess at least a great many performative utterances in a general dimension of correspondence with fact. It may still be said, of course, that this does not make them *very* like statements because still they are not true or false, and that's a little black and white speciality that distinguishes statements as a class apart. But actually—though it would take too long to go on about this— the more you think about truth and falsity the more you find that very few statements that we ever utter are just true or just false. Usually there is the question are they fair or are they not fair, are they adequate or not adequate, are they exaggerated or not exaggerated? Are they too rough, or are they perfectly precise, accurate, and so on? 'True' and 'false' are just general labels for a whole dimension of different appraisals which have something or other to do with the relation between what we say and the facts. If, then, we loosen up our ideas of truth and falsity we shall see that statements, when assessed in relation to the facts, are not so very different after all from pieces of advice, warnings, verdicts, and so on.

We see then that stating something is performing an act just as much as is giving an order or giving a warning; and we see, on the other hand, that, when we give an order or a warning or a piece of advice, there is a question about how this is related to fact which is not perhaps so very different from the kind of question that arises when we discuss how a statement is related to fact. Well, this seems to mean that in its original form our distinction between the performative and the statement is considerably weakened, and indeed breaks down. I will just make a suggestion as to how to handle this matter. We need to go very much farther back, to consider all the ways and senses in which saying anything at all is doing this or that— because of course it is always doing a good many different things. And one thing that emerges when we do do this is that, besides the question that has been very much studied in the past as to what a certain utterance *means*, there is a further question distinct from this as to what was the *force*, as we may call it, of the utterance. We may be quite clear what 'Shut the door' means, but not yet at all clear on the further point as to whether as uttered at a certain time it was an order, an entreaty or whatnot. What we need besides the old doctrine about meanings is a new doctrine about all the possible forces of utterances, towards the discovery of which our proposed list of explicit performative verbs would be a very great help; and then, going on from there, an investigation of the various terms of appraisal that we use in discussing speech-acts of this, that, or the other precise kind—orders, warnings, and the like.

The notions that we have considered then, are the performative, the infelicity, the explicit performative, and lastly, rather hurriedly, the notion of the forces of utterances. I dare say that all this seems a little unremunerative, a little complicated. Well, I suppose in some ways it is unremunerative, and I suppose it ought to be remunerative. At least, though, I think that if we pay attention to these matters we can clear up some mistakes in philosophy; and after all philosophy is used as a scapegoat, it parades mistakes which are really the mistakes of everybody. We might even clear up some mistakes in grammar, which perhaps is a little more respectable.

And is it complicated? Well, it is complicated a bit; but life and truth and things do tend to be complicated. It's not things, it's philosophers that are simple. You will have heard it said, I expect, that over-simplification is the occupational disease of philosophers, and in a way one might agree with that. But for a sneaking suspicion that it's their occupation.

II

PRETENDING[1]

IN a recent paper[2] Mr. Errol Bedford argues that 'anger', like other words which would be said to be words for emotions, is not the name of a feeling, despite the existence of such expressions as 'feeling angry'. 'Anger', he argues, is not a name, nor is anger a feeling: there is no specific feeling that angry men as such feel, nor do we, to be angry, have to feel any feeling at all. With this thesis I am not concerned, but only with some remarks that he makes, quite incidentally, about pretending (and I realize it is hard on him to pick these out for intensive criticism). For he thinks that his view may be countered by referring to the case of someone *pretending* to be angry: is this not parallel to the case of someone *pretending* to be in pain, who precisely does not feel a certain feeling (pain) that the man who *is* in pain *does* feel—a feeling of which 'pain' surely is the name?

'Can we say that being angry is similar to being in pain in this respect? Let us contrast the cases of a man who is angry and another, behaving in a similar way, who is only pretending to be. Now it may well be true that the former feels angry, whereas the latter does not, but in any case it is not this that constitutes the difference between the fact that the one is angry and the fact that the other is only pretending to be. The objection rests on a misconception of what pretence is. There is necessarily involved in pretence, or shamming, the notion of a limit which must not be overstepped: pretence is always insulated, as it were, from reality. Admittedly this limit may be vague, but it must exist. It is a not unimportant point that it is

[1] Reprinted from *Proceedings of the Aristotelian Society*, Supplementary Volume xxxii (1957–8), by courtesy of the editor.
[2] *Proceedings of the Aristotelian Society*, 1956–7.

usually *obvious* when someone is pretending. If a man who is behaving as if he were angry goes so far as to smash the furniture or commit an assault, he has passed the limit; he is not *pretending*, and it is useless for him to protest afterwards that he did not feel angry. Far from this statement being *proof* that he was not angry, it would be discounted even if it were accepted as true. "He was angry, but he did not feel angry" is not self-contradictory, although it is no doubt normally false. If in a particular case it is difficult—as it may be—to settle the question "Pretended or real?" that can only be because the relevant public evidence is inadequate to settle it. What we want is more evidence of the same kind, not a special piece of evidence of a different kind. Our difficulty in resolving the question "Is he really in pain?" on the other hand, arises from the fact that the only decisive evidence is evidence that he alone is in a position to give.

Since pain gets a perhaps undue share of attention in philosophy, and since Mr. Bedford is not shocking us about pretending to be in pain, let us here leave pain out of it, only remarking that if pretending to be in pain and pretending to be angry are actually as different as Mr. Bedford supposes then surely his statements about pretending, designed as they are to fit the case of anger, should be put in less general terms.

Our man, then, is 'behaving as if he were angry'. He scowls, let us say, and stamps his foot on the carpet. So far we may (or perhaps must?) still say 'He is not (really) angry: he is (only) pretending to be angry'. But now he goes further, let us say he bites the carpet: and we will picture the scene with sympathy —the carpet innocent, the bite untentative and vicious, the damage grave. Now he has gone too far, overstepped the limit between pretence and reality, and we cannot any longer say 'He is pretending to be angry' but must say 'He is really angry'. Mr. Bedford's language seems to me on the whole to mean positively that we must say this *because and in the sense that* behaviour of this extreme sort *constitutes* being really angry,[1]

[1] At least the bite 'constitutes the difference' between being really angry and pretending to be angry, the common element being presumably such behaviour as scowling. Some may recall the textbook example, where it is

or is just what we mean by 'being really angry'. If, however, he only means, what he also says, that the extreme behaviour is decisive *evidence* that the man is really angry, that is not only a very different and slightly (if only slightly) more plausible thesis, but also one too weak to serve for his argument: for now we are still not told what really being angry, for which this is only the *evidence*, *is*, nor therefore shown that it does not involve, or even reside in, the feeling of a feeling—the evidence *might* be evidence that he is feeling a certain feeling.

We have primarily to consider whether Mr. Bedford is right in what he says we should *say*, rather than his claims about what is shown by our so speaking, if we do. If the man takes the bite, he *cannot* 'be pretending'—here surely Mr. Bedford carries the philosopher's professional addiction to furniture to a new pitch of positive concern for it. And if he does really mean that the difference in behaviour 'constitutes the difference between the fact that the one is angry and the fact that the other is only pretending to be', then he must be claiming, not only that once he has taken the bite we *cannot* (truly) say 'He is only pretending to be angry', which seems false, but also that if he merely stamps and goes no further we *cannot* (truly) say 'He is really angry', which seems patently false. I think it must on reflection be agreed that in whichever of the ways the man behaves it is open to us to say *either* 'He is angry' *or* 'He is only pretending to be angry', and that either statement can be in fact true, depending on the (other) circumstances of the case at least in addition to these features of his behaviour. It is common enough for someone who is really angry to behave in no way violently or even conspicuously: and if someone is pretending to be angry in some emergency where the success of the pretence matters seriously, more anyway than the integrity of any adjacent furniture (which may not even be his own and may in any case be insured), then surely he

only the hair on a gooseberry that stops it from being a grape: by a 'gooseberry', then, we mean simply a hirsute grape—*and* by a 'grape' likewise simply a glabrous gooseberry.

may hit upon biting the carpet as the very thing to clinch the deception.

Something has gone very wrong. Yet still there are in fact, as we should expect, ways in which limits and the overstepping of limits are relevant to the concept of pretending, as to so many others. On a festive occasion you are ordered, for a forfeit, to pretend to be a hyena: going down on all fours, you make a few essays at hideous laughter and finally bite my calf, taking, with a touch of realism possibly exceeding your hopes, a fair-sized piece right out of it. Beyond question you have gone too far.[1] Try to plead that you were only pretending, and I shall advert forcibly to the state of my calf—not much pretence about that, is there? There are limits, old sport. This sort of thing in these circumstances will not pass as '(only) pretending to be a hyena'. True—but then neither will it pass as *really being* a hyena. The limit overstepped, a limitation upon violence as in the carpet-biting case, is not a boundary between pretending to be a hyena and really being a hyena, but between pretending to be a hyena and behaving like an uncivilized tough, or perhaps between *merely* pretending to be a hyena and pretending to be a hyena *with a difference* of some kind, with knobs on or with ulterior motives. So too if you begin to assault the bric-a-brac when told to pretend to be angry for a forfeit, we need not say that you must be really angry, but only that such antics are too bad and quite uncalled-for when pretending in such circumstances, or perhaps that you are taking advantage of the opportunity to further private aesthetic aims (in which case you may not really be pretending, but only pretending to pretend), or perhaps something else again quite different but still in its way satisfyingly censorious.

The moral is, clearly, that to be not pretending to be, and still more to be not only-pretending to be, is not by any means necessarily, still less *eo ipso*, to be really being. This is so even when the way in which we fail to be (only-) pretending is by

[1] In these circumstances. But if Nero ordered you, in the arena, to pretend to be a hyena, it might be unwisely perfunctory *not* to take a piece right out.

indulging in excessively 'realistic' behaviour: but of course there are also numerous other kinds of case, some to be mentioned later, in which we might be taken to be pretending and so may be said to be not pretending, where the reasons for which we are said not to be (only-) pretending are totally different from this, and such that the notion that not-pretending ⊃ really being could scarcely insinuate itself. We must not allow ourselves to be too much obsessed by the opposition, in which of course there is *something*, between pretending and really being: not one of the following formulae is actually correct:

(1) not really being ⊃ pretending

(2) pretending ⊃ not really being

(3) not pretending ⊃ really being

(4) really being ⊃ not pretending.[1]

So set out these formulae lose, I realize, some of their attractiveness: but arguments like Mr. Bedford's show that they can attract; he has actually, if I am not mistaken, fallen principally for (3), which is not by any means the most tempting, though some of his arguments seem to favour (2), a quite independent matter.

'Pretend' is a verb used in various constructions, of which I have so far only mentioned 'pretend to be' followed by an adjective or adjectival phrase or by a substantive with the article: in such cases excessive behaviour will, as we have seen, commonly not produce the result that the performer 'really is', for example, angry. (I hesitate to say it, but surely the obvious reason is that 'being angry' does not consist merely in behaving publicly in some manner: to say this need not commit us to saying that being angry is the same as feeling angry—it is not, any more than being tired is the same as feeling tired—still less that 'anger' is the name of a feeling.) However, we have to consider also the construction in which 'pretend' is followed by 'to A' or 'to be A-ing', especially in cases where the verb 'A' is one which describes the doing of some *deed* (for example, 'bite' as

---

[1] Actually, 'really' is, like 'actually', really a broken reed in philosophy. See how they twist and turn in example (3) below—the window-cleaner.

opposed to, for example, 'believe'), and more particularly when that deed is of a pretty 'physical' kind (for example, biting as opposed to, for example, giving). If we now consider such a case as this: and if we remember one of the conditions that must be satisfied whenever I am pretending, viz. that there must be something, and something public, that I am actually doing, some action I actually am performing, in pretending and in order to pretend: then we may hope to have found *one* type of case in which what Mr. Bedford claims to hold of pretending in general does in fact hold.

Let us take the case where someone is to 'pretend to take a bite out of your calf'. Here it would be agreed that one thing he must *not* do,[1] however lifelike the pretence, is anything that could be correctly described as '(actually) taking a bite out of your calf': yet plainly too the action he has, in pretending, actually to perform is one which will be up to a point genuinely like the action he is pretending to perform (for what he is pretending is *here* to perform a public physical action), and might, but for precautions, pass over into it.[2] If he goes far enough he *will* have *really* done the thing he was only to pretend to do: and if he does not go so far, he *cannot* have really done *that* thing. Here, then, we seem to have a case on Mr. Bedford's pattern.

It is owing to the special features of cases of this kind that an impasse can arise over pretending to do something, say hole a putt, in circumstances, say in the presence of a surrounding crowd, where there seems to be nothing one can do at all like holing the putt which will not result in the putt's being actually holed.[3] It is easy to pretend to be sitting on a certain chair when

[1] At least intentionally: I neglect complications about the unintentional.

[2] Of course there is too the rarish and quite different case in which a man pretending to be angry actually *becomes* angry—makes himself angry. I do not think this is of comparable interest.

[3] Doubtful, though not inexplicable, cases arise here, because of doubts as to how much is connoted by a putative description of a 'physical' action. Can I pretend to cough? Shall I, if I produce a coughing noise, have actually coughed? Or is 'to cough' different from 'to deliberately cough'?

it is half concealed behind a desk, less easy if it is in full view. (This is different from the less subtle type of case where one cannot pretend to do something because one can do neither it nor, often by the same token, anything even passably like it. Thus you cannot pretend to curl your trunk—though again, of course, if you help yourself to that curious object 'a pretend trunk', i.e. something of which we *pretend that* it is your trunk, you can very likely curl that, and hence also very likely pretend to curl it.)

Is it however the case that at least when we are pretending to do or to be doing a physical action we are *universally* debarred from actually doing that action itself? We will consider three examples:

1. Two miscreants are surprised in the act and hastily agree, the wherewithal being handy, to pretend to be sawing a tree: in a trice the blade is humming to and fro a bare inch away from the bark. How good a pretence is that? And wouldn't they any longer be pretending to be sawing the tree if they allowed the teeth to bite in? Surely if they want the pretence to be convincing they should set about actually sawing the tree?

2. Yet surely again magicians pretend to saw girls, we've all seen one pretending very successfully to saw a girl in half. Would it really be still a pretence, and a more convincing one, if the teeth were biting in? Or wouldn't it rather have been transformed into grim reality?

3. That chap over there, he's all right I suppose, he's cleaning the windows, eh?

Ah, *him*, he's *pretending* to be cleaning the windows right enough, cleaning 'em a treat too: but I seen him taking note of the valuables through 'em all the time.[1]

To unravel these examples, we shall need a few more lemmas: we shall need to bring out more of the full features

[1] Here is another, trick, example, for exercise purposes only:—a man at a party decides, in an attempt to amuse, to pretend to behave vulgarly: the party, however, is of a type at which even to pretend to behave vulgarly is, alas, to behave vulgarly.

of the situation when we are pretending, which is moderately complicated. And first for that goddess fair and free (fairly fair, frailly free), divinest Etymology. *Prae-tendere* in Latin never strays far from the literal meaning of holding or stretching one thing in front of another in order to protect or conceal or disguise it: even in such a figurative use as that in Ovid's 'praetendens culpae splendida verba tuae', the words are still a façade to hide the crime. In English, we do not any longer explicitly refer, in the construction used with 'pretend', to that which the pretender is hiding or dissembling, which in Latin does appear in the dative case.[1] Nevertheless it seems clear that it still is an important feature of pretending, in classic cases if not in all, that the pretender is concealing or suppressing something.

In a case of pretending, then, there will typically be:

(PB) The pretence-behaviour, the actual public performance gone through in pretending, indulged in, as of course it is, for the sake of dissembling.

(Rd) The reality-dissembled, about which the audience is to be hoodwinked. This *may* on occasion include in part, or be wholly identical with

(RBd) Some real-behaviour-dissembled, as for instance when I am really engaged in biting the carpet but disguise this fact by pretending to be kissing it.

Thus when we speak of someone's angry behaviour being only a pretence, *one* thing with which this pretended anger is commonly being contrasted at least in our minds is (Rd) his real emotion, feeling, attitude, or what you will, which, whatever it is, is precisely not 'real anger'. In daily life, indeed, this contrast may be of more interest than the quite different contrast, which has been more stressed by philosophers, between

(PBm) The mere-pretence-behaviour, the actual public

---

[1] Indeed in English even the accusative case after 'pretend', as in, for example, 'He pretended sickness', though a venerable construction is by now archaistic. In the special construction 'pretending not to be' there is however a reference to what is being concealed.

performance gone through in pretending, disregarding its motivation,

and

(GBs) The genuine-behaviour-simulated, which PBm is intended to resemble. This may be related to a further

(Gs) 'Genuinity'[1]-simulated, as genuinely behaving angrily is related, for example, to genuinely being angry.

When some simple contrast between 'pretence' and 'reality' comes up in discussion, it is all too often uncertain which of the things here listed is being contrasted with which.

To return now to our three examples. (2)—the girl-sawing—simply supports the rule suggested by the preceding discussion, that in pretending to do A you must not actually do A, or that PBm must not coincide with GBs. Defending this rule, we are tempted to try some special dodge to get out of (1)—the tree-sawing. The miscreants are 'pretending to be sawing the tree' and also 'they are sawing it' in fact, *but* perhaps they are pretending to 'be sawing' it in a sense that covers times earlier and later than the time during which they 'are sawing' it in fact: so that PBm does differ from GBs, it extends over a shorter stretch of time. Or perhaps we should not allow that they 'are (seriously) sawing' it, for example, in the sense that they are not embarked on an operation designed to terminate in the fall of the tree: but it is not clear what this means—suppose the police are suspicious and continue to hang around indefinitely? The case will then become like that of the man who pretends to be playing golf by playing a few strokes: can he prolong the pretence all round the course and yet not be actually playing golf? It is likely that by introducing 'seriously' (and of course

[1] I am driven to this horrible word because I wish to use throughout the second contrast a different term from 'real', which I have kept for the first contrast.

The Gs may stand to the GBs as, say, its 'motivation': then such an expression as 'pretending to be angry' will commonly run the two together. But where the GBs is something more purely 'physical', such as 'sawing a girl in half', the Gs, if any, is at a discount.

it is true that their heart is not in sawing the tree, they are only doing it at all to cover up something) we are really already on the way to the treatment which we *must* use for example (3)— the window-cleaner.

Here surely no dodge will help us; we must allow that he is indeed actually cleaning the windows, from start to finish and throughout the whole time he is pretending to be cleaning them. But it is still a pretence, because what he is *really* doing all the time is something different, namely noting the valuables: he is only cleaning the windows to disguise and promote this other activity—RBd goes on during the course of PB, which facilitates it and distracts attention from it. (In other cases RBd may actually be incorporated into PB as a camouflaged part of it.) It looks, then, as though it does not matter if PB does coincide with GBs, so long as the contrast between PB and RBd is preserved.[1]

It is worth noting once more that it will seldom be possible to decide with certainty that PBm does coincide exactly with GBs, because in so many cases GBs is apt to be described, and may only be describable, in terms which already import the Gs which underlines it: thus when someone is 'pretending to be angry', the GBs will be 'angry behaviour' or 'the behaviour of an angry man', a description which may be held already to mean that the actions are done 'in anger'. Only when the GBs is describable in pretty purely 'physical' terms which disregard 'motivation' and the like, for example, as 'sawing a girl', shall we be confident of the coincidence.

In the light of example (3), it can now be seen that the supposed rule that in certain cases, such as example (2), PBm must not coincide with GBs, is really only a marginal case of a more general rule. The essence of the situation in pretending is (not so much that my public behaviour must be non-genuine behaviour, as rather) that my public behaviour is meant to

---

[1] Here is one of the similarities between 'pretence' and 'pretext'. A pretext may be not a genuine reason or not your real reason: a pretence may be something you are not genuinely doing or not what you are really doing.

disguise some reality, often some real behaviour. From this it obviously follows, not only that PB must not coincide with RBd, in which case there would be no disguise, but also that PB must not coincide with *not*-RBd, in which case there would be nothing to be being disguised. Now in a case like that of the magician, the RBd precisely is, or includes, *not* actually sawing the girl in half, so that the GBs, sawing the girl in half, is equivalent to not-RBd: hence in such a case it follows directly from the more general rule that PB must stop short of being identical with GBs, as = not-RBd. This type of case, where Gs precisely equals or involves not-Rd, or GBs not-RBd, is of course quite a common one: 'pretending not to be' is a special variety of it.

At least in many cases there seems to be a clear difference in meaning between the expressions 'pretending to A' and 'pretending to be A-ing'. The former seems often to be preferred where it is being pointed out that PBm does not coincide with GBs, while the latter stresses that PB does not coincide with RBd. 'He is only pretending to clean the windows', i.e. what he is doing does not amount to genuinely cleaning the windows: but 'He is only pretending to be cleaning the windows', i.e. what he is really up to is something other than cleaning the windows. Take, again, Potter's gambit, where he makes three random moves and then resigns. If we say 'He's only pretending to play (chess)', we mean that that is not playing chess:[1] but if we say 'He's only pretending to be playing (chess)', we allow that in a way and for all we care he is playing chess, but we mean that he is really up to some deeper game. Children who are ignorant may typically be 'pretending to play chess': children, ignorant or not, who are up to mischief may typically be 'pretending to be playing chess'. The magician who is pretending to saw the girl, i.e. we reassure ourselves, not actually sawing her, may also be said to be 'pretending to be sawing her' if, whether he is or not (and naturally we presume

[1] For some reason. For example, to be genuinely playing chess you must be making your moves with the object of winning, or at least of not losing.

not), he is surreptitiously engaged in something else rather crucial for the success of the illusion.

I should not, however, like to claim that this is the whole story about 'pretending to A' and 'pretending to be A-ing'. For consider two further cases:

4. Someone in the next room out of sight keeps up a string of remarks such as 'Check', 'Your move', &c., and occasionally taps pieces of wood together. We should say 'He is (only) pretending (for the benefit of us in the next room) to be playing chess', but scarcely 'He is (only) pretending to play chess'. Why is this?

5. A boy in an arm-chair is making tugging and twisting movements with his arms, accompanied by gear-change and other raucous noises. He is 'pretending to be driving a racing-car', but scarcely 'pretending to drive a racing-car'. Why? A *possible* answer is this. In neither case is the behaviour of the pretending party sufficiently like the genuine article (GBs) for it to be in point to mark the distinction between the two. To pretend to drive a racing-car, he would need a racing-car: as it is, there is no serious prospect of deception. And in case (4) the deception is worked indirectly, mainly by words: if his actual actions were observed, there would again be no serious chance of deception. It might be urged, too, that both these cases of 'pretending to' have some affinity with 'pretending that', of which more later, which generally requires the continuous present tense after it. On the other hand, the difference between, say, 'pretending to sit' and 'pretending to be sitting' is at least sometimes clearly just the familiar difference between 'he sits' and 'he is sitting', so that it will not do to claim that the two forms of expression are used to mark any one single distinction.

So far we have not strayed very far from our starting-point, a consideration of the limits which must not be overstepped in the pretence-behaviour. Only in special cases is the limit between 'pretending to do A' and 'really doing A' of much interest, and even then it is of minor importance in clarifying the whole notion of pretending. When something claimed to be pretending is ruled out by reason of 'going too far', this will commonly mean something such as 'going beyond what was socially permissible on that occasion' rather than 'slipping into doing the actual thing'. But now further, there are other conditions of a quite general kind to which behaviour must conform if it is to qualify as pretence-behaviour: the following examples may serve to bring out some of them:

6. Trapped on a branch against the moon, we decide to pretend to be owls: you give a colourable hoot while I pull up my legs and hunch my shoulders up to my ears.

7. As I am engaged in filching one of your goats, you return inopportunely through the dusk: with a baffled snarl I bound off into the adjacent bush. Was this 'pretending to be a panther'? Or what if instead I slink about the kraal with menacing grunts?

8. Told to pretend to be a hyena at a party, you recline and appear to sleep.

9. In similar circumstances, you proceed to jump around powerfully on your hind legs, boxing with your fists and fondling something in your pocket.

These are all somewhat facetious cases of 'pretending to be an' animal. It may be worth pointing out that 'pretending to be a hyena' in the let's-pretend, make-believe, party-forfeit way, is a very recent usage, perhaps no older than Lewis Carroll, and the same indeed seems to apply to at least most usages in which we pretend to be something other than ourselves. One of the most conspicuous facts in the history of the word 'pretend' is that of late it has come to be more popular and to be applied more widely than formerly.

In (6) I do better than you. We both *imitate* the owl, you perhaps rather better in voice than I in silhouette: but you stop short of pretending to be an owl, because you fail to attempt to disguise the fact that you are not one—mere imitation does not imply dissembling anything. In (7), while it seems clear that I am pretending if I slink around, this becomes much more doubtful if I bound away, *right* away and *promptly*: for it to be a clear case of pretending I, my human person, must *remain on the scene* to be hidden under the pretence, but as things are it is plainly preferring to be hidden under the bush. If, to startle me, you quack in a passable way from the undergrowth, you are scarcely pretending to be a duck (for you are not on the scene nor in need of disguise), as you would, however, be, very probably, if I trod on you in the dark and you quacked. Of course in all these cases you might be trying to *make me believe* that you were a panther or a duck: but not all such deceptions are achieved by pretending—I can make you believe I am angry by many methods without ever pretending to be angry.

In case (8), at the party, there is of course no question of my trying to convince you *seriously* that I am something other than myself; but still, on the party level, my performance must be convincing, I must dissemble my humanity under a simulated hyenity. I contrive to fail on both counts at once, because my behaviour is as much human as hyenine—how then could it distract attention from my humanity, to which so many other things point, or prompt anyone even to think specially of hyenas? A pretence must be not merely like but *distinctively* like the genuine article simulated: you will hardly pretend to be angry by simulating the behaviour of an angry man in perfect control of himself (though of course it might help if you were to *say* 'I am angry' too).

In (9), you evidently have a wrong idea of what a hyena is. The puzzle, such as it is, is exactly parallel to that about the man who, trying to draw a map of France, draws an outline which is that of Italy: its solution throws no special light on pretending, but rather on doing and intending to do in general —for pretending to be doing something is of course as good a case as another of doing something. You are meaning or trying to pretend to be a hyena, but actually behaving like a kangaroo: this is the correct and the shortest accurate way of describing the situation. There is *no* short answer to the question 'Is he pretending to be a hyena or isn't he?' nor to 'Is he pretending to be a hyena or a kangaroo?' since such simple expressions are not adequate to cope with such a complicated case.

It is quite misleading to handle pretending in the way it is so often handled, as identical with being (or being doing) except that some special feature is left out—and Mr. Bedford is no worse in this respect than those he is attacking, who say, for example, that pretending to be in pain is just the same as being in pain except that you do not feel pain, or that pretending to be angry is behaving like a really angry man only without feeling like one. Even if there were, what there is not, a general bar against PBm being the same as GBs, and even if it were possible, which even then it would not be, to give a *general* account of the precise way in which PBm must *always* fall short of GBs, still such an account would not explain pretending: for there are many situations in which I behave like an angry man without being really angry, which are nevertheless not cases of pretending. For example, I may be a rough diamond, or have odd manners, or be strangely insensitive, or not be attending to what I am doing: or I may be acting or rehearsing, or merely imitating or mimicking. And yet these are only some of the simplest things from which pretending has to be distinguished, much less near to it than, say affecting or shamming or feigning or posing as. To be pretending, in the basic case,[1] I must be trying to make others believe, or to give them the impression, by means of a current personal performance in their presence, that I am (really, only, &c.) *abc*, in order to disguise the fact that I am really *xyz*. To neglect to notice all this is to put in the bathwater without the baby.

Even so, we are far from having a full account of the nuances of pretending. For example, in a pretence there is for preference

---

[1] I neglect here such parasitic cases as let's-pretending and pretending-to-oneself, besides, for the present, pretending-that. Still less have I space to take on 'pretensions', 'the Old Pretender' and the like: but it is not too difficult in fact to fit all these into their appropriate niches in the concept, and sometimes they shed light, as, for example, the contrast between 'affected' and 'pretentious' may help to point the contrast between affecting and pretending.

an element of the extempore, and in the situation that prompts it an element of emergency—there is at least something that has to be hidden. True, there are 'elaborate' pretences: but if there is too much of this, with making-up and dressing-up like an actor rather than a mimic or a diseuse, we begin to prefer to speak of, say, impersonation or imposture or disguise. To pretend to be a bear is one thing, to roam the mountain valleys inside a bearskin rather another. True, there are prolonged pretences—'How long', the cry goes up from the eternal drawing-room, 'must we two go on pretending to one another?'—but still we prefer to say that Col. Barker posed for twenty years as a man rather than that she pretended for twenty years. Again, if there is no sort of urgency to hide what we elect to hide, we may prefer to speak of a leg-pull or of affectation or a pose. Yet these are nuances, for it is probably legitimate enough, in these days, to extend 'pretending' to cover most of these cases if we do not care for precision, just as we can use 'pretended he was going to' to cover those cases where, more specifically, 'he made a feint', i.e. where he made a small movement in one direction to distract his opponent's defence, masking his true *intention*.

There remains, however, more to be said about one essential feature of pretending, namely that the pretender must be present and active in person to effect the deception by dint of his current behaviour. In the example of the panther above, the awkwardness is not merely that what is to be disguised is not 'on the scene' to be disguised, but also that the pretender is not on the scene to do the disguising, features both essential to pretending though of course not essential to many other forms of deception. I may camouflage a factory as a housing estate, in order to deceive the enemy in an emergency, but this is not to pretend that it is a housing estate (still less does it pretend to be a housing estate). I may pretend to have been furious by emerging from the conference room breathing hard and making derogatory remarks about the proceedings: but not by leaving traces in the conference room—bitten carpets, maybe—designed to make you think I was furious at the time. In pretending, *contemporary behaviour* misleads as to *contemporary fact*, here the contemporary fact that I am not one recovering from or still suffering from the after-effects of fury, or mulling over fresh memories of fury.

This brings me to the last point I shall consider, the construction 'pretending that'. It may be the availability of this handy and flexible construction that has led to the ever increasing popularity of 'pretend', since such neighbouring verbs in the family as 'affect', 'feign', 'dissemble', and the like have never acquired a 'that' construction. It may even seem that, equipped with a that-clause, pretending achieves emancipation from some of the limitations inherent in pretending-to: when pretending-to I can deceive only as to *my own* states or activities, and contemporary ones at that, but surely when I 'pretend that it was in the garage yesterday' I deceive as to something other than my own states or activities, and something non-contemporary at that.

However, it is not easy to be certain that there is in fact any systematic difference between pretending-to and pretending-that, let alone that just suggested.[1] What is the difference between pretending to be on your way to Antarctica and pretending that you are on your way to Antarctica? Or between pretending not to remember her face and pretending that you do not remember it? One feels inclined to say: with pretending-that the stress is on the suppression or concealment of knowledge or memory or thought or belief or awareness, in short of some 'cognitive state', and what is simulated is likewise some cognitive state.[2] Thus to pretend that you are in love with her is to dissemble your awareness that you are not, to pretend to be in love with her is to dissemble your indifference or aversion to her. Hence the fact, it might be argued, that in pretending-

[1] It might be relevant, but would take too long, to consider the other verbs ('hope', &c.) which can take both constructions: they are not particularly numerous.

[2] Yet it seems scarcely right to say: 'pretend that' = 'pretend to believe (or the like) that'.

that the pretence-behaviour is particularly liable to take the form of verbal behaviour, since that is particularly apt for creating impressions about our cognitive states. Moreover the apparent emancipation of pretending-that can be on these lines both accounted for and discounted: when I pretend that it was in the garage yesterday I am still only dissembling *my own current* awareness (memory, knowledge, belief) that it was not: but of course awareness can be *awareness* of things other than my own states or activities, and of non-contemporary things.

Moreover it seems possible in this way to account for pretending-to-oneself or let's-pretending, the former of which strongly, if not exclusively, prefers the 'that' construction. Here we have a sort of 'make-believe'—we suppress our actual beliefs and simulate others.

Yet still in all cases of pretending-that, though it may be only a cognitive state that is simulated and though verbal devices may be often employed, it remains true that there is an immediate connexion with non-verbal behaviour. Pretending that I am on top of a mountain may seem a less active affair at first than pretending to be on top of a mountain, yet still it differs very considerably from merely imagining that I am on top of a mountain: pretending-that is a preliminary to or even accompanied by behaviour such as inhaling deeply or pointing downwards ('Let's pretend we're giraffes and eat the leaves'), while imagining-that is a preliminary perhaps only to asking myself certain questions—How should I feel?, &c., while my public behaviour will scarcely go beyond a faraway look, which is certainly no part of the imagining. For this reason I can 'always' imagine, for example, that my prison walls are not there, but it may be 'no good' pretending they are not there, they are solid enough to stop me doing the things that follow on the pretending.

But how far can all this be pressed? Is pretending to be playing chess always so very different from pretending that you are playing chess, or again (perhaps still more) from pretending you are playing chess? Perhaps all that should be said is that the more it is a case of going through the motions the more likely we are to prefer 'to be playing' or 'to play': while the less this is necessary and the more we can put the deception across by verbal means or by simulating a belief the more we shall prefer the 'that' construction.

What, finally, is the importance of all this about pretending? I will answer this shortly, although I am not sure importance is important:[1] truth is. In the first place, it does seem that philosophers, who are fond of invoking pretending, have exaggerated its scope and distorted its meaning. In the second place, in the long-term project of classifying and clarifying all possible ways and varieties of *not exactly doing things*, which has to be carried through if we are ever to understand properly what doing things is, the clarification of pretending, and the assignment to it of its proper place within the family of related concepts, must find some place, if only a humble one.

[1] I dreamt a line that would make a motto for a sober philosophy: *Neither a be-all nor an end-all be.*

12

THREE WAYS OF SPILLING INK[1]

PARTS I, II, and III of the following paper are taken, almost verbatim, from J. L. Austin's longhand draft, found among his papers after his death, of a lecture he gave to the American Society of Political and Legal Philosophy, which met in Chicago in 1958. Authenticity of expression can be claimed for these sections, though no doubt Austin would have changed much had he himself completed his revisions for publication in the yearbook of the Society: *Responsibility* (*Nomos* III), edited by Carl Friedrich (New York, 1960). An outline of this lecture, which was 'distributed at the meeting and available to the participants', was published as an appendix to that volume.

The introductory section was not fully written out in Austin's manuscript, but has been pieced together from notes made on several separate sheets, and with the help also of Austin's notes for seminars he conducted at Oxford, over a period of many years, under the general title 'Excuses.' In these seminars he discussed not only material incorporated in the present paper, but also much on which 'A Plea for Excuses' was based.

The manuscript bears the title 'Responsibility', since this was the general topic of the meeting of the Society at which the lecture was given. The published appendix, however, is entitled 'Three Ways of Spilling Ink', and this is most probably the title Austin himself would have chosen had he published the paper.

The editor is grateful to Mrs. Austin for permission to submit the paper for publication and to Mr. G. J. Warnock, who has read both the manuscript and the present paper and has made many valuable suggestions for its improvement.

L. W. FORGUSON

[1] Reprinted from *The Philosophical Review*, vol. 75, No. 4 (1966), by permission of the editors.

MOST of what I have to say about responsibility in general I have said in another place.[1] But of course the point of what I had to say there was that there isn't much point in discussing it in general terms. I shall repeat it here only in summary. It is a view which I have not so much merely held, but used in practice for some twenty years, and have found it consistently to pay off. Briefly, it is the idea which Aristotle had in a primitive way, without having to fight free of the toils of sophistication that now encumber us: namely, that questions of whether a person was responsible for this or that are prior to questions of freedom. Whatever Aristotle's idea may have been it *worked* this way: to discover whether someone acted freely or not, we must discover whether this, that, or the other plea will pass—for example, duress, or mistake, or accident, and so forth.

We may hope to profit then, in this area of inquiry, from the careful study of what we may call, for the sake of a word, *excuses*—of the different ways, and different words, in which on occasion we may try to get out of things, to show that we didn't act 'freely' or were not 'responsible'. But if we are going to consider this subject and these expressions, we ought to attend as well to what might be called words of *aggravation*—words, that is, that not only don't get us out of things, but may actually make things worse for us, or at any rate may often bring in the very things that excuses, if we had any, would be designed to rule out. I shall concentrate here on a pretty narrow topic, since I don't know enough (or even *think* I know enough) about the whole subject: what follows is a sample only of some contributions that might be of use.

In considering responsibility, few things are considered more important than to establish whether a man *intended* to do *A*, or whether he did *A* intentionally. But there are at least two other familiar words important in this respect. Let us distinguish between acting *intentionally* and acting *deliberately* or on *purpose*, as far as this can be done by attending to what language can teach us.

[1] 'A Plea for Excuses' (1956).

A schoolteacher may ask a child who has spilled the ink in class: 'Did you do that intentionally?' or 'Did you do that deliberately?' or 'Did you do that on purpose (or purposely)?' It appears at first sight to matter little which question is asked. They appear to mean the same or at least to come down to the same in this case. But do they really? There are in fact techniques available for distinguishing between these expressions. I cannot exploit these by any means fully here, but only indicate the resources available. We may consider, for instance, for a start: (i) imagined or actual cases, and (ii) the 'grammar', 'etymology', and so forth of the words.

I

First let us consider some cases. Actual cases would of course be excellent: we might observe what words have actually been used by commentators on real incidents, or by narrators of fictitious incidents. However, we do not have the time or space to do that here. We must instead imagine some cases (imagine them carefully and in detail and comprehensively) and try to reach agreement upon what we should in fact say concerning them. If we can reach this agreement, we shall have some *data* ('experimental' data, in fact) which we can then go on to *explain*. Here, the explanation will be an account of the meanings of these expressions, which we shall hope to reach by using such methods as those of 'Agreement' and 'Difference': what is in fact present in the cases where we do use, say, 'deliberately', and what is absent when we don't. Of course, we shall then have arrived at nothing more than an account of certain ordinary 'concepts' employed by English speakers: but also at no less a thing. And it is not so little. These concepts will have evolved over a long time: that is, they will have faced the test of practical use, of continual hard cases better than their vanished rivals.

Here, then, are some cases.

1. Suppose I tie a string across a stairhead. A fragile relative, from whom I have expectations, trips over it, falls, and perishes.

Should we ask whether I tied the string there intentionally? Well, but it's hard to see how I could have done such a thing unintentionally, or even (what is not the same) not done it intentionally. You don't do that sort of thing—by accident? By mistake? Inadvertently? On the other hand, would I be bound to admit I did it 'on purpose' or 'purposely'? That has an ugly sound. What could the purpose have been if not to trip at least someone? Maybe I had better claim I was simply passing the time, playing cat's cradle, practising tying knots.

2. I needed money to play the ponies, so I dipped into the till. Of course, I *intended* (all the time) to put it back as soon as I had collected my winnings. That was my intention: I took it with the intention of putting it back. But was that my *purpose* in taking it? Did I take it for the purpose of, or on purpose to, put it back? Plainly not.

3. As I drive up, I see that there is broken glass on the roadway outside my home; so I throw it on to the sidewalk, and a pedestrian later stumbles over it and is injured. Very likely I did throw the glass on to the sidewalk intentionally; again, it was not unintentionally—I knew it was the sidewalk all right, etc. But did I do it on purpose, purposely? Did I do it deliberately? Conceivably, but in the way we should naturally imagine the incident, certainly not either.

4. The notice says, 'Do not feed the penguins.' I, however, feed them peanuts. Now peanuts happen to be, and these prove, fatal to these birds. Did I feed them peanuts intentionally? Beyond a doubt: I am no casual peanut shedder. But deliberately? Well, that seems perhaps to raise the question, 'Had I read the notice?' Why does it? Or 'on purpose?' That seems to insinuate that I knew what fatal results would ensue. Again, why?

We may also consider cases that are stereotypes, the ones evoked by clichés. Here are some.

We say that A wounded B with the intention of killing him, or of causing him grave bodily injury; or, more formally, with intent to kill him, and so forth. We do not say, 'A wounded *B* for the purpose of killing him.' Why not? Because the killing and the wounding are 'not sufficiently separate'—are 'too intimately connected'; because there are not '*two things*' that are done? But what does this really mean?

Again, we ask this young man who is paying attentions to our daughter to declare his intentions. What are his intentions? Are his intentions honourable? Here, would it make any difference if we asked him what was the purpose of these attentions, whether he has some purpose in view, whether he is doing these things on purpose or for a purpose? This makes his conduct seem more calculated, frames him as an adventurer or seducer. Instead of asking him to clarify the position, perhaps to himself as well as to us, are we not now asking him to divulge a guilty secret?

Another cliché: we find ourselves fairly often speaking of a 'deliberate intention'; 'with the deliberate intention of forcing the lock', for example. Just as we may speak of a deliberate choice or a deliberate decision. *But* we do not speak of an intentional deliberation; nor (except in special cases which cannot here be discussed) of an intentional decision or an intentional choice.

Perhaps it would help to think of kinds of cases in which a thing is done intentionally but not deliberately, and so forth: cases, that is, where these adverbial expressions are expressly dissociated. The way this happens will commonly reveal some 'opposite' of one of the three expressions which is *not* an 'opposite' of the other two.

For example, suppose I do a thing impulsively, and possibly even on impulse. Then I shall not be doing it deliberately—and indeed to *say* that I did it impulsively (and perhaps even on impulse) would surely be to rule out the suggestion that I did it deliberately. For example, at a certain juncture in the course of our quarrel, moved perhaps by some turn of emotion or memory, I impulsively stretch out my hand to make things up, and exert all my tact to the same end. Now this is intentional enough: I intend to put out my hand, to bury the hatchet.

Actually, I did even stretch out my hand on purpose, purposely. Yet it was not done deliberately: within twenty minutes I may be regretting it. The impulse is strong: I didn't stop to think (but about what?). I act precipitately, so probably not deliberately, but of course I knew what I was doing and meant to do it, even perhaps used my wits in doing it adroitly. (I may have stopped to think about *that*: the impulse may have been merely to make friends, holding out my hand something I thought up to do the trick.) If I acted not even on impulse, but quite *spontaneously* (rather tricky, this), and so even more evidently not deliberately, it is at least plausible to say that I still acted intentionally (cf. Sir Walter Raleigh). Again, a man put into agony of mind and fearful indecision[1] by some crisis may adopt some course such as running back into the blaze. No doubt he runs back into the blaze intentionally enough; he even (*perhaps*) decides to run back—though of course this is not necessary for him to do so 'intentionally'. But I think it might well be agreed he did not do so deliberately. These examples will suffice to show that what is done intentionally and purposely need not be done deliberately. Moreover, they appear to show some common characteristics: there is something 'precipitate' about the act in every case.

On the other hand, it is fully possible to act both deliberately and intentionally yet 'not on purpose', or at least (*if* this is the same thing—there are distinctions here which we shall have to neglect) for no purpose, without any purpose, purposelessly. So to act may be, typically, to act wantonly. A gang of boys decapitates, *seriatim*, every one of the line of young trees newly planted along our street: this is deliberate, wanton damage. But they have, we may say, no interest in killing the trees; very likely they haven't given the matter a thought. Do children pull the wings off flies 'on purpose?' Yet see them at it, and it is patent that they do it intentionally, and also deliberately.

[1] Perhaps owing to someone else's fault: but for reasons given below we will *exclude* this possibility, and suppose it an 'accidental' crisis, such as fire.

So far we have shown that a thing done intentionally need not be done deliberately or on purpose, but what about conversely? Can something be done deliberately or purposely but not intentionally? Can we think of a case in which something is done *deliberately* but not intentionally? Certainly this seems more difficult. However, there are cases.

I am summoned to quell a riot in India. Speed is imperative. My mind runs on the action to be taken five miles down the road at the Residency. As I set off down the drive, my cookboy's child's new gocart, the apple of her eye, is right across the road. I realize I could stop, get out, and move it, but to hell with that: I must push on. It's too bad, that's all: I drive right over it and am on my way. In this case, a snap decision is taken on what is essentially an *incidental* matter. I did drive over the gocart deliberately, but not intentionally—nor, of course, unintentionally either. It was never part of my intention to drive over the gocart. At no time did I intend to drive over it. It was incidental to anything I intended to do, which was simply to get to the scene of the riot in order to quell it. However 'odd' it may sound, I feel little doubt that we should say here that we did run over the gocart deliberately *and* that we should not care to say we ran over it intentionally. We never intended to run over it.

A similar account should probably be given, too, of some things that will, it can be foreseen, follow as consequences or results of our doing certain actions—namely, that these things are 'done' by us deliberately but not intentionally. For example, I realize that by insisting on payment of due debts I am going to 'ruin' my debtor—that is, he will be ruined as a consequence of being compelled to pay. I have absolutely no wish to ruin him, even wish not to: but maybe if I don't get payment both I and others are going to suffer severely; and very likely I think he has been faintly improvident. So I demand payment. He is ruined and, if you like, I ruined him. If this is said—I might resist and resent the imputation a bit— I think it must be admitted that I did ruin him deliberately;

not, however, that I ruined him intentionally. At no time did I intend to ruin him; it was never any part of my intention. (This, if it be admitted, is an especially interesting case: for plainly I am *not* here responsible for his ruin.)

Finally, can a thing be done on purpose, but yet not intentionally? This seems even more difficult, and may actually be impossible. However, the expression 'accidentally on purpose' hints, at least ironically, that something of the sort may be possible; for, if done accidentally, it is not done intentionally. But how ironical is this expression? (Perhaps a case comparable to the debt-collection case could be constructed here.)

II

We now turn to our second general source of information: grammar and philology. Here we find that 'purpose', 'intend', and 'deliberate' exhibit numerous and striking differences.

1. *Deliberate* and *deliberation*, the verb and the noun, differ from both *intend*/*intention* and *purpose*/*purpose* in some ways in which the latter pair resemble each other. Thus, 'I am deliberating' could only be used to describe a process that is going on: but 'I am intending' and (if it exists) 'I am purposing' could not be used to describe a process. In line with this is the fact that deliberations may be protracted, but intentions and purposes cannot be so.

1a. The use of 'I intend' (and, so far as it exists, of 'I purpose') is quite different from 'I deliberate', which if *it* exists could only be a habitual present, describing what I ordinarily do, as in 'I deliberate before I act'. 'I intend to X' is, as it were, a sort of 'future tense' of the verb 'to X'. It has a vector, committal effect like 'I promise to X', and, again, like 'I promise to X', it is one of the possible formulas for making explicit, on occasion, the force of 'I shall X' (namely, that it was a declaration and not, for example, a forecast or an undertaking). We might feel inclined to say: it is almost an 'auxiliary verb'. But the fact of the matter is that terms like 'future tense' and 'auxiliary verb' were not invented with the need to do justice to such a word as 'intend' in mind. A complete reclassification of these archaic terms is needed. That reclassification is needed is shown, for example, by the fact that there is some oddity about the combination 'I shall intend'.

2. If we next consider the adjectival terminations found in 'deliber*ate*', 'intention*al*', and 'purpose*ful*' or 'purpos*ive*' (which are also of course incorporated in the corresponding adverbs), it would seem significant that they are different. 'Deliber*ate*' is of course formed on the Latin past participle: words of this kind commonly mean that something has happened or been done. We should suspect that the process of deliberation, whatever that may be, has been gone through. So consider*ate* behaviour is behaviour which shows that there has been consideration (of the feelings of others, as affected by my proposed activities).

The termination -ful, on the other hand, is commonly used in cases where something may be present or may not be present: an accretion or extra. 'Thoughtful', 'careful', 'purposeful' alike refer to things we may (but equally may not) be doing *when* doing X: we may be taking thought for the interests and feelings of others, taking care to guard against possible accidents, or pursuing a purpose.

The termination -al, as in 'intentional', qualifies, or classifies, as we may say, the act so described much more 'directly' and intimately than -ful or -ate. (Incidental note: -ive, as in 'purposive', would perform a similar function. But of course it is a term of psychological art, and to my mind requires some justification: because all our ordinary terminology, not merely the adjectival termination, certainly suggests that intention is related to our action in a more intimate way than its purpose, and in quite a different way.)

2a. The same lesson is pointed by the negative forms of the adjectives (and adverbs). There is no accepted negative form of 'deliberate'. 'Purpose' takes -less; I may 'have no purpose (whatsoever)' in doing something, just as I may take no care.

But I don't 'have no intention (whatsoever)' in doing something.

Here something of a general justification may be required. Why should we suppose it is significant of anything whatsoever that, for example, these adjectives and their negatives take different forms? Why shouldn't it just be that 'thought', for example, is not a Latin word and so can't readily take the Latin -ate termination, whereas 'consider' can? Why shouldn't it all be 'euphony', or chance, or meaningless luxuriation?

Now we can admit, and indeed positively welcome, all these suggestions, and yet adhere to our superstition that the forms of words and expressions are highly significant for their meaning. Briefly, let us assume, for the sake of argument and because we actually have no right to assume anything else, that 'in origin' speech consisted in any person making any noise in any situation to signify anything. Let us also assume, what in a sense is a tautology, that *in the very long run*, the forms of speech which survive will be the *fittest* (most efficient) forms of speech. Now one general criterion of efficiency[1] is simply this, stated loosely: that any unit of speech U should sound *tanto quanto* like every other unit of speech that 'means' anything like what U means, and unlike *tanto quanto* every other unit of speech that means anything unlike what U means: or that small variations in meaning should be signified by small concomitant variations in sound. This principle will account, on my view, not merely for the phenomenon of the survival of words in groups where similar-sounding words mean similar things (for example, 'fumble', 'tumble', 'stumble', and the like) but for much of what ought to be included in etymology, and for the whole general evolution of morphology, syntax, and grammar.

In this account of the origin of speech forms on evolutionary lines, it will be seen that *allowance* may be—indeed, to some extent is already fully—made for chance, for luxuriance, for

[1] There are others of great importance: brevity, learn-ability, etc. But of these, some are closely connected with the above in a variety of ways.

sound preferences (euphony), and for borrowings. *But still*, in the long run, the expressions which survive will be such that their grammatical and morphological characteristics are of the highest significance for their meaning.

3. The prepositions used with 'intention', 'purpose', and 'deliberation' to form adverbial or other expressions likewise point to distinctions between the three words, and associate them with quite distinct families of words. We say *on* purpose (to), *for* the purpose of, but *with* the intention of: (possibly also *with* the purpose of). It seems clear that 'on' and 'for' (compare 'on the principle', 'on orders', 'for the sake of') *dissociate* or *sever* my purpose from my current action in a way that 'with' does not do. There are many expressions containing 'purpose' ('for the *usual* purposes', 'to good purpose', 'to some purpose', and so forth) which seem to make purpose as it were *im*personal in a way that is never done with intention.

With 'deliberation', perhaps the only, and unexciting, preposition used is 'after'. 'With deliberation' is indeed found, but then the words are used to describe a certain slow style of performance, which makes an impression on the observer. 'Deliberately' is used in the same way, as when someone eats his soup deliberately. (Compare the case where he deliberately eats my soup. Here, if he is well advised, he will make haste over it.) Now this sort of secondary sense is fairly common with adverbs of this kind; and 'purposefully' is in fact also used in this way. We know the kind of performance it describes: a purposeful air is one of getting the preliminaries, the first stages, each stage *over with*, in order to proceed to the next and get the whole business achieved: it is an air of pressing on. Strikingly enough, however, there is no expression connected with 'intentional' which can be used in this manner. The explanation, whatever it is, would seem to lie in the same direction as that of the adjectival terminations referred to above: intention is too intimately associated with ordinary action in general for there to be any *special* style of performance associated with it.

4. Finally, we might consider the trailing etymologies of the three words: for no word ever achieves entire forgetfulness of its origins. The metaphor in 'deliberate' is one from 'weighing' or 'weighing up', that in 'intend' (one which keeps breaking through in many cognate words) is from bending or straining toward (compare 'intent on mischief' and 'bent on mischief'). In 'purpose', the idea is that of setting something up before oneself.

III

Now let us try to understand the three notions of purpose, intention, and deliberation in the light of our investigations so far. We shan't get so far as defining them though, I fear.

The most subtle of our notions is that of intention. As I go through life, doing, as we suppose, one thing after another, I in general always have an idea—some idea, my idea, or picture, or notion, or conception—of what I'm up to, what I'm engaged in, what I'm about, or in general 'what I'm doing'. I don't 'know what I'm doing' as a result of looking to see or otherwise conducting observations:[1] only in rare and perturbing cases do I *discover* what I've done or *come to realize* what I am or have been doing in this way. It is not in such fashion that *I* know what I'm doing when I strike the match in the vicinity of the haystack. (This is the sense in which in general and obviously I know what I'm doing: *contrast* the sense in which you *suppose*, dubiously, that I know what I'm doing when I strike the match so close to the gasoline.) I must be supposed to have *as it were* a plan, an operation-order or something of the kind on which I'm acting, which I am seeking to put into effect, carry out in action: only of course nothing necessarily or, usually, even faintly, so full-blooded as a plan proper. When we draw attention to this aspect of action, we use the words connected with intention.[2]

[1] I profited when I once heard this remarked by Miss G. E. M. Anscombe.
[2] At this point, the manuscript contains the unfinished sentence, 'When we use the great majority of 'active' verbs, e.g., 'kick' . . .' What Austin

Now although I say that the 'intention' words are connected with this notion of my idea of what I'm doing, it should not be supposed that it will always make sense to stick in 'intentionally' after every verb of action in every ordinary sentence with an active personal verb. Only when there is some suggestion that it might have been unintentional does it make non-misleading sense to say, for example, 'I ate my dinner intentionally'. To this extent, it is true that 'intentionally' serves to rule out 'unintentionally'. What would be wholly untrue is to suggest that 'unintentionally' is the word that 'wears the trousers'—that is, that until we have grasped certain specific ways of doing things unintentionally, and except as a way of ruling these out, 'intentionally' has no positive meaning. There are words of this description: 'real', for example, is one. But in the present case, to mention nothing more, there is the verb 'intend' to take into account, and it must obviously have a highly 'positive' sense; it cannot just be used to rule out 'don't (or didn't) intend'.

Although we have this notion of my idea of what I'm doing —and indeed we have as a general rule such an idea, as it were a miner's lamp on our forehead which illuminates always just so far ahead as we go along—it is not to be supposed that there are any precise rules about the extent and degree of illumination it sheds. The only general rule is that the illumination is always *limited*, and that in several ways. It will never extend indefinitely far ahead. Of course, all that is to follow, or to be done thereafter, is not what I am intending to do, but perhaps consequences or results or effects thereof. Moreover, it does not illuminate *all* of my surroundings. Whatever I am doing is being done and to be done amidst

probably had in mind was the fact that most 'active' verbs include, as part of their sense, some notion of a design or plan to be carried out. Thus, it is generally a mistake to consider them as purely 'behaviouristic'. That I kick someone does not mean merely that my foot moves sharply into contact with his shin. Perhaps this is why, in normal contexts, adding the adverb 'intentionally' is somewhat redundant. This point was suggested to me by G. J. Warnock. (L. W. F.)

a background of *circumstances* (including of course activities by other agents). This is what necessitates *care*, to ward off impingements, upsets, accidents. Furthermore, the doing of it will involve *incidentally* all kinds of minutiae of, at the least, bodily movements, and often many other things besides. These will be below the level of any intention, *however* detailed (and it need not of course be detailed at all), that I may have formed.

There is a good deal of freedom in 'structuring' the history of someone's activities by means of words like 'intention', just as when we consider a whole war we can divide it into campaigns, operations, actions, and the like; but this is fairly arbitrary except in so far as it is based upon the plans of the contestants. So with human activities; we can assess them in terms of intentions, purposes, ultimate objectives, and the like, but there is much that is arbitrary about this unless we take the way the agent himself did actually structure it in his mind before the event. Now the word 'intention' has from this point of view a most important *bracketing effect*: when the till-dipper claims that he *intended all along* to put the money back, what he is claiming is that his action—the action that he was engaged upon—is to be judged *as a whole*, not just a part of it carved out of the whole. Nearly always, of course, such a contention as this will carry with it a contention that his action (as a whole) is not to be described by the term chosen to describe (only a part of) it: for example, here, it was not 'robbing' the till, because the action taken as a whole would not result in the absence of any money from the till. *Reculer pour mieux sauter* is not to retreat.

Quite distinct is the use of the word 'purpose'. Certainly, *when* I am doing something for a purpose, this will be known to me, like my intentions, and will guide my conduct. Indeed, like an objective, a purpose will influence the forming of intentions. But my purpose is something to be achieved or effected as a result of what I'm doing, like the death of my aunt, or the sickness of the penguins if I did indeed feed them peanuts on purpose. (Very commonly my purpose is to put myself into a position to be able to go on with the next action, the next operation in the campaign.) I need not, however, have any purpose in acting (even intentionally);[1] just as I need not take care or thought. I act for or on (a) purpose, I achieve it; I act with the intention, I carry it out, realize it.

I act *deliberately* when I have deliberated—which means when I have stopped to ask myself, 'Shall I or shan't I?' and then decided to do X, which I did. That is to say, I weighed up, in however rudimentary (sometimes almost notional or fictional) a fashion, the pros and cons. And it is understood that there must be some cons, even when what I do deliberately is something unexceptionable, such as paying my taxes. The pros and cons are not confined to *moral* pros and cons, nor need I decide in favour of what I think best or what has the most reasons in favour of it. (Nor, of course, when I have decided to do it, *must* I necessarily carry it out.) Deliberation is not just *any* kind of thinking prior to action: to act with forethought or with premeditation, or to think about ways and means—all these show that we *took thought*, perhaps over a period of time, but none of these shows that we were acting deliberately, and indeed are quite distinct matters from deliberation. Ways and means are a matter for the planning staff; decision is a matter for the commander. That there should be slowness in moving into action or conducting it (so much relied on by lawyers) is the merest symptom.

I will close by adding a general word of warning: there are overriding considerations, which may be operative in any situation in which I act, which may put all three words out of joint, in spite of the other standard conditions for their use being satisfied. For instance, I may be acting under a threat: however much I weigh up the pros and cons, if I act under the influence of a threat I do not do that act deliberately. This

---

[1] E.g. feeding starving children: I need have no purpose here.

sort of overriding consideration must always be allowed for in any case.[1]

[1] The manuscript contains a few further remarks, but not enough to reconstruct a conclusion that could claim to reflect at all adequately Austin's own intentions for a conclusion. It can be said from these remarks, however, that *one* thing Austin most likely had in mind was this: we should not only compare and contrast these three expressions—'intentionally', 'deliberately', 'on purpose'—with each other, but each should be compared and contrasted with other expressions as well (e.g. 'motive' with both 'intention' and 'purpose', 'premeditation' with 'deliberation', and 'to mean' with 'to intend'). These are Austin's own examples, reproduced also, though inaccurately, in the *Nomos* Appendix. (L. W. F.)

13

THE LINE AND THE CAVE IN PLATO'S *REPUBLIC*

THIS reconstruction of Austin's views is based on three sources. There are notes dating from the 1930s for a reply to a paper (so far as I know unpublished) by W. D. Ross on the metaphysics of the *Republic* and the *Phaedo*. These notes are very full and the first half of the printed paper is very faithful to them; alterations are mainly excisions of comments on Ross which cannot be read profitably without Ross's paper and which do not advance Austin's argument. The later parts of these notes rely heavily on the view that Plato, like Aristotle, always used the word 'hypothesis' to mean an existential postulate; Austin came to doubt this at a later date. For the second half of the paper I have therefore made considerable use of Austin's own notes for a class held at Oxford in the late 1940s, and of notes taken at this class by Professor Hugh Lloyd-Jones, with a modified thesis about the nature of hypothesis. I am grateful to Professor Lloyd-Jones for allowing me to see his notes. I transliterate and translate what Austin left in Greek; I, not he, am responsible for the English names given to the segments of the line.

J. O. URMSON

TOO much has already been written on the interpretation of the Line and Cave in Plato's *Republic* (509–18). In Britain in the present century, to omit other references, there have been elaborate discussions in Adam's edition of the *Republic*; in Ferguson's articles in the *Classical Quarterly* of 1921, 1922, and 1934; by Stocks in the *Classical Quarterly* of 1911; by Murphy in the *Classical Quarterly* of 1934; by Paton in the *Proceedings of the Aristotelian Society* of 1921–2; and by Hardie in his *Study in Plato* of 1936. In this paper I shall assume that the reader is

A	Aa
gnosis—knowledge of *noeta*— intelligibles by philosopher	*episteme*—science of *eide*—forms by dialectician

A

	Ab
	dianoia—thought of ? by mathematician

B	Ba
doxa—belief of *doxasta*— objects of belief by *philotheamon*— lover of sights	*pistis*—conviction of animals, &c. by natural philosopher

B

	Bb
	eikasia [see p. 298] of shadows, &c. by ordinary man

acquainted with this literature. But I shall not discuss it; rather I shall attempt to present Plato's doctrines as accurately as possible.

We may start by obeying Plato's instruction and drawing the line. It should be vertical, not horizontal, and of a decent length.

The first main segment of the line, A, symbolizes *gnosta* (knowables), *noeta* (intelligibles), or *onta* (realities). The second, B, symbolizes what are variously called *gignomena* (becoming), *aistheta* (perceptible), *doxasta* (objects of belief), or *horata* (visible). Some have made great play with the fact that the objects of B are actually called visible when the line is first drawn (509d8). But a reading of 507a–c shows clearly that 'sight' is used metaphorically to include our belief about the good and the beautiful; the 'visible' is the whole domain of what was distinguished in Book V as *doxa* (belief). Again, in 534a the lower main segment B of the line is explicitly said to symbolize the *doxasta* (objects of belief).

Having divided the line into the two main segments, we are next required to divide each of these segments in the same way as the line was originally divided. It will thus be seen that we have on our hands six segments, grouped in pairs, in every pair a longer and a shorter in the same ratio. It is quite essential to bear this in mind and not to speak casually of the line 'being divided into four segments'. Let us impress this on our minds by using the nomenclature of the diagram, which I think is apt and easy to follow. The large original segments I call A and B: A is subdivided into Aa and Ab: B is subdivided into Ba and Bb. When two segments are in the ratio mentioned I shall say that they are in the AB ratio and that the things they symbolize are in the AB relation: similarly I shall speak of 'an A segment', 'a class of A objects', and 'an A state of mind'.

Let me here mention a point which has often been discussed. If the pairs Plato mentions and is interested in are all to be in the same ratio, it is a simple mathematical consequence that the so-called 'two middle subsections', Ab and Ba, should be equal in length. From this fact, unmentioned by Plato, no inferences should be drawn. No doubt Plato, being a mathematician, noticed the point, but so far as as we know he attached no special importance to it. Some, such as Sir David Ross, have thought this equality a defect which Plato would, if he had noticed it, have wished to eliminate; but this is utterly unwarrantable, for if Plato's symbol were so inadequate he could easily have chosen another. Two reasons advanced for the view by Ross are wrong in important ways. First, he thinks that the 'continuous advance in clearness as we pass from *eikasia* through *pistis* and *dianoia* to *noesis*, and in reality as we pass from the objects of each to the objects of the next', would not be adequately represented in the line unless this equality, which opens a door to Ferguson's heresy, were eliminated.

Now I do not quite understand what this problem is about continuity, but it seems clear that Ross thinks that the continuity is broken if ever we come to a cut in the line which has not got, on either side of it, two segments in the AB ratio. But the line is already satisfactory in this respect, without there being any need for Ab and Ba to stand in that ratio. For the middle cut in the line is the cut between, not indeed Ab and Ba, but A and B. This is emphasized by the 'Cave' allegory which Plato, at 517b, says must be attached to the preceding account, and which I take to be parallel, in the old sense, to the Line: for although the progress in a man's education is continuous enough, it is evident that there is no special relation between the statuettes carried through the cave, which are parallel to segment Ba, and the reflections on the surface of the earth, which are parallel to segment Ab. We must not think of the man, at this stage, passing from looking at statuettes to looking at reflections on the earth's surface, but as passing from the realm of objects illuminated by the fire to the realm of objects illuminated by the sun. The passage is not from conviction (*pistis*) to thought (*dianoia*), but from belief (*doxa*) to knowledge (*gnosis*). In the résumé in Book VII at 534a, just as clearly as in the account of the line in Book VI, the grouping is only into the pairs belief and knowledge, science and thought, conviction and *eikasia*; at 534a, indeed, the relation of thought to conviction is significantly omitted—significantly since here Plato mentions rather the analogy between thought and *eikasia*.

Secondly, Ross has a more specific reason for his view that the equality of Ab and Ba is unfortunate. He seems to think that what Plato actually tells us about the relation between thought and conviction corresponds exactly to what he tells us about the relations between the members of each of the other pairs of states of mind (*pathemata*) which stand in the AB relation. This seems to me false and to have bad consequences. What Plato tells us is that the man in the state of thought (*dianoia*) *uses as* images (*eikones*) those very objects of which the objects in segment Bb *are* images. But we are never told that the man in a state of conviction *uses* the objects of Bb as images, only that they are in fact images. Thus no verbal parallel is here drawn between the relations *thought–conviction* and *conviction–eikasia*. However, I shall not press this point, for the following reason: that I think it very highly probable that Plato did think that the man in an A state of mind (*pathema*) does use the corresponding B objects as images. We shall shortly see that the reason why little prominence is given to this fact is that, in the case of at least two of the three pairs of states of mind in the AB relation, the upper state of mind must be left more or less obscure. Why then does Plato mention the fact that in thought the objects of conviction are used as images? It is not in order to relate thought and conviction, but, as the context makes obvious, in order to contrast science and thought. This is borne out, if that is necessary, by other facts. For example, if Plato had wished carefully to relate thought and conviction in the AB relation, he could scarcely have failed to notice that a Bb object would do just as well as a diagram for the mathematician as would a Ba object. Again at 511d and 533d thought is said to be intermediate between belief and knowledge; but if the AB relation held between thought and conviction he quite clearly should have said 'conviction' not 'belief'.

In short then I see no necessity whatever for supposing that Plato held that Ab and Ba are in the AB ratio or regarded their equality as significant. It is therefore unfortunate that so many people use the relation between these two segments, which seems to them the most easy and familiar, to explain the AB relation itself and so the whole symbolism of the line. This is a fatal error; the relation between these two segments in no way explains the AB relation.

What then is the AB relation? Here it is important to grasp that the AB ratio between each pair of segments of the line has a *double* symbolic significance, as Plato himself says. The segments of the line are of course symbolic both of classes of objects and of states of mind. What we must discover, then, is what the AB ratio symbolizes, first in the case of the objects, secondly in the case of the states of mind. The relation between the A and B objects is comparatively clear: they are related as 'original' to 'copy' or 'image' (*eikasthen* to *eikon*). It is evident that, in the case of each AB pair, this metaphorical language of *eikon* and *eikasthen* will have a different precise meaning, but the positions occupied by the A objects and B objects in respect to each other will be always analogous and recognizably describable as those of 'original' and 'image' respectively. The metaphor is of course most directly applicable in the case of Ba and Bb. At 510a Socrates asks permission to treat the metaphor as applicable also to the relation between the objects in the main segments A and B. Clearly the extension to the case of the objects in Aa and Ab, which are certainly none of them visible, must be more metaphorical still. What these objects all are I shall not discuss at this stage; but the line must make sense here, however we interpret it.

The next problem is what the relation is between the A and B states of mind. It seems to be supposed commonly that this needs no explanation: the A state of mind is that which concerns itself with the A class of objects, the B state of mind that which concerns itself with the B class of objects. But Plato tells us much more and other than that.

In the first place, as Hardie points out in his *A Study in Plato*, we must understand the metaphor, constantly recurring, of dreaming. It was first used and carefully explained in Book V, to which we are later referred back emphatically; it is in Book V that the relation between knowledge (*gnosis*) and belief (*doxa*), symbolized as A and B in the line, was described in detail. What Plato does in Book VI is to subdivide each of them into states of mind related in the same way as knowledge and belief. In Book V that relation is metaphorically named that of waking to sleeping and is carefully described as consisting in this, that the man in the B state of mind makes a certain complicated *mistake*, which the man in the A state of mind does not make. That this relation is intended to apply throughout the Line can be proved by the text throughout: but I shall simply mention enough evidence to clinch the matter.

(1) At 510a8 the main A–B division of the line is described as being in truth as the believed is to the known.

(2) With regard to the two subordinate pairs: Aa and Ab are described, as in Book V, as related as waking to sleeping at 533c, as Hardie notes.

(3) As for the Ba–Bb relation, at 515a–c the prisoners in the cave, who are in the Bb state of mind, are carefully described as making a mistake of just the kind described in Book V as being made by sleepers. Moreover, this sort of mistake is described again, with special regard to sensible objects, in the *Theaetetus* at 158, and called there once again the mistake made in *dreaming*. I shall not use evidence from elsewhere, but shall give reasons later why the *Theaetetus* not only may but should be used in interpreting the *Republic*.

What is the mistake in question, which is typical of the man in the B state of mind? It is compound, as carefully described in Book V. Granted that there are two sorts of objects related as originals to copies:

(i) He thinks that there is only one set, namely the one which is most obvious and 'before' him. If it were put to him, he would deny that there was a second set at all.

(ii) He thinks that this set is what we, who distinguished two sets, would call the originals; that is, he ascribes to the set before him, which he thinks is the only set, the properties which we would ascribe to the originals, and which we should refuse to ascribe to the set which he recognizes, as being only copies.

A man in this state is said 'not to understand about' (*noun ouch echein*), a constantly recurring phrase, the objects which he seeks to describe, those that are truly original.

It will be seen then that it is quite incorrect to say that the B state of mind is distinguished as being concerned with the B class of objects. It is in a way concerned with both classes of objects, confusing them in a certain definite manner.

Now what of the A state of mind, called a state of being awake? The man in this state recognizes that there are two classes of objects, related as originals to copies. Further, he recognizes that the objects which are obviously before him are the copies only. And, I *think*, he is *not* then able to turn away from the copies and 'look at' the originals, but what he can do is to use the copies simply as copies in order to infer about that he is really interested in, the originals. But this is not quite certain.

Why does Plato describe the former state as dreaming? Because the mistake made is precisely typified by the mistake we make in dreams, when, having before us dream-images, we not only do not distinguish between them and material things, but take it for granted that what is passing before us is material things. This Plato describes in the *Theaetetus*, when he discusses dreams on page 158.

So then, we have six segments of the line, grouped in three pairs; each pair symbolizes first two sets of objects, related as originals to copies, or as more to less real, secondly two states of mind, related as being awake to being asleep.

We now come to the second main point: the detailed interpretation of the symbolism in the case of each of the three pairs of segments.

About its interpretation in the case of the pair A and B I shall not say much. The classes of objects are those which *are* (*onta*) and those which *become* (*gignomena*), as Plato repeatedly says. The mistake made by the ordinary man is that he does not distinguish perceptible *gignomena* from *onta*, but thinks there is only one set of objects, the visible ones, to which, however, he ascribes properties, such as 'reality', which properly belong only to *onta*. Not much is told us about the two states of mind in detail, because Plato intends to point out later that this is an over-simplification and that each state of mind requires subdivision.

Let us rather consider the pair Ba and Bb, conviction (*pistis*) and *eikasia*. No doubt the purpose of the line is primarily to distinguish between thought (*dianoia*) and science (*episteme*), and that is why not so much attention is devoted to *eikasia* and *pistis* in Book VI. But the distinction between Ba and Bb is none the less important, particularly in connection with the interpretation of the Cave. For it seems to me certain that the Line and the Cave are in the traditional sense parallel; and therefore it is as certain as can be that the ordinary man, in default of philosophical education, lives all his life in a state of *eikasia*, while *pistis* is a merely short-lived and unsatisfactory first stage when he starts his education. Perhaps those who think that the elucidation of the Ba–Bb relation is unimportant do so because they do not realize that there lies ready to hand an interpretation on which it would turn out to be important. But such an interpretation is ready to hand and I shall develop this shortly.

As I intend to use certain doctrines from the *Theaetetus* I shall explain why I think this legitimate, despite the fact that this dialogue is probably later than the *Republic*. The doctrines in question, about sense-data, are doctrines of the Heracliteans, notably of Cratylus. Now Cratylus was Plato's own teacher in his youth, perhaps even before he came under the influence of Socrates. Whatever may be thought of Aristotle's account of Plato's development, that much is surely unquestionable. Therefore these doctrines were certainly known to Plato when, and since long before, he wrote the *Republic*. Moreover they are doctrines which no one, once trained in them, readily forgets. Therefore we may take it as highly probable that Plato had them in mind when he wrote the *Republic*.

In the *Theaetetus* then (153–8) a quite traditional account of sense-data, not unlike that of Descartes, is given: all that we sense is on a level—dreams are on the same level as our waking sensations. Material objects are *perhaps* only groups of sensations (*athroismata*), but no account of them is decided on; what is made clear is that we do not, contrary to our ordinary opinion, sense material objects, since, as far as what we sense goes, it is just the same whether we are awake or asleep. I do not say that Plato was right in this, but merely that he believed it. Similar doctrines are found in the *Timaeus* at pages 45, 61, and 67.

Now let us return to the *Republic*: what are the two sets of objects corresponding to Ba and Bb? Ba consists of animals, trees, &c.—material objects. What of Bb? This consists of shadows, echoes, reflections in smooth objects, and 'everything of that sort'. What is the sort? I say, plainly 'sense-data'. The examples are chosen because they are the very examples which modern philosophers use when they want, if they do, to suggest to pupils that they do not sense material objects! They take as examples hallucinations, noises, mirror images, and the like. That Plato was well aware of the doctrine of sense-data is shown in, for example, Book X, where we are told that the painter does not copy the material bed but only an appearance of it. Now it seems to me that the relation between sense-data and material objects has often been held, especially by those who rely on the argument from dreaming, to be that between copy and original. By such philosophers the ordinary man is thought to live in a state of 'naïve realism', mistaking sense-data for material objects and failing to distinguish between them in precisely the way described as typical of a man in a state of dreaming and represented at 515a–c as awareness only of shadows and echoes, which are taken to be the only reality.

As for the upper state of mind, conviction (*pistis*), there is a difficulty here, in that Plato did not himself believe in the existence of physical objects like the sense-data: hence we have only 'statuettes' in the light of the fire in the Cave; hence, too, no one stays looking at the statuettes, although to distinguish between them and the shadows on the wall is a necessary first stage in education. Certainly Plato does not believe that it is possible to refrain from looking at sense-data and look at material objects instead: even the guardian, when he returns to the Cave, looks at the shadows and not the statuettes. But the fact that the upper state of mind here is not wholly genuine explains why Plato tells us so little about it; but one assumes that the man with conviction does use sense-data as images from which to draw inferences about material objects.

Regarding the names *pistis* and *eikasia*, of which I have translated *pistis* as 'conviction' and left *eikasia* untranslated, it is not reasonable to make too much of the ordinary Greek (or English) meanings of these words. It would be very surprising if ordinary Greek had four words forming just such a scale as Plato means to describe. *Eikasia* does not mean 'conjecture', as is often thought, but is a rare and artificial word, connected with the verb εἰκάζειν, and that does not mean 'to conjecture'; in fact it has no exact English equivalent. The root idea is 'to treat a thing as like another'; it thus can mean 'to compare', and in some contexts, such as the phrase ὡς εἰκάσαι, it can mean 'to conjecture' in the sense of 'to go by likenesses'. The word *pistis* is used elsewhere by Plato, almost in a technical sense. It is nearer to 'faith' than 'belief'. Its use in the *Timaeus* is almost technical; see, for example, the beginning of the account of the physical world in the *Timaeus*, where the account is said to be not knowledge but only *pistis*. At 29c we are told that 'what being is to becoming, that truth is to *pistis*'; at 49c there is a reference to a '*pistos* account'; at 37b we are told that an 'account of the perceptible' yields only 'opinions and *pisteis*', whereas an 'account of the intelligible' yields 'reason and science'. Therefore in the *Timaeus pistis* is the best state about the physical world that we can get ourselves into.

We now turn to the upper segment of the line, where the difficulties are of a very different kind. It is not these difficulties which have led Ferguson and others to deny the parallelism of the Line and Cave. The distinction between the two upper segments Aa and Ab is painstakingly stated at the end of Book VI. But even so Plato finally says that he has not succeeded in making the distinction really clear; in fact he has repeated himself about five times in almost identical terms. He is thus not doing what he ought to do if he is to apply the symbolism of the Line straightforwardly. He ought first to explain the distinction between two classes of objects, and then show how the man in the Ab state of mind confuses and the other distinguishes them. But there is nothing about two classes of objects, and nothing about how the mathematician confuses and the dialectician distinguishes them. What then does he say at the end of Book VI? There are two things that he says again and again about the mathematician: first, that he uses hypotheses in order to proceed from them to draw conclusions; secondly, that he continually makes use of sensible diagrams. By contrast, Plato says that if a man is to gain true knowledge he will have to destroy the hypotheses, using them as starting-points in the search for an *arche anhypothetos*—an unhypothesized starting-point.

First we must explain the word 'hypothesis'. In his *A Study in Plato* Hardie points out that in Aristotle it is a more or less technical term, meaning an existential postulate. When Aristotle sets out the *archai* or starting-points of the sciences he includes *theseis* which are definitions and *hypotheseis* which are postulates to the effect that objects corresponding to certain of these definitions exist. Euclid does not use Aristotle's precise terminology, but does follow his procedure. He does not need to postulate that objects corresponding to all his definitions exist, because he can prove by constructions that some exist when he has assumed the existence of the rest.

I should like to say that the word 'hypothesis' meant the same in *Plato*, and in a way I shall, but it does not have this precise meaning. Plato often uses it in just this way, but in other cases more loosely, so that it means 'an assumption', 'a suggested definition', or something of that kind. The passage in *Meno* (86–7), for example, does not fit the sense of 'existential postulate'. Perhaps it was this imprecision which led to Aristotle and Euclid being so careful in their use of the word 'hypothesis'. Plato's examples are not what we should call hypotheses but 'the odd, the even, and the three kinds of angle'. I believe that he means that the mathematician gives definitions of these three things and then proceeds to his demonstrations. But what Plato wants to point out is that he has assumed and not proved that objects of these three types really exist. The mathematician of Plato's day apparently did not state his assumptions, as Euclid did, but just gave definitions. Presumably it was Plato's criticism here that was responsible for this change.

We can now see the force of Plato's criticism of the use made by mathematicians of sensible diagrams. What he has in mind is that the mathematician says: 'I am demonstrating the nature and properties of the circle', and then says, pointing to his diagram, 'I do not mean this, but it will do to go on with.' The fact that he has the sensible diagram enables him to overlook the necessity of showing that his demonstrations are about something real to a still greater degree. Plato complains that though the mathematician purports to tell us about non-sensible realities, all he, in fact, has to show is his definitions and his sensible diagrams. But nothing is real knowledge except what is about something real. Thus we can see that Plato believed that the mathematician confused the *logos* that he had with an undemonstrated being which he did not have, and was thus dreaming about reality also, but within the realm of the intelligible.

Thus we require another account of the objects of mathematics to supplement the one given by the mathematician. He has only *logos*, definitions, and has no real knowledge, and this we cannot have unless we can show by a new method that supra-sensible objects do really exist. The unhypothesized starting-point is that which requires no existential postulate. How we are to attain it Plato does not profess to see, but he insists that it must be attained if any pursuit designed to acquire knowledge of the supra-sensible is to be justified. The traditional argument for the forms 'from the sciences' assumes that mathematical knowledge is real, and argues that therefore its objects must exist. Plato is here saying, in effect, that this argument puts the cart before the horse. The reality of the objects must be proved first in order to show that mathematics is science.

The mathematician resembles the dreamer in failing to realize the distinction between the *logos* and the form itself. Plato regards the *logos* as the image (*eikon*, *eidolon*) of the form, and he often uses this language. Nowhere does he speak with such rigour on this subject as here, but one should compare the remarks in the important *Cratylus* at 423–32 and 438–9 on realities (*onta*) and the names (*onomata*) and *logoi* that are their images (*eikones*). In the *Seventh Letter* (343) Plato says that in getting to know about anything there are five factors—the name, the *logos*, the illustration (*eidolon*), the thing itself (*on*), and the science (*episteme*). The circle is his example, one relevant to our present interest. This is a very important passage, partly because it is not in a dialogue but a statement by Plato in his own person.

We can therefore make sense of what Plato says about the Aa–Ab relation in the upper line. My exposition of the Line is thus complete. But there are three other points to be considered.

First, some think that the two sets of objects between which Plato distinguishes in the upper line are the *mathematica*, a belief in which is ascribed to Plato by Aristotle in the *Metaphysics*, and the forms; Hardie and Adam both hold this view. Certainly in the abstract respect of being ontologically between forms and perceptible things, and of being many where the forms are unitary, the *mathematica* seem to fulfil some of the necessary conditions. But there are many difficulties. (*a*) This doctrine is a great deal more obscure and difficult than editors and commentators allow. Cook Wilson and his followers were too hasty, for Aristotle's statements on this subject are very obscure. Cook Wilson says that the *mathematica* were postulated because in mathematical demonstrations we talk, for example, of two circles intersecting, but there is no evidence for this. (*b*) We have no evidence outside this passage that Plato held this doctrine at the time he wrote the *Republic*. Those who try to show that remarks in other dialogues might imply it strain their interpretations. (*c*) If Plato had meant to allude to them he would have been perverse to use in describing the objects of mathematics language at least equally appropriate to the forms themselves. (*d*) How can those who think that Plato was interested in pointing out that the mathematician was concerned only with *mathematica* explain why he says so much about hypotheses and diagrams at the end of Book VI? What have these to do with the distinction between forms and *mathematica*? What is the relation between relying on existential postulates and the doctrine of *mathematica*?

Secondly, when Plato denounces the mathematicians for their reliance on sensible diagrams, he does observe that the sensible diagrams used are from the segment Ba and thus exhibits a relation between the objects of Ab and Ba. This fact is apt to be misleading because people think that the relation between the objects of the mathematician and the objects of Ba ought to be typical of the AB relation. But Plato never implies this. To suppose that we can take the mathematician's use of diagrams as typical of the AB relation is wrong. Plato mentions the point only in order to bring out the contrast between thinking (*dianoia*) and science (*episteme*).

Finally, I want to point out that other philosophers have felt similar difficulties about mathematics. Descartes, who is the modern philosopher most akin to Plato, says in his account of the method of doubt things closely analogous to what Plato says in the *Republic*. Descartes begins by saying that the testimony of the senses is valueless, and both agree on this. Descartes then turns to mathematics, where at least our ideas are 'clear and distinct'. Descartes says that what is such cannot be doubted as the testimony of the senses can be doubted. But in spite of this Descartes does raise doubts about mathematics; who is to say whether there is any reality corresponding to these ideas? It might be that an arch-deceiver contrives that our ideas differ from reality. Both Plato and Descartes have to find some starting-point whose very nature guarantees the existence of something real corresponding to it; we know where Descartes found it and how he used it to validate mathematics. We know too that Plato held that the starting-point without postulates was the Form of the Good; but in the *Republic* he does not profess to lead us to that starting-point.

INDEX

Numbers in bold type refer to papers, numbers in roman type to pages